LESLIE BECK'S
HEALTHY KITCHEN

LESLIE BECK'S HEALTHY KITCHEN

250 QUICK AND DELICIOUS RECIPES PLUS ESSENTIAL KITCHEN TIPS

LESLIE BECK RD

WITH MICHELLE GELOK RD
RECIPE DEVELOPMENT AND NUTRITIONAL ANALYSIS

PENGUIN
an imprint of Penguin Canada

Published by the Penguin Group

Penguin Group (Canada), 90 Eglinton Avenue East, Suite 700, Toronto, Ontario, Canada M4P 2Y3 (a division of Pearson Canada Inc.)

Penguin Group (USA) Inc., 375 Hudson Street, New York, New York 10014, U.S.A.
Penguin Books Ltd, 80 Strand, London WC2R 0RL, England
Penguin Ireland, 25 St Stephen's Green, Dublin 2, Ireland (a division of Penguin Books Ltd)
Penguin Group (Australia), 250 Camberwell Road, Camberwell, Victoria 3124, Australia (a division of Pearson Australia Group Pty Ltd)
Penguin Books India Pvt Ltd, 11 Community Centre, Panchsheel Park, New Delhi – 110 017, India
Penguin Group (NZ), 67 Apollo Drive, Rosedale, Auckland 0632, New Zealand (a division of Pearson New Zealand Ltd)
Penguin Books (South Africa) (Pty) Ltd, 24 Sturdee Avenue, Rosebank, Johannesburg 2196, South Africa

Penguin Books Ltd, Registered Offices: 80 Strand, London WC2R 0RL, England

First published 2012

2 3 4 5 6 7 8 9 10 (WEB)

Manufactured in Canada.

LIBRARY AND ARCHIVES CANADA CATALOGUING IN PUBLICATION

Beck, Leslie (Leslie C.)
   Leslie Beck's healthy kitchen.

Includes index.
ISBN 978-0-14-317186-7

1. Cooking. 2. Diet. 3. Cookbooks. I. Title.

TX714.B43 2011   641.5'63   C2011-906197-X

Visit the Penguin Canada website at **www.penguin.ca**

Special and corporate bulk purchase rates available; please see **www.penguin.ca/corporatesales** or call 1-800-810-3104, ext. 2477.

ALSO BY LESLIE BECK

PENGUIN

LESLIE BECK'S HEALTHY KITCHEN

LESLIE BECK, a registered dietitian, is a leading Canadian nutritionist and the bestselling author of 11 nutrition books. Leslie writes a weekly nutrition column in *The Globe and Mail*, is a regular contributor to CTV's *Canada AM* and can be heard one morning a week on CJAD Radio's *The Andrew Carter Show* (Montreal).

Leslie has worked with many of Canada's leading businesses and international food companies and runs a thriving private practice in Toronto. She also regularly delivers nutrition workshops to corporate groups across North America.

Visit Leslie's website at www.lesliebeck.com.

MICHELLE GELOK is a Canadian registered dietitian currently based in Abu Dhabi, United Arab Emirates. Michelle writes health and nutrition articles and develops recipes for a variety of publications and corporate clients in Canada and internationally. Her work has appeared in *Chatelaine*, *CBC Online*, *My Yoga Online*, *Aquarius* magazine and *The National* newspaper. Michelle has collaborated extensively with Leslie Beck since 2004, developing recipes for her last four books, including *The No-Fail Diet*, *Foods That Fight Disease*, *Heart Healthy Foods for Life* and *Leslie Beck's Longevity Diet*. Visit Michelle's website at www.michellegelok.com.

Contents

Introduction

I'm often asked by clients and friends if I cook my meals. That might sound like a strange question, but it's actually not. Consider that more and more time-crunched Canadians are relying on prepared foods to serve at meal time. Grocery stores offer plenty of choices for people too busy to cook: frozen and refrigerated entrées, hot entrées and side dishes at the deli counter—even a sushi bar. And, of course, you can order take-out from almost any type of restaurant.

Our busy lifestyle is certainly one barrier to preparing meals from scratch. It can be hard to find the motivation—and energy—to cook after a long day spent working and chauffeuring kids to extracurricular activities. And, without a plan, it's easy to give in to the temptation of an effortless meal that requires only heating and serving.

But lack of time isn't the only obstacle. Some people don't feel comfortable in the kitchen because they haven't learned how to cook. Baking salmon, cooking quinoa or even steaming vegetables are tasks that can intimidate beginner cooks. Many of my private practice clients ask me to design a meal plan that's as simple as possible to follow—one that requires very little preparation.

Yes, I do cook my meals. I eat breakfast at home, bring my lunch to work and prepare dinner from scratch seven days a week. (Okay, once in a while we order in a thin-crust pizza.) It's not just because I'm a dietitian that I cook my meals. Sure, I understand that home-prepared meals are typically more nutritious—and tasty—than a meal you buy at the supermarket or from a local restaurant. But I cook because I enjoy doing so. My mother taught me how to cook when I was in grade school. While she was at work, I took on the task of preparing dinner when I arrived home from school. I experimented with different recipes and had fun in the process.

I was also fortunate to have home economics classes offered in high school. It's a shame that home ec is no longer part of the school curriculum for so many kids today. To me, learning how to cook has equal—or even more—importance to learning world history or mathematics. It's a life skill, after all.

My goal in writing this book is to help you incorporate healthy and great-tasting meals and snacks into your family's menu plan. Even better, the majority of the recipes in this book are quick and easy to make. I hope my quick tips and recipes will also encourage your family to gather for meals as often as possible.

Research shows that kids who participate in regular family meals—five or more meals together each week—have more healthful diets and meal patterns than their peers who eat few family meals. What's more, kids who report eating as a family on a regular basis are more likely to have a higher intake of vegetables, fibre, calcium, magnesium, potassium and iron when they are older. But family meals are not just about nutrition. Studies also show that the more often families eat together, the less likely kids are to smoke, drink, do drugs or develop eating disorders—and the more likely they are to excel academically.

I know it can be challenging to find time for everyone to sit down together for the evening meal, especially five times per week. If your schedule gets in the way, eat breakfast together or gather for lunch on the weekend to encourage healthy eating habits. I've included plenty of delicious breakfast, brunch and lunch recipes to help you do so!

HOW TO USE THIS BOOK

Leslie Beck's Healthy Kitchen is different from my previous books about health and nutrition. While my focus remains on healthy eating, this book is intended to be used as a hands-on resource in your kitchen. Unlike my previous books, I spend very little time giving you background information—why certain foods are good for you, what studies have found and so on. Instead, this book is a tool to help you eat a nutritious diet. It's a cookbook with practical tips and recipes to help you plan and prepare healthy, delicious meals.

Before you delve into the recipes, take a few moments to read "Eight Steps to Prime Your Kitchen for Healthy Eating." This section gives you essential tips for incorporating "power" foods into your diet, portion control, menu planning and grocery shopping. I've also included a handy food storage guide in case you're wondering about the shelf life of certain foods in the fridge, freezer and pantry. Even canned foods don't last forever! You can also read my list of must-have cooking aids—nutrition-friendly tools and gadgets—as well as healthy cooking methods. Finally, you'll find fundamental food safety tips to help prevent foodborne illness.

The bulk of the book is devoted to 250 recipes—recipes that are easy to follow and turn out great-tasting food that's also good for you. Each recipe in this book was developed, tested and analyzed by Michelle Gelok, a dietitian who has worked with me for the past seven years. Many of the recipes are family and client all-time favourites from my previous books. Some have been tweaked to make them even better than they were before.

But there are plenty of brand-new recipes to tempt you, too. You'll find recipes ranging from Egg White Frittata with Goat Cheese and Red Pepper, to Easy Fish Tacos with Tomato and Avocado Salsa, to Chocolate Ginger Cake. Each recipe is accompanied by a per serving nutrient analysis: a breakdown of its calories, fat, protein, fibre and so on.

I hope *Leslie Beck's Healthy Kitchen* will help you build your repertoire of healthy, quick meals that you and your family will love. I hope it finds a permanent place in *your* kitchen.

Yours in good health,

Leslie Beck, RD
Toronto, Canada, 2012

ACKNOWLEDGMENTS

There are a number of people whose hard work, support and constant encouragement brought *Leslie Beck's Healthy Kitchen* to life.

- The talented Michelle Gelok, a dietitian I have had the pleasure of working with and becoming friends with for the past seven years. She spent months in her kitchen developing, testing and analyzing the recipes in this book. Quite a task, I must say—and she managed to gain only a few pounds in the process of tasting all of them! I am grateful for her collaboration on this project—her creativity and love of good, wholesome foods shines as always.

- Laura Hanson, my amazingly enthusiastic, kind, efficient and professional assistant, who helped manage my busy private practice while I worked on this book.

- My private practice clients, who have adopted many of my recipes into their diets. Their feedback and questions about healthy eating have allowed me to grow professionally and prompted me to write my books on nutrition and health.

- Andrea Magyar, and the entire team at Penguin Group (Canada), who continue to support my vision and bring my books—now 11 in total—to the public. Thank you for your ongoing support and cheerleading.

- To Darrell, my husband and best friend, who supports any project I undertake and makes sure I laugh and have fun during the journey. Thank you for bringing such incredible balance to my life.

Eight Steps to Prime Your Kitchen for Healthy Eating

Wouldn't it be wonderful to come home from work each day to find a delicious, healthy meal waiting for you? Between the demands of work, family and social obligations, it can be challenging to drum up the energy—and time—to prepare nutritious meals day after day. I'm sure many of us would agree having a personal chef would seem like a dream come true.

The good news: preparing healthy meals doesn't have to be a labour-intensive, time-consuming task. Sitting down to a healthy meal that's ready within 30 to 40 minutes is absolutely within your reach! The key is being organized. Planning your family's meals in advance will prevent the stress of not knowing what to make for dinner. And, believe it or not, planning ahead will actually save you time later on. (Even take-out food can take longer to arrive at your door than it takes to make a pre-planned home-cooked meal!)

Being organized in the kitchen requires more than planning menus. It requires a series of strategies that any novice cook can master. You need to read labels and shop wisely in order to have the right ingredients on hand. And you need to have a properly equipped kitchen that helps you cook efficiently and with good nutrition in mind. Finally, you need the right recipes. And you'll find 250 of those recipes on the very pages of this book!

First, it's time to prime your kitchen for healthy eating! The advice that follows will give you the know-how and tools to prepare great-tasting, healthy meals even on the busiest weekdays.

STEP ONE
Add Leslie's 15 power foods to your diet

The foods you are going to read about are some of the healthiest foods on the planet. They're foods you will want to add to your grocery list and build your meals around. They are unprocessed, nutrient-rich and packed with disease-fighting antioxidants and phyto (plant)-chemicals. Antioxidants like vitamins C and E, beta carotene, selenium and countless phytochemicals defend your body's cells from harm caused by free radicals. Free radicals are unstable oxygen molecules that arise normally in our bodies during metabolism and from pollution, sun exposure and cigarette smoke. The problem: if free radicals become excessive—or if antioxidants are unavailable—cell damage can occur. And this damage accumulates over time and can lead to health problems.

The power foods below are also incredibly low in saturated and trans fats, the two fats that can cause unhealthy levels of LDL (bad) cholesterol in your bloodstream. Over time, LDL cholesterol can deposit in your blood vessels, making it more difficult for oxygen-rich blood to flow through them. In fact, most of the foods below are virtually fat free! And because they're all naturally low in sodium, they help keep your blood pressure in check. You'll find these power foods featured in many of my recipes.

Take a moment to familiarize yourself with each of these foods—and their relatives, which offer similar nutrients and health benefits (they're listed in alphabetical order). You'll learn what makes them so good for you and how they can help you stay healthy. Some of them might already be a regular part of your diet. That's great! For those that aren't on your menu, try my quick tips to help you eat more.

ALMONDS

Notable nutrients: Monounsaturated fat (heart healthy), fibre, vitamin E, calcium, manganese, potassium

Guard against: High LDL cholesterol, high blood pressure, cardiovascular disease, type 2 diabetes, Alzheimer's disease

Eat these too: Brazil nuts, cashews, hazelnuts, macadamia nuts, peanuts, pecans, pine nuts, pistachios, pumpkin seeds, sunflower seeds, walnuts

Tips to eat more

- Add slivered almonds to oatmeal, yogurt and stir-fries.
- Blend ground almonds into a smoothie.
- Spread almond butter on apple slices.
- Snack on *Tamari Roasted Almonds*, page 101

BLUEBERRIES

Notable nutrients: Fibre, vitamin C, folate, potassium, anthocyanins (potent antioxidants), lutein (a phytochemical that keeps your eyes healthy)

Guard against: Cancer, heart disease, memory loss, Alzheimer's disease, cataracts, macular generation (an age-related eye disease that leads to central vision loss)

Eat these too: Açai berries, blackberries, red cherries, cranberries, strawberries, raspberries

Tips to eat more

- Toss fresh blueberries into a bowl of breakfast cereal.
- Add fresh or frozen blueberries to muffin, pancake and waffle batters.
- Use dried blueberries to make a homemade trail mix.
- For breakfast, try my *Blueberry Raspberry Smoothie*, page 67

BROCCOLI

Notable nutrients: Fibre, vitamin C, folate, calcium, potassium, beta carotene, sulforaphane (an anti-cancer phytochemical)

Guards against: Cancer, stroke

Eat these too: Bok choy, broccoflower, broccoli sprouts, broccolini, Brussels sprouts, cabbage, cauliflower, rapini, turnip

Tips to eat more

- Add steamed broccoli florets to a homemade pizza.
- Top a baked potato with chopped, steamed broccoli florets.
- Snack on raw broccoli with hummus (chickpea dip).
- Serve *Roasted Broccoli* for an easy side dish, page 307

DARK CHOCOLATE (70% cocoa solids or more)

Notable nutrients: Magnesium, iron, copper, flavonoids (a class of phytochemicals)

Guards against: High blood pressure, heart disease

Eat these too: Cocoa powder

Tips to eat more

- Enjoy a small portion (1 ounce/30 grams) of dark chocolate after lunch to curb sweet cravings. Keep in mind that 30 grams of 70% dark chocolate—about 3 squares—has 160 calories and 8 grams of sugar (2 teaspoons' worth).
- Sip on a mug of homemade hot dark chocolate. (Mix cocoa powder with skim or soy milk. Sweeten with a teaspoon of sugar, if desired.)
- Add chopped dark chocolate to muffin, loaf and cookie batters.
- Try my *Chocolate Fruit Fondue* for a healthy dessert, page 354

GRAPEFRUIT

Notable nutrients: Fibre, vitamin A, vitamin C, folate, potassium, naringenin (an anti-cancer phytochemical), hesperidin (an anti-inflammatory phytochemical)

Guards against: Cancer, heart disease, stroke, obesity

Eat these too: Lemons, limes, oranges, pummelos, tangerines

Tips to eat more

- Start the day with a small glass of freshly squeezed grapefruit juice.
- Skewer grapefruit segments with grapes and strawberries for a delicious fruit kebab.
- Add grapefruit segments to a spinach salad. (The vitamin C will enhance your body's absorption of iron from the spinach leaves.)
- Try my *Grapefruit and Raspberry Smoothie with Toasted Coconut,* page 70

GREEN TEA

Notable nutrients: Water, epigallocatechin or EGCG (a potent antioxidant)

Guards against: Cancer, high LDL (bad) cholesterol, heart disease, arthritis, dental cavities

Drink these too: Black tea, oolong tea

Tips to eat more

- Start your day with a cup of freshly brewed green tea.
- Use brewed green tea to sauté or stir-fry vegetables.
- Use loose green tea leaves in rubs as a coating for meat, fish and poultry.
- Quench your thirst with my *Lemon Green Iced Tea,* page 73

KALE

Notable nutrients: Fibre, vitamin C, vitamin E, vitamin K, calcium, manganese, beta carotene, lutein

Guards against: Cancer, cataracts, macular degeneration, osteoporosis, age-related memory loss

Eat these too: Arugula, beet greens, collard greens, dandelion greens, mustard greens, rapini (broccoli raab), Romaine lettuce, spinach, Swiss chard, turnip greens

Tips to eat more
- Sauté chopped kale with minced garlic and red chili flakes; drizzle with roasted sesame oil just before serving.
- Add raw kale leaves to any soup—homemade or store-bought—and simmer until leaves are tender.
- Toss steamed kale leaves into a pasta salad.
- Snack on *Kale Chips with Sea Salt*, page 90

LENTILS

Notable nutrients: Protein, fibre, folate, iron, magnesium, potassium

Guard against: Cancer, high blood pressure, high LDL cholesterol, heart disease, type 2 diabetes

Eat these too: Black beans, chickpeas (garbanzo beans), fava beans, kidney beans, lima beans, navy beans, pinto beans, soybeans (see section below), split peas

Tips to eat more
- Toss cooked lentils into a marinara pasta sauce for a protein- and fibre-rich meal.
- Add canned lentils, drained and rinsed, to any soup or stew.
- Add cooked lentils to sautéed greens like kale or Swiss chard.
- Try *Lentil Salad with Citrus Yogurt Dressing*, page 161

OATS (large-flake and steel-cut)

Notable nutrients: Whole grain, fibre, magnesium, selenium, avenanthramides (a type of antioxidant)

Guard against: High LDL cholesterol, heart disease, stroke, type 2 diabetes, obesity

Eat this too: Oat bran

Tips to eat more

- Enjoy a bowl of oatmeal for breakfast made with large-flake or steel-cut oats.
- Stir raw large-flake oats into muffin, pancake and waffle batters.
- Mix oats—cooked or raw—into lean ground beef or turkey when making burgers, meatballs or meat loaf.
- Snack on a slice of *Applesauce Oat Loaf*, page 332

QUINOA

Notable nutrients: Whole grain, protein, fibre, folate, iron, magnesium, potassium

Guards against: Cancer, heart disease, stroke, type 2 diabetes, obesity

Eat these too: Amaranth, barley, brown rice, buckwheat, flaxseed, kamut, millet, whole rye, rye berries, whole spelt, whole wheat, wheat berries, wild rice

Tips to eat more

- Enjoy hot quinoa topped with nuts and fresh fruit for a healthy hot breakfast.
- Serve steamed quinoa instead of rice for a quick whole-grain side.
- Toss chilled cooked quinoa with chopped vegetables, herbs and a vinaigrette salad dressing for a tasty whole-grain salad.
- Try *Salmon Quinoa Salad with Spicy Ginger Dressing*, page 168

RED BELL PEPPERS

Notable nutrients: Vitamin C, folate, vitamin B6, potassium, beta carotene

Guard against: Heart disease, stroke, Alzheimer's disease, osteoarthritis, cataracts

Eat these too: Green, yellow and orange bell peppers

Tips to eat more
- Add diced red pepper to scrambled eggs, omelets and frittatas.
- Serve grilled or roasted red peppers drizzled with balsamic vinegar for dinner. Make extra to use in sandwiches.
- Snack on raw red pepper strips with hummus or a bean dip.
- Try *Quinoa Stuffed Red Bell Peppers*, page 205

SALMON

Notable nutrients: Protein, omega-3 fatty acids (DHA and EPA), niacin, vitamin B12, vitamin D, selenium

Guards against: Heart attack, stroke, cancer, Alzheimer's disease, rheumatoid arthritis, macular degeneration

Eat these too: Anchovies, Arctic char, herring, mackerel, sablefish, sardines, trout (these fish are high in omega-3 fats and low in mercury)

Tips to eat more
- Add cooked or smoked salmon to scrambled eggs, frittata and Eggs Benedict.
- Substitute cooked salmon for tuna in a salad Niçoise recipe.
- Grill or bake an extra salmon fillet and save it to serve over a bed of greens for lunch the next day.
- Try *Maple-Glazed Salmon* for a healthy, quick dinner, page 219

SOYBEANS

Notable nutrients: Protein, fibre, folate, calcium, iron, magnesium, potassium, isoflavones (anti-cancer phytochemicals)

Guard against: Cancer, high LDL cholesterol, heart attack, stroke, type 2 diabetes

Eat these too: Soy beverages (unflavoured), tempeh, tofu

Tips to eat more

- Add canned soybeans, drained and rinsed, to salads, soups and chilis.
- Snack on steamed edamame, young green soybeans. (You'll find these in the freezer section of most grocery stores.)
- Enjoy unsalted roasted soybeans (soy nuts) and dried fruit as a midday snack.
- Try my *Zesty Edamame*, page 105

SWEET POTATOES

Notable nutrients: Fibre, vitamin C, vitamin B6, potassium, beta carotene

Guard against: Cancer, heart disease

Eat these too: Carrots, winter squash (acorn, buttercup, butternut, Hubbard pumpkin, spaghetti)

Tips to eat more

- Mash cooked sweet potato with a few tablespoons of orange juice and a dash of cinnamon.
- Make sweet potato chips. Thinly slice sweet potato, brush with olive oil, and sprinkle with salt, pepper and paprika. Bake at 400°F (200°C) until golden and crisp.
- Add puréed cooked sweet potato to muffin, quick bread and pancake batters.
- Serve *Spicy Sweet Potato Wedges* with roasted chicken or meat, page 314

STEP TWO
Practise portion control

The average number of calories in the Canadian diet has increased over the past 20 years. What's more, the portion sizes of many foods—chocolate bars, potato chips, desserts, restaurant meals—have practically doubled in the past two decades. With restaurants, supermarkets and convenience stores selling food in larger-than-life portions, it's no wonder so many people have lost touch with what is an appropriate amount of food to eat.

Portion control is an important part of healthy eating. It's key to maintaining a healthy weight. Even foods that are good for you, like salmon and brown rice, can add excess calories if you overeat. Learning portion control isn't as difficult as you think. Simply translate serving size information into something visual that's easy to remember. Use this guide to help you eyeball an appropriate serving of whatever you eat.

3 oz (90 g) meat, fish, chicken	=	1 deck of playing cards
1.5 oz (45 g) hard cheese	=	3 dominos
1/2 cup (125 ml) cooked pasta or rice	=	1/2 tennis ball
1 small muffin	=	1 large egg
1/2 bagel	=	1 hockey puck
1 pancake	=	a compact disc
1/2 cup (125 ml) cooked vegetables	=	1/2 tennis ball
1 cup (250 ml) salad greens	=	1 tennis ball
1 medium-sized fruit	=	1 tennis ball
1 small baked potato	=	a computer mouse
1 tsp (5 ml) butter, margarine	=	the tip of your thumb or 1 dice
2 tbsp (25 ml) peanut butter	=	1 Ping Pong ball
1/4 cup (50 ml) nuts	=	1 golf ball

MORE PORTION CONTROL TIPS

1. **Use the plate model.** To eat less, you've got to put less food on your plate. Period. Divide your plate into four sections, or quarters. Fill one quarter with protein such as meat, chicken, fish or tofu. Fill another quarter with a whole-grain starchy food like cooked rice, pasta, potato or quinoa. The remaining half of your plate should be filled with vegetables.

2. **Use smaller dishware.** Instead of filling a dinner plate, serve your meal on a luncheon-sized plate (7–9 inches/18–22 cm in diameter). Use small glasses (6–8 ounces/175–250 ml) for milk, juice and other caloric beverages and large glasses for water.

3. **Keep seconds out of sight.** Don't serve "family style." Seeing dishes of food on the table encourages overeating. Keep seconds out of sight. Ideally, cook only one serving. If there's extra food sitting on the stove, you'll be tempted to go back for seconds. If you do make extra food for leftovers or the next day's lunch, store it in the fridge before you sit down to your meal.

4. **Slow down.** It takes roughly 20 minutes for appetite-related hormones to kick in and tell your brain you've had enough to eat. Eating quickly can cause you to eat too much before you're fully aware of it. After every bite, put down your knife and fork, chew thoroughly and sip water. Do not pick up your utensils until your mouth is 100% empty.

5. **Plate your snacks.** Don't snack directly from the package. To see how much you're eating, measure or count out one serving and put it on a plate. Read the Nutrition Facts box to learn how many crackers, potato chips, cookies and so on equal one serving.

STEP THREE
Plan meals in advance

Have you ever skipped breakfast in a rush to get out the door and ended up grabbing a 500-calorie muffin mid morning? Or come home from work, tired and hungry, to an empty fridge and picked up the phone to order in dinner—or grazed your way through the evening? Chances are you've fallen into these traps on occasion. But if your usual approach to eating is to "play it by ear," your diet is probably not as healthy as you'd like. When your stomach growls, it's too easy to grab whatever's fast and convenient—often at the expense of good nutrition.

The key to successful long-term healthy eating is *planning ahead* to make sure you're fuelling your body with nutritious foods. And if you're trying to lose weight, having a meal plan will help ensure your success. Studies show that having a menu plan results in better adherence, more regular meals and fewer snacks, and, of course, having healthier foods in the home.

Nutrition aside, there are other benefits to meal planning. Knowing what you're going to eat takes the stress out of having to figure it out at the end of a hectic day. If the whole family knows what's for dinner in advance, last-minute meal battles can be averted. Planning your meals also saves time and money. Devising a plan means fewer last-minute trips to the grocery store. It also means you'll rely less on restaurant and take-out meals.

You don't have to have a family to reap the benefits of meal planning. As a dietitian in private practice, I have many clients who cook for one and rely on menu planning to stick to their diet. Designating what you're going to eat and when you're going to eat it prevents you from making on-the-fly poor decisions.

I know what you're thinking. Who has the time for what seems like such an overwhelming chore? Planning a week's worth of meals implies time-consuming effort when there's already so much to do juggling the demands of work and family. The truth is, the busier you are, the more important meal planning becomes. And the more often you do it, the easier it gets.

TIME SAVERS: MENU PLANNING TIPS

The following tips will help make your healthy eating efforts easier.

1. **Plan for a week.** Write down a week's worth of dinners. I encourage you to plan breakfasts and lunches too, if appropriate. When planning, consider your family's schedule of extracurricular activities and social events and make allowances for days you don't have a lot of time or get home late.

2. **Create a template.** Make a meal planner form on the computer with columns for each day of the week and boxes for meals. Develop two to four weeks' worth of menus and then rotate them. If breakfast, lunch and snacks could use some improvement, plan these meals as well.

3. **Plan ahead on more leisurely days.** Establish a time and day of the week to plan your weekly menu when you won't be interrupted too much and have time to flag recipes you'd like to try. Meal planning will seem less like a chore and will become part of your weekly routine.

4. **Get input.** Engage your family and partner in the meal planning process to get their buy-in. When everyone has a say about which meals they'd like to eat, they're more likely be open to eating other people's selections. Post your weekly meal plan in a visible spot (e.g. the kitchen fridge) to ward off complaints by reminding everyone what's been agreed upon for dinner.

5. **Make a grocery list.** Once you have your meals planned out, write a grocery list that you can stick to. Having a list means you'll buy only what you need, not extra food you won't use. Grocery shopping once a week saves time and money. Although you might need to restock fresh produce mid week, try to buy all the essentials once weekly. If you don't have time to grocery shop—or just don't enjoy it—consider using a grocery delivery service.

6. **Think convenience.** If you don't mind spending a little extra money, take advantage of time savers at the grocery store—pre-washed salad greens, pre-cut fresh vegetables and fruit, grated cheese, even minced garlic and ginger.

     Or do it yourself in advance to save money. Wash and spin a head of lettuce once you get it home and then store it in a vegetable bag. On the weekend, spend 15 minutes chopping vegetables to have handy for snacks and salads during the week.

7. **Plan for leftovers.** As you plan, think about how you can cook once and make two or more meals out of it. Batch-cook soups, casseroles, pasta sauce or chili on the weekend and freeze to serve on a busy weeknight. Cook an extra portion of chicken at dinner for a simple, no-prep lunch the next day.

STEP FOUR
Shop right to eat healthfully

With your list in hand, you're ready for the grocery store. Going to any large supermarket can be overwhelming. With so many products to choose from—so many labels calling out to you—knowing what to buy can be challenging. Use the quick tips below to make the right choices in the grocery store.

1.   **Shop on a full stomach.** If you shop with a growling stomach, you'll come home with more items than you planned, not all of them good for you. If you can't shop soon after a meal, have a snack before you go.

2.   **Shop the perimeter.** Spend most of your time in the outer aisles of the grocery store. That's where all the healthy foods are—the fruits, vegetables, dairy products, lean meats, poultry and fish and whole-grain breads. Visit only the central aisles for staples such as breakfast cereals, cooking oils, vinegars, spices, flour and canned goods such as beans, tomatoes and tuna fish. Resist the temptation to browse the cookie and snack food aisles.

3.   **Buy perishable foods last.** The order in which you place foods in your grocery cart plays a role in keeping foods safe to eat. Shop for non-perishable items first and save refrigerated and frozen foods for last. At the check-out, ask that meat, poultry and seafood be bagged separately. Raw meat may contaminate other foods if it leaks, which may lead to food poisoning.

4.   **Check expiration dates.** The "packaged on" date is the date the item was packaged by the manufacturer. It's mandatory for meats and tells you when the fresh food was packaged in the store. "Best before" dates refer to quality, not safety. They tell you how long an unopened product will retain its freshness, flavour and high quality. Once opened, best before dates no longer apply. "Use by" and "expiry" dates mean the product should be eaten by the date listed. If these dates on a food have passed, it's safer to discard them.

5. **Buy in season.** Fresh fruit and vegetables taste best when they are bought in season. This usually means they're grown locally. They not only cost less than imported produce but also taste superior.

6. **Buy frozen produce.** When produce is out of season—or out of your budget—don't discount frozen. Frozen fruits and vegetables can actually be higher in nutrients than their fresh counterparts because they're flash-frozen immediately after picking. The fact that some produce arrives at the grocery store up to two weeks after harvest, and often sits on the shelf (or in your refrigerator) for some time thereafter, results in nutrient loss.

7. **Choose low-fat dairy.** To limit your intake of cholesterol-raising saturated fat, buy skim or 1% milk, yogurt and cottage cheese. When buying hard cheese, look for part skim (20% milk fat/MF or less) or skim (7% MF or less). Choose sour cream labelled 7% MF or less.

8. **Select lean meats.** Buy lean cuts of meat such as sirloin, flank steak, eye of the round, beef tenderloin, lean and extra-lean ground beef, pork tenderloin and centre-cut pork chops. Keep in mind that any cut of meat that comes from an animal's stomach area—for example, rib eye steak, rib chops, spareribs—will be high in saturated fat.

    Lean poultry choices include chicken breast, turkey breast and lean and extra-lean ground chicken and turkey.

9. **Use the Nutrition Facts table.** Always choose products lower in sodium, saturated and trans fats and sugars. Look for products that provide more fibre per serving. If you're looking for a lower-calorie product, read the serving size information. If your usual portion is more than the stated serving size, you're consuming more calories than you think.

    Look at the % Daily Value (%DV) to see whether a product has a little or a lot of a specific nutrient. Percent DVs are given for fat, saturated and trans fats (combined), sodium, carbohydrate, fibre, vitamin A, vitamin C, calcium and iron. Foods with a daily value of 5% or less are considered low in a nutrient. That's a good thing for sodium and saturated and trans fats. But for fibre, vitamins and minerals you'll want to choose a brand that supplies at least 15% of the daily value.

10. **Look for 100% whole grains.** When buying bread, crackers and breakfast cereals, look for the claim 100% whole grain on the front of the package. That means the product does not contain any refined flours. If you don't see this statement, read the ingredient list. Look for the words "whole-grain whole wheat flour," whole rye, rye meal, whole oats, brown rice, whole barley and so on as the first ingredient listed. Ingredients are listed in descending order by weight.

   While 100% bran cereals aren't made from the entire grain kernel, you can consider them whole grain since they're a concentrated source of bran that's missing from refined grains. Other whole grains to stock your grocery cart with include whole wheat pasta, brown rice, quinoa, millet, large-flake or steel-cut oats, kasha (buckwheat groats) and ground flaxseed.

11. **Pick foods with less sugar.** An excessive intake of added (refined) sugars has been linked with a higher blood triglyceride (fat) level, a greater calorie intake, a higher body weight and a lower intake of vitamins and minerals. The grams of sugar disclosed on a nutrition label include both refined sugars added during food processing (e.g. sucrose, glucose-fructose, honey, corn syrup) *and* naturally occurring sugars (e.g. fruit or milk sugars).

   Choose breakfast cereals that have no more than 6 to 8 grams of sugar per serving. Exceptions include cereals with dried fruit. When buying packaged baked goods or granola bars, choose products with no more than half the total carbohydrate from sugars. Look for yogurt with no more than 20 grams of sugar per 3/4 cup (175 g) serving. (Remember that some of the sugar in yogurt is lactose, the naturally occurring milk sugar.)

12. **Look for foods low in saturated and trans fat.** A food product with a higher amount of *total* fat grams isn't necessarily unhealthy. Higher-fat foods like vinaigrette salad dressings, packages of nuts and nut butters contain heart-healthy unsaturated fats. What's most important is to look at the grams of combined saturated and trans fats—the two fats linked to a higher risk of heart disease because they raise LDL cholesterol.

   The most saturated and trans fat you should consume in a day depends on your calorie intake. Current guidelines recommend consuming no more than 10% of daily calories from these so-called bad fats. For a 2000-calorie diet, that means no

more than 22 grams of saturated plus trans fat per day (The math: 2000 calories ×
10% = 200 calories; since 1 gram of fat = 9 calories, then 200/9 = 22 grams.) Choose
products with a low %DV for saturated plus trans fats, ideally no more than 10%.

13. **Buy healthy oils.** Choose heart-healthy unsaturated oils such as extra virgin olive,
canola, grapeseed, sunflower and safflower. If you buy margarine, choose a non-
hydrogenated product that is low in saturated fat and free of trans fat. Look for
commercial salad dressings made with extra-virgin olive oil or canola oil. Limit
butter, hard margarine and shortening.

14. **Stock up on healthy canned goods.** Staples worth adding to your grocery cart
include stewed tomatoes, tomato sauce, canned beans, canned tuna and salmon and
canned fruit (in its own juice, not syrup). Look for canned goods low in sodium
or with no salt added. If they are not available in your supermarket, compare brands
to find one lower in sodium. Or ask your grocer to stock them.

15. **Choose prepared foods with fewer ingredients.** When buying prepared foods, look
for ones with shorter ingredient lists. Fewer ingredients usually means fewer synthetic
additives.

STEP FIVE
Store foods right for maximum quality

Once you get your groceries home, it's important to store them properly to retain their highest quality—their freshness, their taste and, of course, their nutrient levels. It's a good idea to clean out your fridge, freezer and pantry at least once a year to discard any products that are past their prime. The tips below will help you store food products with quality and safety in mind.

THE FRIDGE

Check the temperature of your fridge. In order to keep your foods safe when they are being stored, make sure your fridge is set at 40°F (4°C) or colder. And don't crowd the contents of your fridge—air circulation is key to keeping foods cold.

Time limits for storage

Food	Time Limit
Milk	4 to 6 days, opened 7 days after "best before" date, unopened
Yogurt	Check best before date or 7 to 10 days, opened or unopened
Cheese, hard	3 to 4 weeks, opened 3 to 6 months, unopened
Butter	2 to 3 weeks
Eggs	4 weeks
Fresh meat	2 to 4 days
Fresh ground meat	1 to 2 days
Deli meats	3 to 4 days
Fresh chicken, turkey (whole, pieces)	2 to 3 days
Fresh ground poultry	1 to 2 days
Cooked chicken	3 to 4 days
Fresh fish	2 to 3 days
Fresh shellfish (e.g. clams, crab, lobster)	12 to 24 hours
Fresh shellfish (e.g. shrimp, scallops)	1 to 2 days
Leftovers (e.g. soups, stews, casseroles)	3 to 4 days
Jams and jellies	3 to 4 months, opened 12 months, unopened
Mayonnaise	2 to 3 months, opened
Mustard	6 to 8 months, opened
Ketchup	4 months, opened
Salad dressing, bottled	3 months, opened
Salsa	3 months, opened

THE FREEZER

Keep your freezer set at 0°F (–18°C). Like the fridge, don't crowd foods to maintain good air circulation.

Time limits for storage

Butter	6 to 9 months
Cheese, hard, unopened	6 months
Ice cream, sherbet, frozen yogurt	1 to 2 months
Fresh meat, roasts	10 to 12 months
Fresh meat, steaks	10 to 12 months
Fresh meat, pork chops	8 to 10 months
Fresh meat, veal	4 to 5 months
Fresh ground meat	2 to 3 months
Cooked meat	2 to 3 months
Deli meats, unopened	1 to 2 months
Fresh poultry, pieces	6 months
Fresh poultry, whole	12 months
Fresh poultry, ground	2 to 3 months
Cooked poultry	1 to 3 months
Fresh fish, white (e.g. sole, tilapia)	6 months
Fresh fish, fatty (e.g. salmon, trout)	2 to 3 months
Shellfish	2 to 3 months
Soups, stews, casseroles	2 to 3 months

THE PANTRY

Although canned goods have a long shelf life, keep in mind that canned and packaged foods can lose 5% to 20% of their nutritional content every year. Label your canned goods with the date they were purchased. When putting your groceries away, rotate your stock. Move older cans to the front so they are used first and keep newer ones in the back. Store canned foods in a cool, dry, dark place and use within one year of purchasing.

Time limits for storage

Canned fish or shellfish	12 months
Honey	12 months
Jams and jellies	12 months, unopened
Ketchup, barbecue sauce	12 months, unopened
Mustard	2 years, unopened
Salsa	18 months, unopened
Salad dressing, bottled	10 to 12 months, unopened
Vegetable oil	12 months opened, 2 years unopened
Nuts, in shell	4 months, unopened
Peanut butter	9 months, unopened
Ready-to-eat cereal	6 to 12 months (check expiry date on the box), unopened; 3 to 4 months, opened
Oatmeal	12 months, unopened 2 to 3 months, opened
Pasta, dried	2 years
Rice, white	2 years
Rice, brown	1 year
Rice, mixes	6 months

Popcorn, unpopped	2 years
Flour, white	6 to 12 months
Flour, whole wheat	6 to 8 months in the fridge
Sugar, brown	4 months
Sugar, white	2 years
Syrup	12 months
Tea, bags	18 months
Tea, loose leaf	2 years
Spices, whole (e.g. cloves)	1 year opened, 2 years unopened
Spices, ground	6 months opened, 1 to 2 years unopened
Herbs, dried	6 months opened, 1 to 2 years unopened

STEP SIX
Have the right tools for the job

Now that your fridge, freezer and kitchen cupboards are stocked with nutritious foods, it's time to take inventory of your kitchen equipment. Your workspace should be equipped with tools that make healthy meal preparation efficient and enjoyable. I am sure you can think of a piece of cookware or a gadget that you can't be without. Here are some that I recommend:

Nonstick pots, pans and baking sheets—Make sure you buy good quality. I know they're expensive, but they'll last you for years and years. Be sure to use plastic utensils so you don't scratch the surface.

Wok, electric or stovetop—The round bottom allows food to be stir-fried with a minimum of oil. Choose a wide (14 inches/35 cm is good), deep wok so you can keep foods moving while stir-frying.

Steamer baskets—I couldn't be without my steamer baskets. In fact, I have three: two made of stainless steel and one made from bamboo. I steam everything from vegetables to fish to tofu. Steamers are also great for reheating brown rice or quinoa that was cooked in advance.

Blender—A convenient tool for whipping up a quick breakfast smoothie, preparing healthy fruit shakes or puréeing soups.

Food processor—An invaluable tool if you need to shred, chop or grate a large amount of food. They're also great for making hummus and other bean dips.

Stock pot—A must-have for making large batches of soup and chili.

Hot air popper—An essential piece of equipment for making a low-calorie, fat-free popcorn snack.

Sharp knives—If you don't own any, do yourself a favour and invest in a few good knives. You will be amazed at how efficient you become in the kitchen. For me, nothing is more frustrating than using a dull knife to chop foods. It makes for harder work and a slower prep time.

Grater—Buy a multi-plane grater for versatility. Use it for carrots and zucchini, lemon and orange zest and Parmesan cheese.

Digital instant-read meat thermometer—This tool allows you to cook your meat to just the way to like it, and safely too.

Food scale—You'll want a good kitchen scale to help you keep your food portions in check. The only way to know exactly how much meat or chicken you're eating is to weigh it.

Larger appliances—I take full advantage of the *barbecue* in the warmer weather. Many people can't live without their *microwave oven*. A microwave will allow you to reheat or defrost in minutes, and it's handy to have for cooking vegetables and fish. A *slow cooker* is also a handy appliance to have. It allows you to enjoy a hot, home-prepared meal with minimal effort.

If you're cooking for one, you might invest in a *toaster oven*. I have many clients who toast, bake and grill foods in this space-saving appliance. Portable *indoor electric grills* are popular too. They come in many shapes and sizes; some wipe up easily, while cleaning other models can be cumbersome. Do your homework before you invest.

STEP SEVEN
Use healthy cooking methods

Eating healthfully goes beyond selecting the right foods to eat. It also requires cooking foods in such a way that maintains their nutritional value while not adding excessive amounts of calories and fat. Consider, for example, that one tablespoon (15 ml) of oil adds 120 calories to a meal. A 2000-calorie diet shouldn't get more than 700 calories from fat each day (no more than 30% to 35% of daily calories from fat). The cooking techniques described below seal in flavour while reducing or eliminating the need for fat.

Braising. This cooking method is usually used for meats that need longer cooking times to become tender. Once meat is browned, it is then cooked in a small amount of liquid in a covered container at a low heat, typically 300°F to 325°F (150°C to 160°C). Foods can be braised in the oven or on the stovetop.

The amount of liquid used will vary but generally covers one-third to two-thirds of the food. Water or low-sodium broth can be used. Braising can also be used for vegetables.

Grilling. This is a low-fat way to prepare meat, poultry and fish as the fat drips away from the food. Foods can be grilled on the barbecue or an indoor grill. Before grilling, trim away visible fat from meat. If you're planning to grill vegetables on the barbecue, I recommend using a grill basket to prevent smaller pieces from falling through the rack.

One drawback exists with this cooking method: Grilling (and broiling and frying) meat at high temperatures creates compounds called heterocyclic amines (HCAs) that have been linked with cancer in animal studies. They're formed when amino acids (the building blocks of protein) and creatine (a natural compound found in muscle meats) react at high temperatures. I'm not suggesting you ban grilled meat from your diet. It wouldn't be summer without the taste of barbecued foods. You need to consider how often you grill, the types of foods you grill, how well done you cook meat and what other foods you add to your plate. Practise the following tips to help minimize the formation of HCAs when you barbecue.

Safe Grilling Tips

Keep portions small. For safer grilled meats, keep meat portions small to cut down on grilling time. Instead of grilling a whole steak, make kebabs since they cook more quickly.

Pre-cook meats. For meats that require longer cooking times, partially cook in the microwave, drain away the juices and then finish on the barbecue. Research has shown that microwaving meat for two minutes prior to grilling can result in a 90% reduction in HCA content.

Marinate meats. Briefly marinating meat for 10 minutes before grilling can reduce the formation of HCAs substantially. A marinade may act as a barrier, keeping flames from touching the meat. Certain ingredients in a marinade— vinegar, citrus juice, vegetable oil or spices—may also prevent carcinogen formation.

Lower the temperature. Cooking at a lower temperature will decrease the formation of HCAs. Turn the gas down or wait for the charcoal to become low-burning embers.

Flip burgers often. Research has shown that burgers cooked at a lower temperature and turned every minute while cooking had 75% to 95% fewer carcinogens than burgers turned only once after five minutes of cooking. Beef burgers must be cooked to an internal temperature of 160°F (71°C) and poultry burgers to 175°F (80°C).

Add fruit to your burgers. Research from Michigan State University determined that adding one cup (250 ml) of mashed cherries to a pound (454 g) of ground meat suppressed carcinogen formation by 90%. Flavonoids, natural compounds found in cherries and berries, can block the formation of HCAs.

Poaching. I highly recommend this cooking method for fish. Poaching results in a tender, moist piece of fish. To poach foods, gently simmer ingredients in water, low-sodium broth or fruit juice until they're cooked through. The liquid should just cover the food. Never let the liquid boil. Keep the pan partially uncovered so steam can escape and the liquid does not boil.

Roasting. Dry heat cooking, like roasting, is another cooking method with nutrition in mind. Fat does not need to be used, and if you place the meat or poultry on a rack in the roasting pan, fat in the food can drip away. Sometimes, food will need to be basted to prevent it from drying out. Use lemon juice, fruit juice, low-sodium broth or wine to baste foods.

Sautéing. This method is most often used for vegetables, but you can also sauté small, thin pieces of meat and chicken. Sautéing means cooking food quickly in a minimal amount of oil—you want to use just enough oil to prevent sticking. Preheat the pan before adding food. Don't overcrowd the pan so foods cook evenly and quickly. You may use cooking spray, low-sodium broth or water in place of oil.

Steaming. This is by far the best way to cook vegetables—it retains colour, flavour, nutrients and antioxidants and does not require any fat! In fact, steaming retains significantly more nutrients in vegetables than boiling or microwaving.

To steam, place a steamer basket with food in a pot with a little boiling water and cover. Cook until the vegetables are just tender. Watch the cooking time to prevent overcooking. If you want to add flavour to the food you are steaming, use a flavourful liquid instead of water or add herbs to the water.

Stir-frying. This method cooks uniformly small-sized foods quickly over high heat in a small amount of oil. The high heat and constant stirring of the food prevent it from sticking and burning. Stir-frying does a great job of preserving the crisp texture and bright colour of vegetables.

For best results, coat the wok or large nonstick frying pan with a small amount of oil such as canola, peanut or grapeseed oil. (These oils have what's called a high smoke point, meaning they're well suited for high-heat cooking; extra-virgin olive oil has a lower smoke point and starts to burn at a lower temperature.) Preheat the pan to a high temperature and then add the food. Stir foods rapidly during cooking. When the meat is almost done, add the vegetables. Don't overfill the pan or wok.

STEP EIGHT
Handle foods safely

Foodborne illness has been a growing concern over the past decade, with reports of contaminated spinach, tomatoes, apple juice, berries, bean sprouts and deli meats. While food processing has been blamed for many of these outbreaks, the fact remains that the majority of food safety issues occur at home—and many can be prevented by handling foods safely.

Food poisoning is caused by bacteria, bacterial toxins and moulds in foods. Bacteria are normally present everywhere—in the air, soil and water and in people and animals. Food usually becomes contaminated from poor hygiene practices and sloppy food preparation. Food stored at the wrong temperature also increases the likelihood of contamination. Once introduced into food, bacteria flourish at temperatures between 40°F (4°C) and 140°F (60°C), a temperature range known as the "danger zone."

Common symptoms of food poisoning include stomach cramps, nausea, vomiting, diarrhea and sometimes chills and fever. Symptoms can appear a few hours after eating the food or after several days, when they are no longer clearly linked to a particular food. That's why many cases are never reported—people often pass symptoms off as the stomach flu, stress or overeating. Because you can't see or smell food poisoning bacteria, there are no clues as to a harmful food. The only strategy to prevent food poisoning is to handle foods safely in the first place.

Repeatedly, we've been advised to wash our hands thoroughly, rinse fresh produce, check best before dates and cook burgers to a safe temperature. But knowing about safe food-handling practices and putting them into practice are two different things. Research suggests that many of us are not putting these instructions into practice. Take a moment to review the food safety motto: clean, separate, chill, cook!

CLEAN

Guarding against foodborne illness starts with proper hygiene. Practise the following tips in your kitchen every day:

- Always wash your hands for 20 seconds with soap and hot water before you handle food, repeatedly while preparing food and again once you've finished. Ditto for utensils and cooking surfaces.

- Use a disinfectant cleaner or a mixture of bleach and water on countertops and cutting boards for added protection against bacteria (1 tsp/5 ml bleach per 3 cups/750 ml water). Use paper towels to wipe kitchen counters or change dishcloths daily to avoid the prospect of spreading bacteria.

- Wash fresh produce (even packaged prewashed produce!) thoroughly under cool running water to remove dirt and residue.

- Scrub fruits and vegetables that have firm surfaces such as oranges, melons, cucumbers, potatoes and carrots.

- Cut away any damaged or bruised areas on produce; these are places where bacteria can thrive.

SEPARATE

Bacteria can be unknowingly spread from food to people, from people to food or from one food to another. The spread of bacteria from one thing to another is called cross-contamination. Here's how to prevent it from occurring in your kitchen:

- Separate raw meat, poultry and seafood from other foods in your shopping cart and in your fridge.

- Use one cutting board for fresh produce and another one for raw meat, poultry and seafood.

- To prevent juices from raw meat, poultry and seafood from dripping onto other foods in the fridge, store them in plastic bags or sealed containers on the bottom shelf.

- Never put cooked food back on the same plate or cutting board that previously held raw food.

- Sauce that's been used to marinate raw meat, poultry or seafood should not be used on cooked foods. Boil leftover marinade for one minute or prepare extra for basting cooked food.

CHILL

Storing foods at the correct temperature will help keep them safe. You learned earlier that your fridge should be set at 40°F (4°C) or colder and the freezer at 0°F (–18°C). Foods should not be left in the danger zone (40°F to 140°F/4°C to 60°C) for more than two hours. In hot weather (90°F/32°C), don't leave foods sitting out for more than one hour.

- Refrigerate or freeze perishables, prepared foods and leftovers within two hours or less.

- Cool hot food as quickly as possible by storing food in shallow containers and stirring hot foods occasionally to speed up cooling. You don't need to cool hot food before you put it in the fridge, but very hot food (e.g. simmering soup) can be left out for 30 minutes before refrigerating.

- Always marinate foods in the refrigerator.

- Defrost foods in the refrigerator, in cold water or in the microwave if you will be cooking it right away. Never defrost at room temperature.

- Don't crowd the contents of your fridge—air circulation is important for keeping foods cold.

- When eating outdoors, keep all perishable foods chilled right up until serving time. Pack foods in a well-insulated cooler with plenty of ice or frozen gel packs. Pack foods first that you're likely to use last. Take two coolers—one for cold drinks and another for perishable foods. Transport the cooler in the back seat of an air-conditioned car, not in the hot trunk.

COOK

The only way to kill harmful bacteria is to cook foods to the proper internal temperature. To keep foods out of the danger zone (40°F to 140°F/4°C to 60°C), serve them immediately after cooking.

- When serving hot foods buffet-style, use chafing dishes, crock pots and warming trays. Use a food thermometer to keep hot foods at 140°F/60°C or higher. Keep buffet portions small and refill from back-up dishes stored in the oven or fridge.

- Make sure soups, chilis and hot dips are piping hot before serving.

- When using a microwave, cover food, stir and rotate to ensure thorough cooking.

- Use a digital instant-read meat thermometer to check the doneness of foods near the end of cooking. These thermometers give a temperature reading rather than just a doneness range. Leave the thermometer in the meat for at least 30 seconds.

Recommended internal cooking temperatures

Ground beef, pork, veal (e.g. burgers)	160°F (71°C)
Ground chicken, turkey	176°F (80°C)
Beef, rare	140°F (60°C)
Beef, medium	160°F (71°C)
Beef, well done	170°F (77°C)
Pork chops	160°F (71°C)
Pork roasts	160°F (71°C)
Cooked ham, to reheat	140°F (60°C)
Chicken/turkey, whole, stuffed	180°F (82°C)
Chicken, whole, unstuffed	180°F (82°C)
Turkey, whole, unstuffed	170°F (77°C)
Chicken/turkey, pieces	170°F (77°C)
Stuffing, cooked alone	165°F (74°C)
Egg dishes	160°F (71°C)
Leftovers, reheated	165°F (74°C)

Source: Canadian Partnership for Consumer Food Safety Education, www.canfightbac.org

Breakfast & Brunch

Almond and Berry Yogurt Breakfast Parfait

I like to make this parfait the night before and refrigerate it overnight for a quick and healthy breakfast to start my busy day. This recipe can also double as a light dessert. Substitute Greek yogurt for extra protein.

Serves 4

2 cups (500 ml) low-fat (1% MF or less) plain or vanilla yogurt

1 tbsp (15 ml) honey

1 tbsp (15 ml) lemon zest

2 cups (500 ml) mixed fresh berries, such as blueberries, sliced strawberries or raspberries

1/2 cup (125 ml) slivered almonds

In a small bowl, whisk together yogurt, honey and zest.

In 4 parfait glasses (or tall glasses), layer berries, almonds and yogurt mixture.

Refrigerate until ready to serve.

NUTRITION
Per serving: 222 cal, 11 g pro, 9 g total fat (1 g saturated fat), 27 g carb, 4 g fibre, 2 mg chol, 93 mg sodium

Apple Cinnamon Oatmeal

This high-fibre, high-protein breakfast will keep you feeling satisfied for hours, especially after a morning workout. It doesn't require much cooking time and it's an excellent source of cholesterol-lowering soluble fibre.

Serves 2

1 cup (250 ml) low-fat (1% MF or less) milk or soy milk

1/2 cup (125 ml) quick cooking oats

1 apple, peeled and finely diced

1 tbsp (15 ml) honey

1/2 tsp (2 ml) cinnamon

1/4 tsp (1 ml) vanilla extract

In a small saucepan, combine milk, oats, apple, honey, cinnamon and vanilla. Bring to a boil; reduce heat to minimum and continue to stir until oatmeal has thickened, about 90 seconds. Remove from heat and serve immediately.

NUTRITION
Per 3/4 cup (175 ml) serving: 207 cal, 8 g pro, 3 g total fat (1 g saturated fat), 39 g carb, 3 g fibre, 6 mg chol, 57 mg sodium

Banana Flax Pancakes

This recipe makes a very thin batter, similar to that of crepes. The trick to these pancakes is to get the pan good and hot before adding the batter. They have a nutty flavour thanks to the flaxseeds. Top them with fresh berries, vanilla low-fat yogurt and a drizzle of maple syrup.

Makes 4 large pancakes

1/2 cup (125 ml) all-purpose flour

1/2 cup (125 ml) whole wheat flour

1/4 cup (50 ml) quick cooking oats

2 tbsp (25 ml) ground flaxseed

2 tbsp (25 ml) whole flaxseed

1/4 tsp (1 ml) salt

2 tsp (10 ml) baking powder

1 cup (250 ml) low-fat (1% MF or less) milk or soy milk

2 medium eggs

1 banana, mashed

1 tsp (5 ml) vanilla extract

4 tsp (20 ml) canola oil

In a large mixing bowl, combine all-purpose and whole wheat flour, oats, ground flaxseed, whole flaxseed, salt and baking powder.

In a separate bowl, whisk together milk, eggs, banana and vanilla.

Add dry ingredients to wet ingredients. Briskly whisk batter for 10 to 15 seconds until mixed thoroughly.

Heat 1 tsp (5 ml) canola oil in a skillet over high heat.

Add one-quarter of the batter to the hot pan and reduce heat to medium-high. Quickly tilt the skillet to spread out the batter as thinly as possible. When bubbles appear on the surface of the batter, about 90 seconds, flip and continue to cook until golden brown, about another 90 seconds.

Heat 1 tsp (5 ml) of oil before adding batter for each remaining pancake.

NUTRITION

Per pancake: 307 cal, 11 g pro, 12 g total fat (2 g saturated fat), 40 g carb, 6 g fibre, 85 mg chol, 357 mg sodium

Blueberry Walnut Muesli with Rolled Oats and Flax

This hearty muesli is delicious when combined with plain or vanilla yogurt and fresh blueberries. Make the muesli ahead of time and store in an airtight container. For a nuttier flavour, first toast the oats, rye flakes, wheat germ and walnuts for five to seven minutes at 350°F (180°C) on a baking sheet until lightly brown and fragrant.

Serves 6

1 cup (250 ml) large-flake rolled oats

1/2 cup (125 ml) rye flakes, such as Bob's Red Mill Creamy Rye Flakes

1/2 cup (125 ml) wheat germ

1/2 cup (125 ml) dried cranberries

1/4 cup (50 ml) whole flaxseed

1/4 cup (50 ml) coarsely chopped walnuts

1 tsp (5 ml) cinnamon

3 cups (750 ml) low-fat (1% MF or less) plain or vanilla yogurt

1-1/2 cups (375 ml) fresh blueberries

In a large mixing bowl, toss together rolled oats, rye flakes, wheat germ, cranberries, flaxseed, walnuts and cinnamon.

Store in an airtight container for up to a month, or serve immediately with yogurt and fresh blueberries.

NUTRITION
Per 1/2 cup (125 ml) serving of dry muesli: 285 cal, 11 g pro, 9 g total fat (1 g saturated fat), 43 g carb, 9 g fibre, 0 mg chol, 3 mg sodium
Per 1/2 cup (125 ml) serving of muesli with 1/2 cup (125 ml) yogurt and 1/4 cup (50 ml) blueberries: 368 cal, 18 g pro, 9 g total fat (1 g saturated fat), 57 g carb, 10 g fibre, 2 mg chol, 92 mg sodium

Breakfast Banana Split with Toasted Oats and Coconut

This banana split has everything you need for a healthy start to the day—whole grains, fresh fruit and low-fat dairy. Toasting the oats and coconut may seem like extra work, but it's worth the effort as it gives this breakfast a delicious nutty flavour. If you're short on time, toast the oats and coconut the night before and store them in an airtight container.

Serves 1

2 tbsp (25 ml) quick cooking oats

1 tbsp (15 ml) shredded unsweetened coconut

1 banana, peeled and cut in half lengthwise or sliced

1/2 cup (125 ml) low-fat (1% MF or less) plain or vanilla yogurt

1/2 cup (125 ml) sliced strawberries

1 tsp (5 ml) honey

Preheat oven to 350°F (180°C).

Place oats and coconut on a baking sheet; place in oven and toast for 5 minutes, or until lightly brown. Remove from heat and cool.

Meanwhile, in a small bowl top banana with yogurt and strawberries; sprinkle with toasted oats and coconut. Drizzle with honey. Serve immediately.

NUTRITION
Per serving: 310 cal, 10 g pro, 7 g total fat (5 g saturated fat), 56 g carb, 6 g fibre, 7 mg chol, 91 mg sodium

Tip: Mix it up! Use other grains instead of oatmeal, such as rolled spelt flakes or rye flakes.

Cinnamon Flax French Toast

French toast was my favourite weekend breakfast growing up. This easy recipe uses egg whites instead of a whole egg, making it virtually cholesterol free! Choose 100% whole-grain bread for extra fibre.

Serves 2

4 egg whites, whisked

2 tbsp (25 ml) low-fat (1% MF or less) milk or soy milk

2 tbsp (25 ml) ground flaxseed

2 tsp (10 ml) cinnamon

1 tsp (5 ml) orange zest

2 tsp (10 ml) canola oil

4 slices whole-grain bread

In a shallow dish, whisk together egg whites, milk, flaxseed, cinnamon and orange zest until frothy.

Meanwhile, heat oil in a skillet over medium heat.

Dip slices of bread into egg mixture and place in hot skillet. Cook over medium heat until lightly brown, turning once.

NUTRITION
Per 2 slices: 281 cal, 15 g pro, 10 g total fat (1 g saturated fat), 35 g carb, 7 g fibre, 1 mg chol, 425 mg sodium

Tip: A drizzle of maple syrup and fresh blueberries, or no-added-sugar jam, taste great on this French toast.

Cranberry Apple Granola

My clients love this recipe. The ginger gives this granola extra zing. Enjoy this whole-grain cereal for breakfast with milk or soy beverage or sprinkle it over yogurt as a midday snack.

Serves 18

4 cups (1 L) large-flake rolled oats

1/4 cup (50 ml) slivered almonds

1/4 cup (50 ml) sunflower seeds

1/2 cup (125 ml) unsweetened applesauce

1/3 cup (75 ml) honey

2 tsp (10 ml) cinnamon

2 tsp (10 ml) canola oil

1/2 tsp (2 ml) ground ginger

1 cup (250 ml) dried apples, chopped

1/2 cup (125 ml) dried cranberries

Preheat oven to 375°F (190°C).

In a large mixing bowl, combine oats, almonds and sunflower seeds.

In a separate bowl combine applesauce, honey, cinnamon, oil and ginger. Pour over oat mixture and mix well, until coated evenly.

Evenly spread mixture on a baking sheet and bake for 15 to 20 minutes. Gently shake pan; bake an additional 5 to 10 minutes or until dry.

When granola is cool, toss with dried apples and cranberries.

Store in an airtight container.

NUTRITION
Per 1/3 cup (75 ml) serving: 201 cal, 7 g pro, 5 g total fat (1 g saturated fat), 34 g carb, 5 g fibre, 0 mg chol, 6 mg sodium

Egg White Frittata with Goat Cheese and Red Pepper

This colourful frittata uses egg whites instead of whole eggs, so it's very low in saturated fat and virtually cholesterol-free. This dish makes for a delicious breakfast, lunch or dinner. I also like to use roasted red pepper in this recipe—it goes so well with the goat cheese.

Serves 4

2 tsp (10 ml) canola oil

1/2 cup (125 ml) chopped red onion

1 cup (250 ml) asparagus spears, cut into 1-inch (2.5 cm) pieces

1 clove garlic, crushed

1 cup (250 ml) chopped red bell pepper

6 egg whites

1/4 tsp (1 ml) sea salt

1/4 cup (50 ml) crumbled goat cheese

Preheat oven to 375°F (190°C).

Heat oil in a 10-inch (25 cm) ovenproof skillet over medium heat. Add onions; sauté about 4 to 5 minutes or until soft. Add asparagus spears; sauté another 4 to 5 minutes. Add garlic and red pepper; sauté 1 minute.

Meanwhile, in a mixing bowl, whisk egg whites and salt until frothy and white, about 30 seconds.

Add egg whites and goat cheese to skillet; stir for 30 seconds.

Place skillet in oven and bake for 10 to 12 minutes or until eggs are set.

NUTRITION
Per serving: 90 cal, 8 g pro, 4 g total fat (1 g saturated fat), 7 g carb, 2 g fibre, 3 mg chol, 252 mg sodium

Field Berry Almond Pancakes

These hearty, stick-to-your-ribs pancakes are packed with oats, almonds and berries. As a result, they're fibre-rich and will help you feel satisfied all morning long. Their small size means they're ideal for freezing and popping in the toaster for a quick weekday breakfast before you dash out the door.

Serves 4

3/4 cup (175 ml) whole wheat flour

1/4 cup (50 ml) all-purpose flour

1/3 cup (75 ml) quick cooking oats

1/4 cup (50 ml) sliced almonds

1 tsp (5 ml) baking powder

1/4 tsp (1 ml) baking soda

1/4 tsp (1 ml) nutmeg

1/8 tsp (0.5 ml) salt

4 egg whites

3/4 cup (175 ml) low-fat (1% MF or less) plain yogurt

1/4 cup (50 ml) low-fat (1% MF or less) milk or soy milk

1/2 tsp (2 ml) almond extract

1-1/2 tsp (7 ml) canola oil

1/2 cup (125 ml) blueberries

1/2 cup (125 ml) raspberries

In a large mixing bowl, combine flours, oats, almonds, baking powder, baking soda, nutmeg and salt. Set aside.

In another mixing bowl, whisk together egg whites till white and fluffy, about 30 seconds. Add yogurt, milk and almond extract; whisk to combine. Add dry ingredients to bowl, and whisk together until ingredients are just combined.

Heat oil in a large skillet over medium-high heat. When pan is hot, reduce heat to medium and pour 1/4 cup (50 ml) batter into pan to make each pancake. Sprinkle each pancake with 2 tbsp (25 ml) berries. When bubbles start to appear at edges of pancakes, about 4 to 5 minutes, flip and continue cooking for another 4 to 5 minutes or until pancakes are brown.

Remove from heat and serve immediately.

Makes 8 pancakes.

NUTRITION
Per 2 pancakes: 255 cal, 13 g pro, 7 g total fat (1 g saturated fat), 38 g carb, 6 g fibre, 2 mg chol, 401 mg sodium

Tip: Fresh or frozen berries work equally well in this recipe.

Fresh Fruit Salad with Ginger and Mint

The combination of fruit, ginger and mint is so delicious. Serve this fruit salad for brunch, or make it ahead of time for a quick breakfast during the week. Be creative—any type of fresh fruit works well, including pears, oranges and bananas.

Serves 4

1 cup (250 ml) sliced strawberries

1 cup (250 ml) fresh blueberries

1 cup (250 ml) diced apple (with skin on)

1 cup (250 ml) sliced kiwi

1 tbsp (15 ml) freshly squeezed lime juice

2 tsp (10 ml) minced fresh ginger root

1 tbsp (15 ml) finely chopped fresh mint

In a large bowl, combine strawberries, blueberries, apple, kiwi, lime juice and ginger. Garnish with chopped mint. Serve cold.

NUTRITION

Per 1 cup (250 ml) serving: 76 cal, 1 g pro, 1 g total fat (0 g saturated fat), 19 g carb, 4 g fibre, 0 mg chol, 3 mg sodium

Fruit Cocktail with Orange Ginger Marinade

The sauce for this fruit cocktail is made by boiling orange juice, honey, ginger and vanilla. So easy and so delicious! If you have time, make this a day in advance and let the fruit marinate overnight. Substitute any other fresh fruit you like if you don't have kiwi, pineapple or mango.

Serves 4

1 cup (250 ml) unsweetened orange juice

2 tbsp (25 ml) honey

2 pieces of ginger, peeled (about 1/4-inch/0.5 cm thick and 2 inches/5 cm long)

1/8 tsp (0.5 ml) vanilla extract

2 cups (500 ml) sliced kiwi

2 cups (500 ml) diced pineapple

2 cups (500 ml) sliced mango

1 sprig fresh mint

In a small saucepan, combine orange juice, honey, ginger and vanilla. Bring to a boil over high heat; continue to boil for 5 minutes. Set aside to cool.

In a large bowl, combine kiwi, pineapple and mango. Drizzle with orange ginger sauce; garnish with mint. Serve cold.

NUTRITION
Per 1-1/2 cup (375 ml) serving: 159 cal, 2 g pro, 1 g total fat (0 g saturated fat), 40 g carb, 4 g fibre, 0 mg chol, 4 mg sodium

Mushroom and Arugula Mini Frittatas

These mini frittatas are a crowd pleaser at brunch but they also double as easy hors d'oeuvres. They have a tendency to stick to the pan, so be sure to liberally oil the muffin cups as suggested. They also work well with finely diced ham and crumbled goat cheese.

Serves 8

1 tbsp (15 ml) olive oil

1/2 cup (125 ml) thinly sliced leek, white part only (about 1 medium leek)

2 cups (500 ml) sliced brown mushrooms, such as cremini

4 cloves garlic, crushed

1 cup (250 ml) tightly packed arugula

8 medium eggs

1/4 tsp (1 ml) sea salt

Freshly ground black pepper, to taste

Preheat oven to 350°F (180°C).

Generously grease a muffin tin (with 8 large muffin cups).

Heat oil in a skillet over medium heat. When pan is hot, add leeks and mushrooms; sauté for 10 minutes until mushrooms begin to dry out. Add garlic and arugula; continue to sauté for another minute until arugula is wilted and garlic is fragrant. Remove from heat and set aside.

In a large mixing bowl, whisk together eggs until light and frothy, about 30 seconds. Add salt, pepper and the arugula-mushroom mixture; stir to combine.

Using a ladle, gently scoop contents into prepared muffin tin.

Bake for 18 minutes, or until eggs are set and begin to puff up. Using a rubber spatula or knife, gently loosen the edges of the frittatas as soon as they come out of the oven; serve immediately.

NUTRITION
Per mini frittata: 100 cal, 7 g pro, 6 g total fat (2 g saturated fat), 4 g carb, 1 g fibre, 164 mg chol, 132 mg sodium

Mushroom Leek Omelet

Leeks are a great substitute for onions. I really like the mild flavour they add to dishes. Here they're combined with brown mushrooms and Swiss cheese for a decadent-tasting morning meal that's packed with vitamins E and K and potassium.

Serves 2

2 medium eggs

2 medium egg whites

1/8 tsp (0.5 ml) sea salt

Freshly ground black pepper, to taste

1 tbsp (15 ml) canola oil

1 cup (250 ml) thinly sliced leek, white part only

1 cup (250 ml) sliced brown mushrooms, such as portobello or cremini

2 cloves garlic, crushed

1/4 cup (50 ml) shredded low-fat Swiss cheese

In a large mixing bowl, whisk together eggs, egg whites, salt and pepper until slightly frothy, about 30 seconds. Set aside.

Heat oil in a skillet over medium heat. When pan is hot, add leeks and mushrooms; sauté for 8 to 10 minutes. Add garlic; sauté for another minute.

Pour egg mixture over leeks and mushrooms. Gently lift the edges of the omelet with a spatula to let uncooked egg run underneath. Continue to cook until eggs are set, about 4 to 5 minutes. Run a spatula around the edges of the omelet and under it to loosen it from the pan. Sprinkle half of the omelet with cheese, and then gently fold in half. Continue to cook for 3 to 4 minutes, or until eggs are firm.

Remove from heat and serve immediately.

NUTRITION
Per 1/2 omelet: 230 cal, 17 g pro, 12 g total fat (2 g saturated fat), 13 g carb, 2 g fibre, 170 mg chol, 310 mg sodium

Poached Eggs with Sautéed Mushrooms and Spinach

Making poached eggs can be a bit daunting if you've never tried it before. But once you get the hang of it, it's one of the healthiest ways to enjoy eggs since they require no added fat. You can also use an egg poacher if you prefer. This recipe is great for brunch when you're entertaining, but I also make it for a quick lunch or dinner.

Serves 4

1 tbsp (15 ml) white vinegar

1 tbsp (15 ml) olive oil

4 green onions, sliced

2 cups (500 ml) sliced brown mushrooms, such as cremini

4 cloves garlic, crushed

4 cups (1 L) coarsely chopped spinach

Pinch sea salt, or to taste

Pinch red pepper flakes, or to taste

4 medium eggs

4 slices whole-grain bread, toasted

Freshly ground black pepper, to taste

Fill a saucepan with 4 inches (10 cm) of water and vinegar. Bring to a boil over high heat.

Meanwhile, heat oil in a skillet over medium heat. When pan is hot, add onions and mushrooms; sauté for 6 to 8 minutes until mushrooms begin to dry out. Add garlic, spinach, salt and red pepper flakes; sauté for another 3 to 4 minutes, or until spinach is wilted. Remove from heat; set aside.

When water is boiling, reduce heat to medium-low to a gentle simmer. Break one egg at a time into a small heat-proof bowl or metal measuring cup. Gently tip bowl (or measuring cup) into water and carefully slip egg into water. Use a spoon to gently push the whites toward the yolk. Quickly repeat with remaining eggs.

Cook eggs for 3 to 5 minutes, or until desired doneness (3 minutes will yield runny yolks; 5 minutes results in a poached egg with a firmer yolk). Remove eggs from pan with a slotted spoon, allowing water to drain off eggs.

Evenly distribute the spinach-mushroom mixture among the four pieces of toast.

Place each egg on top of spinach-mushroom mixture on toast. Season with black pepper. Serve immediately.

NUTRITION
Per poached egg and piece of toast: 202 cal, 12 g pro, 9 g total fat (2 g saturated fat), 20 g carb, 3 g fibre, 164 mg chol, 319 mg sodium

Tip: For an almost effortless breakfast, make the sautéed mushrooms and spinach a day in advance. That way all you have to do is poach the eggs and toast the bread the next morning.

Red Pepper and Asparagus Omelet

Sautéed red bell pepper, red onion and asparagus team up to deliver plenty of flavour and colour in this low-calorie omelet. One serving has only 150 calories and is an excellent source of vitamins C, E and K. Make it for breakfast, or enjoy it as a quick weeknight dinner when you're short on time.

Serves 2

2 medium eggs

2 medium egg whites

1/8 tsp (0.5 ml) sea salt

Freshly ground black pepper, to taste

2 tsp (10 ml) canola oil

1/4 cup (50 ml) finely chopped red onion

1/2 cup (125 ml) thinly sliced red pepper

1/2 cup (125 ml) bite-sized pieces of asparagus stems and spears

2 cloves garlic, crushed

In a large mixing bowl, whisk together eggs, egg whites, salt and pepper until slightly frothy, about 30 seconds. Set aside.

Heat oil in a skillet over high heat. When pan is hot, add onions and reduce heat to medium; sauté for 8 to 10 minutes. Add red pepper and asparagus; sauté for another 4 to 5 minutes. Add garlic; sauté for another minute.

Pour egg mixture over vegetables. Cook over medium heat, lifting the edges of the omelet to let uncooked egg run underneath. Continue to cook until eggs are set, about 4 to 5 minutes. Run a spatula around the edges of the omelet and under it to loosen it from the pan. Using the edge of a spatula, cut omelet in half; gently flip each half and continue to cook for another 3 to 4 minutes or until eggs are firm.

Remove from heat and serve immediately.

NUTRITION
Per serving (1/2 omelet): 150 cal, 10 g pro, 9 g total fat (2 g saturated fat), 7 g carb, 2 g fibre, 164 mg chol, 255 mg sodium

Rye Breakfast Bars with Flaxseed and Cranberries

If you need a portable breakfast to go, this recipe is for you! Make it on the weekend and store these high-fibre breakfast bars in the fridge (they'll keep for five days). Rye flakes give these bars a nutty flavour I really like, but other grains like spelt flakes or large-flake rolled oats work just as well.

Serves 12

1-1/2 cups (375 ml) rye flakes, such as Bob's Red Mill Creamy Rye Flakes

1/2 cup (125 ml) all-purpose flour

1/2 cup (125 ml) brown sugar

1/4 cup (50 ml) ground flaxseed

2 tbsp (25 ml) whole flaxseed

2 tsp (10 ml) cinnamon

1 tsp (5 ml) ground ginger

1/2 tsp (2 ml) baking powder

1/2 tsp (2 ml) baking soda

1/4 tsp (1 ml) salt

1 cup (250 ml) sweetened applesauce

3 tbsp (50 ml) canola oil

1 medium egg

2 tsp (10 ml) vanilla extract

1/3 cup (75 ml) dried cranberries

1/4 cup (50 ml) sliced almonds

Preheat oven to 350°F (180°C).

Lightly grease a 9 × 9 inch (2.5 L) metal cake pan.

In a large mixing bowl, combine rye flakes, flour, brown sugar, ground flaxseed, whole flaxseed, cinnamon, ginger, baking powder, baking soda and salt.

In another mixing bowl, combine applesauce, oil, egg and vanilla.

Pour wet ingredients over dry ingredients and mix well to combine. Add cranberries and almonds; stir to combine.

Pour batter into cake pan. Bake for 30 minutes, or until cooked through, and a knife inserted in the centre comes out clean.

Serve warm or cold.

NUTRITION
Per bar: 198 cal, 4 g pro, 7 g total fat (1 g saturated fat), 31 g carb, 4 g fibre, 14 mg chol, 125 mg sodium

Smoked Salmon and Dill Frittata

Taste-testers love this recipe! I love to serve this for brunch when I have overnight guests at my cottage. If you don't have fresh dill on hand, substitute 1 tbsp (15 ml) dried dill. The recipe also works well with canned salmon if you don't have smoked salmon.

Serves 6

8 medium eggs

Freshly ground black pepper, to taste

1 tbsp (15 ml) olive oil

1 small onion, cut into thin wedges

7 oz (200 g) smoked salmon, cut into 1/2-inch (1 cm) pieces

1/3 cup (75 ml) fresh dill, finely chopped

Preheat oven to 350°F (180°C).

In a large mixing bowl, vigorously whisk eggs until frothy—about 15 to 20 seconds. Add pepper; whisk another 5 seconds to combine. Set aside.

Heat oil in a 10-inch (25 cm) ovenproof skillet over medium heat. When pan is hot, add onions and sauté for 8 to 10 minutes. Add salmon and continue to sauté until salmon is opaque, about 2 to 3 minutes.

Add eggs and dill to skillet, and then immediately place skillet in oven. Bake for 18 to 20 minutes, or until eggs are set and the top of the frittata begins to puff up. Remove from heat, and immediately run a knife or rubber spatula around the edge of the skillet to loosen the edges of the frittata. Serve warm.

NUTRITION
Per serving: 155 cal, 14 g pro, 10 g total fat (2 g saturated fat), 3 g carb, 0 g fibre, 226 mg chol, 334 mg sodium

Soft Scrambled Eggs with Fresh Chives

Substituting egg whites for whole eggs, or using a combination of the two, is an easy way to cut calories, cholesterol and saturated fat from a recipe. Unlike egg yolks, egg whites are fat- and cholesterol-free and deliver a hefty dose of protein, riboflavin and selenium.

Serves 2

2 medium eggs

2 medium egg whites

1 tbsp (15 ml) low-fat (1% MF or less) milk or soy milk

1 tbsp (15 ml) chopped fresh chives

1/8 tsp (0.5 ml) coarse sea salt, or to taste

Freshly ground black pepper, to taste

1 tsp (5 ml) canola oil

In a large mixing bowl, whisk together eggs, egg whites, milk, chives, salt and pepper until slightly frothy, about 30 seconds.

Heat the oil in a skillet over medium heat. When pan is hot, add the egg mixture. Once eggs begin to set, about 1 minute, gently draw a spatula through the eggs to form large curds. Continue cooking until the eggs are cooked through, but still moist, about 5 to 7 minutes.

Serve immediately.

NUTRITION

Per serving: 103 cal, 9 g pro, 7 g total fat (2 g saturated fat), 1 g carb, 0 g fibre, 164 mg chol, 255 mg sodium

Tofu Scramble

My vegetarian clients gave this recipe a thumbs-up. Here, tofu replaces the eggs to yield a high-protein breakfast that's very low in saturated fat.

Serves 4

1 tsp (5 ml) canola oil

1/2 cup (125 ml) chopped onion

2 cloves garlic, crushed

1 pkg (12 oz/350 g) extra firm tofu

1 tsp (5 ml) turmeric

1/2 tsp (2 ml) chili powder

1 tsp (5 ml) cumin seeds

1 tbsp (15 ml) sodium-reduced soy sauce

Freshly ground black pepper, to taste

Heat oil in a skillet over medium heat. When pan is hot, add onion; sauté for 4 to 5 minutes or until golden brown. Add garlic; sauté for another minute.

With your hands, crumble tofu into 1-inch (2.5 cm) pieces; add to skillet. Stir in turmeric, chili powder, cumin seeds and soy sauce. Season with black pepper.

Continue to cook over medium heat for 8 to 10 minutes or until most of the moisture from the tofu has evaporated and the tofu begins to brown.

NUTRITION
Per serving: 166 cal, 15 g pro, 9 g total fat (1 g saturated fat), 10 g carb, 2 g fibre, 0 mg chol, 139 mg sodium

Tip: For added colour, add freshly chopped chives just before serving.

Smoothies & Other Beverages

Banana Flax Smoothie

Ground flaxseeds give this smoothie a slightly nutty flavour and a boost of heart-healthy omega-3 fatty acids.

Serves 2

2 cups (500 ml) low-fat (1% MF or less) milk or soy milk

1 cup (250 ml) mixed berries, such as strawberries, blueberries or raspberries, fresh or frozen

1 medium banana

2 tbsp (25 ml) ground flaxseed

In a blender, combine milk, berries, banana and flaxseed; purée until smooth.

NUTRITION
Per 1-1/2 cup (375 ml) serving: 225 cal, 10 g pro, 6 g total fat (2 g saturated fat), 35 g carbohydrate, 5 g fibre, 10 mg chol, 127 mg sodium

Tip: Store ground flaxseeds in the fridge to extend their shelf life.

Blackberry Yogurt Shake

You can substitute any 100% unsweetened fruit juice for the orange juice in this recipe. Pomegranate juice works especially well, and gives the smoothie a deep crimson colour.

Serves 2

1 cup (250 ml) blackberries, fresh or frozen

1 cup (250 ml) low-fat (1% MF or less) plain or vanilla yogurt

2 cups (500 ml) unsweetened orange juice

In a blender, combine blackberries, yogurt and orange juice. Purée until smooth. Serve cold.

NUTRITION

Per 1-1/2 cup (375 ml) serving: 212 cal, 8 g pro, 1 g total fat (0 g saturated fat), 44 g carb, 4 g fibre, 2 mg chol, 90 mg sodium

Blueberry Almond Smoothie

Almonds are an excellent source of monounsaturated fat, vitamin E and magnesium—all of which promote heart health. While the recipe calls for blueberries, you can substitute any type of berry, fresh or frozen, such as raspberries or strawberries.

Serves 2

1 cup (250 ml) low-fat (1% MF or less) milk or soy milk

1/2 cup (125 ml) unsweetened orange juice

1/4 cup (50 ml) blueberries, fresh or frozen

2 tbsp (25 ml) sliced almonds

2 tsp (10 ml) maple syrup

1 medium banana

1/2 tsp (2 ml) vanilla extract

In a blender, combine milk, orange juice, blueberries, almonds, maple syrup, banana and vanilla. Purée until smooth. Serve cold.

NUTRITION

Per 1 cup (250 ml) serving: 242 cal, 9 g pro, 9 g total fat (1 g saturated fat), 35 g carb, 3 g fibre, 6 mg chol, 62 mg sodium

Blueberry Banana Smoothie

Nothing says summer like a basketful of fresh, locally grown blueberries. If you don't have fresh blueberries on hand, frozen berries work just as well.

Serves 2

1/2 cup (125 ml) blueberries, fresh or frozen

2 small bananas

2 cups (500 ml) low-fat (1% MF or less) milk or soy milk

In a blender, combine blueberries, bananas and milk. Purée until smooth. Serve cold.

NUTRITION
Per 1-1/2 cup (375 ml) serving: 228 cal, 10 g pro, 3 g total fat (2 g saturated fat), 44 g carb, 3 g fibre, 10 mg chol, 125 mg sodium

Blueberry Raspberry Smoothie

Berries are well recognized as superfoods, and for good reason. Studies suggest eating plenty of antioxidant-rich berries can help ward off cancer and heart disease, and keeps our memory sharp. Fresh or frozen berries work equally well in this recipe.

Serves 2

1/2 cup (125 ml) blueberries, fresh or frozen

1/2 cup (125 ml) raspberries, fresh or frozen

1/2 cup (125 ml) low-fat (1% MF or less) plain yogurt or soy yogurt

1/2 cup (125 ml) low-fat (1% MF or less) milk or soy milk

1/2 cup (125 ml) unsweetened orange juice

1/2 tsp (2 ml) grated fresh ginger root

Combine all ingredients in a blender and purée until smooth. Serve cold.

NUTRITION
Per 1 cup (250 ml) serving: 122 cal, 6 g pro, 1 g total fat (0 g saturated fat), 23 g carb, 3 g fibre, 4 mg chol, 72 mg sodium

Tip: Swap the blueberries for blackberries or the raspberries for strawberries for a delicious variation.

Cranberry Smoothie

This tasty and very vibrantly coloured smoothie is so easy to make. I like to drink this as my post-workout snack on the weekend. The protein and carbohydrates help my muscles recover after a long run.

Serves 2

2 cups (500 ml) pure cranberry juice

1-1/2 cups (375 ml) low-fat (1% MF or less) plain or vanilla yogurt

1/2 cup (125 ml) blueberries, fresh or frozen

In a blender, combine cranberry juice, yogurt and blueberries. Purée until smooth. Serve cold.

NUTRITION
Per 1-3/4 cup (425 ml) serving: 194 cal, 10 g pro, 0 g total fat (0 g saturated fat), 38 g carb, 1 g fibre, 3 mg chol, 169 mg sodium

Creamy Strawberry Smoothie

If you prefer your smoothies on the thicker side, add a few more strawberries or increase the proportion of yogurt to milk.

Serves 2

1 cup (250 ml) sliced strawberries, fresh or frozen

1 cup (250 ml) low-fat (1% MF or less) plain or vanilla yogurt

2 cups (500 ml) low-fat (1% MF or less) milk or soy milk

In a blender, combine strawberries, yogurt and milk. Purée until smooth. Serve cold.

NUTRITION
Per 1-1/2 cup (375 ml) serving: 173 cal, 15 g pro, 1 g total fat (0 g saturated fat), 27 g carb, 2 g fibre, 7 mg chol, 215 mg sodium

Grapefruit and Raspberry Smoothie with Toasted Coconut

Lightly toasted coconut gives this smoothie a wonderful rich, nutty flavour that is sure to make you think of white sandy beaches and palm trees! The grapefruit juice makes this smoothie refreshingly tart, but if you prefer your smoothies on the sweeter side, I suggest you double up on the honey.

Serves 2

2 tbsp (25 ml) shredded unsweetened coconut

2 cups (500 ml) pure grapefruit juice

1 cup (250 ml) raspberries, fresh or frozen

1 banana

1 tbsp (15 ml) honey

Preheat oven to 350°F (180°C).

Place coconut on a baking sheet; put in oven for 5 minutes, or until fragrant and lightly toasted. Remove from heat and cool.

In a blender, combine grapefruit juice, raspberries, banana, honey and toasted coconut; purée until smooth. Serve cold.

NUTRITION
Per 1-1/2 cup (375 ml) serving: 248 cal, 3 g pro, 5 g total fat (3 g saturated fat), 53 g carb, 7 g fibre, 0 mg chol, 6 mg sodium

Tip: Instead of tossing out overripe bananas, peel and freeze them for a quick addition to smoothies like this one.

Honeydew and Lime Smoothie

This refreshing smoothie is great for those long, hot summer days—perfect for drinking poolside. I like to refrigerate the melon for a few hours before making the smoothie so it's nice and cold. Serve it on its own, or garnish each glass with a sprig of mint and slice of lime.

Serves 2

2 cups (500 ml) diced honeydew melon

1 cup (250 ml) unsweetened orange juice

2 tbsp (25 ml) freshly squeezed lime juice

1 tsp (5 ml) honey

In a blender, combine melon, orange juice, lime juice and honey; purée until smooth. Serve cold.

NUTRITION
Per 1-1/4 cup (300 ml) serving: 132 cal, 2 g pro, 1 g total fat (0 g saturated fat), 33 g carb, 2 g fibre, 0 mg chol, 33 mg sodium

Lemon Ginger Infusion

This soothing drink is ideal when you're feeling under the weather or just wanting a caffeine-free alternative to tea or coffee. Serve it warm or hot, and double the ginger for a spicier version.

Serves 2

2 cups (500 ml) water

3 tbsp (50 ml) freshly squeezed lemon juice

1 tbsp (15 ml) chopped fresh ginger root (large chunks)

In a small saucepan, combine water, lemon juice and ginger root. Bring to a boil, cover, and simmer for 3 to 5 minutes. Remove from heat and scoop out the pieces of ginger. Serve warm.

NUTRITION
Per 1 cup (250 ml) serving: 8 cal, 0 g pro, 0 g total fat (0 g saturated fat), 3 g carb, 0 g fibre, 0 mg chol, 8 mg sodium

Lemon Green Iced Tea

This refreshing iced tea has very little sugar, making it a much healthier alternative to most store-bought versions. For variety, use different types of green or black teas, including tea leaves blended with dried fruit or flowers.

Serves 6

6 cups (1.5 L) boiling water

6 green tea bags

1/4 cup (50 ml) freshly squeezed lemon juice

2 tbsp (25 ml) honey

Fresh mint leaves, as garnish

Pour boiling water over tea bags in a large pitcher. Steep for 5 to 10 minutes, depending on desired strength.

Remove tea bags. Stir in lemon juice and honey. Allow the tea to cool before pouring into 6 large ice-filled glasses. Garnish with fresh mint leaves. Serve immediately.

NUTRITION

Per 1 cup (250 ml) serving: 30 cal, 0 g pro, 0 g total fat (0 g saturated fat), 8 g carb, 0 g fibre, 0 mg chol, 3 mg sodium

Orange Ginger Smoothie

Fresh ginger gives this smoothie a refreshing and delicious taste—my taste-testers couldn't seem to get enough of it!

Serves 2

1 cup (250 ml) unsweetened orange juice

1 cup (250 ml) low-fat (1% MF or less) milk or soy milk

1 tsp (5 ml) grated or minced fresh ginger root

1 cup (250 ml) mixed berries, such as strawberries, blueberries or raspberries, fresh or frozen

In a blender, combine orange juice, milk, ginger root and berries. Purée until smooth. Serve cold.

NUTRITION
Per 1-1/2 cup (375 ml) serving: 148 cal, 6 g pro, 2 g total fat (1 g saturated fat), 30 g carb, 2 g fibre, 6 mg chol, 60 mg sodium

Tip: When fresh berries are plentiful in the summer, freeze 1-cup (250 ml) portions in a freezer bag to use year-round in smoothies and baked goods.

Pomegranate Power Shake

Ground flaxseed adds a boost of fibre to this antioxidant-rich smoothie. If you prefer your smoothies on the thinner side, add 1/4 cup (50 ml) skim milk or low-fat soy milk. Or, add a few ice cubes before you purée.

Serves 2

2 cups (500 ml) pure pomegranate juice, such as POM

1 cup (250 ml) sliced strawberries, fresh or frozen

2 small bananas

2 tbsp (25 ml) ground flaxseed

In a blender, combine pomegranate juice, strawberries, bananas and flaxseed. Purée until smooth. Serve cold.

NUTRITION

Per 1-1/2 cup (375 ml) serving: 313 cal, 3 g pro, 4 g total fat (1 g saturated fat), 71 g carb, 5 g fibre, 0 mg chol, 13 mg sodium

Pumpkin Orange Banana Smoothie

Canada's Food Guide recommends eating at least one bright orange vegetable, such as pumpkin, each day. Smooth and creamy, this unconventional smoothie is as delicious as it is nutritious. Its deep orange colour is a clear sign this smoothie is brimming with antioxidants—it's packed with beta carotene and vitamin C.

Serves 2

1 cup (250 ml) low-fat (1% MF or less) milk or soy milk

1/2 cup (125 ml) pure pumpkin purée

1/2 cup (125 ml) unsweetened orange juice

1 medium banana, sliced

4 ice cubes, optional

Combine all ingredients in a blender and purée until smooth. Serve cold.

NUTRITION
Per 1 cup (250 ml) serving: 153 cal, 6 g pro, 2 g total fat (1 g saturated fat), 31 g carb, 3 g fibre, 6 mg chol, 58 mg sodium

Tip: Pure pumpkin purée is sold in a can in grocery stores. Unlike pumpkin pie filling, pure pumpkin purée does not have added sugar, fat or spices and has about one-third of the calories.

Raspberry Kefir Smoothie

This recipe works well with any berry, not just raspberries. Try blueberries, strawberries or blackberries. You'll find kefir, a fermented milk product, in the dairy section of most grocery stores and natural food stores.

Serves 2

2 cups (500 ml) plain kefir

1 cup (250 ml) raspberries, fresh or frozen

2 small bananas

In a blender, combine kefir, raspberries and bananas. Purée until smooth. Serve cold.

NUTRITION
Per 1-1/2 cup (375 ml) serving: 257 cal, 10 g pro, 6 g total fat (3 g saturated fat), 45 g carb, 5 g fibre, 14 mg chol, 123 mg sodium

Strawberry Kiwi Smoothie

My taste-testers loved this delicious vitamin C–rich smoothie. You can't go wrong with the combination of strawberries, kiwifruit and mango juice. One serving of this smoothie contains more than twice the recommended daily intake of vitamin C!

Serves 2

1 cup (250 ml) sliced strawberries, fresh or frozen

1 cup (250 ml) 100% pure mango juice

1/2 cup (125 ml) low-fat (1% MF or less) plain yogurt or soy yogurt

2 kiwifruit, peeled

4 ice cubes, optional

Combine all ingredients in a blender and purée until smooth. Serve chilled.

NUTRITION
Per 1-1/4 cup (300 ml) serving: 166 cal, 5 g pro, 1 g total fat (0 g saturated fat), 38 g carb, 4 g fibre, 1 mg chol, 53 mg sodium

Tip: Choose a brand of mango juice with no added sugar, such as Ceres Fruit Juices mango juice.

Two Berry Smoothie

It's hard to beat the nutrition that's packed into one serving of this yummy smoothie—disease-fighting antioxidants called anthocyanins and plenty of vitamin C.

Serves 2

1 cup (250 ml) low-fat (1% MF or less) milk or soy milk

1 cup (250 ml) low-fat plain or vanilla yogurt

1-1/2 cups (375 ml) sliced strawberries

1 cup (250 ml) blueberries, fresh or frozen

In a blender, combine milk, yogurt, strawberries and blueberries; purée until smooth. Serve chilled.

NUTRITION
Per 1-1/2 cup (375 ml) serving: 192 cal, 11 g pro, 2 g total fat (1 g saturated fat), 34 g carb, 5 g fibre, 7 mg chol, 154 mg sodium

Snacks

Almond Lemon Biscotti

Biscotti get their signature crunchy texture from the fact that they are baked twice. These biscotti are no exception—they're hard and crunchy if you eat them on their own, but dipped into a cup of tea or coffee they become deliciously soft. Store these cookies in an airtight container for up to a week.

Makes 16 biscotti

2 cups (500 ml) all-purpose flour

1 cup (250 ml) granulated sugar

1 cup (250 ml) coarsely chopped plain almonds

1-1/2 tsp (7 ml) baking powder

1/4 tsp (1 ml) salt

2 medium eggs

1 tbsp (15 ml) freshly squeezed lemon juice

1 tsp (5 ml) lemon zest (about 1 lemon)

1 tsp (5 ml) vanilla extract

3/4 tsp (4 ml) almond extract

Preheat oven to 350°F (180°C). Lightly grease a baking sheet; set aside.

In a large mixing bowl, combine flour, sugar, almonds, baking powder and salt.

In another mixing bowl, whisk together eggs, lemon juice, lemon zest, vanilla and almond extract.

Add egg mixture to flour mixture and stir ingredients together. When dough becomes thick, use clean hands to fold ingredients together until all the flour is absorbed and dough becomes sticky.

Divide dough in half; form each portion into a log about 7 inches (18 cm) long. Place both logs on the baking sheet and press down until they are about 2-1/2 inches (6 cm) wide and 3/4 inch (2 cm) tall.

Place in oven and bake for 35 minutes. Remove from oven and let cool for 5 minutes.

Using a very sharp knife, slice biscotti into 3/4-inch (2 cm) slices. Lay biscotti flat on the baking sheet and bake another 8 minutes. Remove from oven, flip biscotti and bake another 8 minutes.

Cool before serving.

Store in an airtight container for up to a week.

NUTRITION
Per biscotti: 167 cal, 4 g pro, 5 g total fat (1 g saturated fat), 26 g carb, 2 g fibre, 21 mg chol, 71 mg sodium

Black Bean Hummus

Hummus has a long history in the Middle East, where it's traditionally made with chickpeas. This version uses black beans instead. Gram for gram, black beans have 15% more fibre and 25% fewer calories than chickpeas. And they beat out other beans when it comes to antioxidants. This hummus is a delicious dip for vegetables and also makes a tasty spread on whole-grain crackers.

Serves 8

1 can (19 oz/540 ml) black beans, drained and rinsed well

1/4 cup (50 ml) tahini

3 tbsp (50 ml) freshly squeezed lemon juice

2 tbsp (25 ml) olive oil

1 clove garlic, crushed

1/8 tsp (0.5 ml) red pepper flakes, or to taste

1 tbsp (15 ml) finely chopped parsley, optional

In a food processor, combine black beans, tahini, lemon juice, olive oil, garlic and red pepper flakes; pulse until smooth or desired consistency. Alternatively, use the back of a fork to mash ingredients until smooth or desired consistency.

Place in a serving bowl and garnish with fresh parsley. Serve cold or at room temperature.

NUTRITION
Per 1/4 cup (50 ml) serving: 130 cal, 5 g pro, 8 g total fat (1 g saturated fat), 12 g carb, 3 g fibre, 0 mg chol, 3 mg sodium

Bruce Trail Mix

Whether it's for the West Coast Trail, the Cabot Trail or the Bruce Trail, this trail mix is the perfect snack to keep you energized while hiking.

Serves 6

1/2 cup (125 ml) slivered almonds

1/4 cup (50 ml) walnut halves

2 tbsp (25 ml) dried cranberries

2 tbsp (25 ml) dark chocolate chips

1/2 cup (125 ml) large-flake rolled oats

In a large mixing bowl, toss together almonds, walnuts, cranberries, chocolate chips and rolled oats. Store in an airtight container.

NUTRITION
Per 1/4 cup (50 ml) serving: 159 cal, 5 g pro, 11 g total fat (2 g saturated fat), 12 g carb, 3 g fibre, 0 mg chol, 4 mg sodium

Cashew Mango Trail Mix

Keep this tasty snack on hand for those days when you need a mid-afternoon energy boost.

Serves 4

1/2 cup (125 ml) unsalted cashews

1/4 cup (50 ml) shelled unsalted sunflower seeds

1/4 cup (50 ml) shredded unsweetened coconut

2 strips dried mango, cut into chunks

1/3 cup (75 ml) dried banana chips

In a large mixing bowl, toss together cashews, sunflower seeds, coconut, dried mango and banana chips. Store in an airtight container.

NUTRITION
Per 1/3 cup (75 ml) serving: 222 cal, 5 g pro, 17 g total fat (6 g saturated fat), 17 g carb, 3 g fibre, 0 mg chol, 16 mg sodium

Creamy Dill Dip

This dip is great with sliced fresh vegetables, or it can be used as a salad dressing or as a condiment for grilled salmon.

Serves 4

1 cup (250 ml) low-fat (1% MF or less) plain yogurt

2 tbsp (25 ml) chopped fresh dill

1 tbsp (15 ml) freshly squeezed lemon juice

1 clove garlic, crushed

In a small bowl, combine yogurt, dill, lemon juice and garlic. Cover and refrigerate until ready to serve.

Makes 1 cup (250 ml).

NUTRITION
Per 1/4 cup (50 ml) serving: 33 cal, 3 g pro, 0 g total fat (0 g saturated fat), 5 g carb, 0 g fibre, 1 mg chol, 44 mg sodium

Tip: If you don't have fresh dill, you can substitute 1/2 tbsp (7 ml) dried dill.

Guacamole

This recipe turns ripe avocados into a tasty appetizer or mid-afternoon snack with baked tortilla chips. If you have avocados that aren't quite ripe yet, you can quicken the ripening process by storing them in a paper bag with a tomato. They should be ready to use within a day or two. Serve this guacamole with Herbed Pita Chips (page 89).

Serves 6

3 avocados, mashed

2 cloves garlic, crushed

3 tbsp (50 ml) freshly squeezed lime juice

1 small jalapeno, finely chopped

1/4 tsp (1 ml) coarse sea salt, or to taste

In a small bowl, combine avocado, garlic, lime juice, jalapeno and salt. Mash to desired consistency.

Makes about 3 cups (750 ml).

NUTRITION

Per 1/2 cup (125 ml) serving: 165 cal, 2 g pro, 15 g total fat (2 g saturated fat), 9 g carb, 5 g fibre, 0 mg chol, 110 mg sodium

Tip: Since most of the heat in a jalapeno comes from the seeds, leave them in if you prefer spicy guacamole; otherwise carefully discard them for a milder version.

Herbed Pita Chips

These pita chips are so easy to make and are a healthier alternative to most store-bought chips. Eat them on their own, or serve them with hummus, guacamole or dip.

Serves 8

4 6-inch (15 cm) whole wheat pitas, cut into 8 wedges

1-1/2 tbsp (22 ml) extra-virgin olive oil

2 tsp (10 ml) Herbes de Provence

1/2 tsp (2 ml) coarse sea salt

Preheat oven to 350°F (180°C).

In a large bowl, toss together sliced pita, olive oil, herbs and sea salt. Using clean hands, rub the oil and spice mixture into the bread, until coated evenly.

Lay pita chips in a single layer on a baking sheet; bake for 8 to 10 minutes, or until chips are crispy. Let cool before serving.

NUTRITION
Per serving (4 chips): 109 cal, 3 g pro, 3 g total fat (1 g saturated fat), 18 g carb, 3 g fibre, 0 mg chol, 317 mg sodium

Tip: Herbes de Provence is traditionally a mix of dried spices, including thyme, rosemary, savory, lavender and tarragon. You can substitute any dried herb for Herbes de Provence in this recipe, including basil, oregano or rosemary. Alternatively, use ground cumin, paprika, garlic powder or freshly ground black pepper.

Kale Chips with Sea Salt

These yummy "chips" are a much more nutritious alternative to potato chips. Kale is an exceptional source of lutein, a phytochemical that helps maintain our vision. What's more, one serving of these chips provides more than a day's worth of vitamins C and K. Kale's sturdy leaves are ideally suited to making these crispy chips. I suggest making extra—they won't last long!

Serves 4

4 cups (1 L) kale, washed, trimmed and torn into bite-sized pieces

1 tbsp (15 ml) olive oil

1/2 tsp (2 ml) sea salt

Freshly ground black pepper, to taste

Preheat oven to 350°F (180°C).

In a large mixing bowl, toss together kale, olive oil, salt and pepper. Use clean hands to gently rub oil into kale.

Spread kale on a large baking sheet. Bake for 15 minutes, or until kale is crispy. Cool and serve.

NUTRITION
Per 1 cup (250 ml) serving: 63 cal, 2 g pro, 4 g total fat (1 g saturated fat), 7 g carb, 2 g fibre, 0 mg chol, 321 mg sodium

Lemon Ginger Fruit Dip

This dip is an excellent accompaniment to Roasted Fruit Kebabs (page 370), or to slices of your favourite fresh fruit.

Serves 6

1-1/2 cups (375 ml) low-fat (1% MF or less) vanilla yogurt

2 tbsp (25 ml) honey

1 tsp (5 ml) minced fresh ginger root

Zest of 1/2 lemon

In a bowl, combine yogurt, honey, ginger root and lemon zest. Cover and refrigerate until ready to serve.

Makes 1-1/2 cups (375 ml).

NUTRITION
Per 1/4 cup (50 ml) serving: 57 cal, 3 g pro, 0 g total fat (0 g saturated fat), 11 g carb, 0 g fibre, 1 mg chol, 44 mg sodium

Lemon Hummus

This creamy hummus is a crowd pleaser—serve it with carrot sticks or whole-grain crackers at parties and get-togethers. It also makes for a tasty spread on burgers and sandwiches, especially when paired with sliced tomatoes and baby spinach leaves.

Serves 6

1 can (19 oz/540 ml) chickpeas, drained and rinsed well

1/3 cup (75 ml) tahini

1/4 cup (50 ml) freshly squeezed lemon juice

2 tbsp (25 ml) extra-virgin olive oil

1 tbsp (15 ml) water

1/4 tsp (1 ml) coarse sea salt

In a food processor or blender, combine chickpeas, tahini, lemon juice, olive oil, water and salt; pulse to a smooth consistency.

Makes 1-1/2 cups (375 ml).

NUTRITION
Per 1/4 cup (50 ml) serving: 205 cal, 7 g pro, 13 g total fat (2 g saturated fat), 18 g carb, 4 g fibre, 0 mg chol, 117 mg sodium

Lemon Pepper Salmon Dip

This creamy dip is excellent with cut raw vegetables or whole-grain crackers. It also makes a tasty sandwich spread that's low in saturated fat.

Serves 12

1 pkg (8 oz/226 g) light cream cheese

1 can (7-1/2 oz/213 g) salmon, drained

1 tbsp (15 ml) prepared horseradish

2 tbsp (25 ml) fresh dill

1 tbsp (15 ml) freshly squeezed lemon juice

2 tbsp (25 ml) chopped green onion

2 tbsp (25 ml) low-fat (1% MF or less) milk

1/4 tsp (1 ml) coarsely ground pepper, or to taste

In a mixing bowl, beat cream cheese with an electric mixer until smooth. Add salmon, horseradish, dill, lemon juice, green onion, milk and pepper. Mix until combined.

Cover and refrigerate until ready to serve.

NUTRITION
Per 2 tbsp (25 ml) serving: 71 cal, 6 g pro, 4 g total fat (2 g saturated fat), 2 g carb, 0 g fibre, 18 mg chol, 148 mg sodium

Tip: To store fresh dill, absorb any excess moisture with a towel and place the dill in a resealable freezer bag in the crisper of the fridge. Do not wash the dill before storing because moisture will cause the leaves to deteriorate.

Lime and Black Pepper Popcorn

Movie theatre and store-bought brands of microwave popcorn are often packed with calories, fat and sodium. I was shocked to find out how many calories are in a large, unbuttered movie theatre popcorn—1100! This recipe uses heart-healthy olive oil and lime zest for a healthy take on an old favourite.

Serves 5

2 tbsp (25 ml) extra-virgin olive oil

3/4 cup (175 ml) popping corn

1 lime wedge

Non-aerosol olive oil spray bottle (about 40 sprays, equivalent to 10 ml olive oil)

4 tsp (20 ml) finely chopped lime zest (about 4 limes' worth)

1/4 tsp (1 ml) salt

Freshly ground black pepper, to taste

Heat oil and three corn kernels in a large saucepan with a tight-fitting lid over high heat.

When the corn kernels pop, remove lid just enough to pour remaining corn kernels into pan. Cover and continue to shake the pan over high heat until most of the corn has popped. (Use a tea towel or oven mitts to protect your hands and arms from steam escaping from the pan.)

When popping sound subsides, remove the pan from heat.

Rub a lime wedge on the inside of a large mixing bowl.

Empty popcorn into bowl; spray with olive oil and season with lime zest, salt and pepper.

Serve immediately.

NUTRITION

Per 3 cup (750 ml) serving: 154 cal, 3 g pro, 8 g total fat (1 g saturated fat), 19 g carb, 4 g fibre, 0 mg chol, 119 mg sodium

Tip: The key to evenly coating the popcorn with olive oil is to use a non-aerosol spray bottle for cooking oils. Look for bottles already filled at specialty food stores or purchase a refillable bottle, available at most kitchen supply stores.

Orange Fig Granola Bars

These wholesome bars are perfect for a midday energy booster or a light dessert.
Swap the oats for other whole grains, such as rye or spelt flakes, for an easy variation.

Serves 16

FILLING

2 cups (500 ml) finely chopped dried figs (stems removed)

3/4 cup (175 ml) freshly squeezed orange juice

1 tbsp (15 ml) orange zest

CRUST AND TOPPING

1 cup (250 ml) all-purpose flour

1/2 cup (125 ml) whole wheat flour

1 cup (250 ml) quick cooking oats

1/2 cup (125 ml) brown sugar

1/2 cup (125 ml) non-hydrogenated margarine

1 tbsp (15 ml) low-fat (1% MF or less) milk or soy milk

1 tsp (5 ml) vanilla extract

1 tsp (5 ml) cinnamon

1/4 tsp (1 ml) salt

Preheat oven to 350°F (180°C).

Lightly grease and flour a 9 × 9 inch (2.5 L) metal cake pan.

In a saucepan, combine figs, orange juice and orange zest. Cover and bring to a boil; reduce heat and simmer for 10 minutes.

Remove from heat and, using the back of a fork, mash the figs until they begin to break apart. Set aside.

In a large mixing bowl combine all-purpose and whole wheat flour, oats, brown sugar, margarine, milk, vanilla, cinnamon and salt. Using clean hands, combine ingredients until the mixture resembles a dry dough that holds together when squeezed. Set aside 3/4 cup (175 ml) oat mixture for the topping.

Firmly press the oat mixture onto the bottom of the prepared cake pan. Spread fig and orange mixture overtop. Sprinkle with 3/4 cup (175 ml) reserved oat mixture.

Bake for 25 to 30 minutes or until top begins to brown.

Remove from oven, and while still hot use a knife or metal spatula to gently press along the edges to remove squares from side of pan.

NUTRITION
Per serving: 193 cal, 3 g pro, 6 g total fat (2 g saturated fat), 33 g carb, 3 g fibre, 0 mg chol, 119 mg sodium

Tip: Use a clean pair of sharp kitchen scissors to quickly chop the dried figs. Unsweetened bottled orange juice can be substituted for freshly squeezed juice.

Roasted Squash and Garlic Dip

This dip takes a little longer to prepare than others, but it's worth the effort. It pairs well with raw vegetables and crackers. It's also a great low-fat alternative to butter, margarine, or mayonnaise on sandwiches. This dip can be made in advance and refrigerated for up to five days.

Serves 8

1 medium acorn squash

1/2 cup (125 ml) water

1 apple, peeled, cored and halved

2 tbsp (25 ml) freshly squeezed orange juice

2 bulbs garlic

1 tsp (5 ml) extra-virgin olive oil

1/2 tsp (2 ml) coarse sea salt, or to taste

Freshly ground black pepper, to taste

Preheat oven to 375°F (190°C).

Cut squash in half lengthwise, removing seeds. Place squash cut side up in a shallow casserole dish. Pour water into the bottom of the dish.

Place an apple half into the hollow of each squash half. Drizzle 1 tbsp (15 ml) of the orange juice onto each squash half. Cover casserole dish with foil and set aside.

Cut off the top eighth of each bulb of garlic and remove any loose skin. Drizzle with olive oil. Wrap each garlic bulb in foil or place in a clay garlic roaster.

Place squash and garlic in the oven and bake for 55 to 60 minutes or until the squash is tender when pricked with a fork. Remove squash and garlic from oven and cool slightly.

Gently scoop out squash flesh and apple and place in a mixing bowl. Unwrap garlic bulbs and gently squeeze the garlic pulp from the cloves into the mixing bowl.

Mash squash, apple and garlic with a fork until smooth and combined. Season with salt and black pepper.

Makes about 2 cups (500 ml).

NUTRITION
Per 1/4 cup (50 ml) serving: 49 cal, 1 g pro, 1 g total fat (0 g saturated fat), 12 g carb, 2 g fibre, 0 mg chol, 153 mg sodium

Sesame Ginger Edamame

While often served at Japanese restaurants as an appetizer, edamame is a quick and easy dish to make at home. I like to keep a few bags of edamame in the freezer for a satisfying protein-rich snack—they're a great alterative to potato chips and popcorn.

Serves 4

1-1/2 tbsp (22 ml) sesame seeds

1 bag (1.1 lb/500 g) frozen edamame

1 tbsp (15 ml) grated fresh ginger root

2 tsp (10 ml) sesame oil

1/2 tsp (2 ml) coarse sea salt, or to taste

Preheat oven to 350°F (180°C).

Place sesame seeds on a baking sheet. Bake for 5 to 7 minutes, or until seeds begin to brown and become fragrant; remove from heat and set aside.

Meanwhile, bring a saucepan full of water to a boil. Add edamame and cook for 4 to 5 minutes. Remove from heat and drain water.

In a mixing bowl, toss edamame with ginger, sesame oil, salt and toasted sesame seeds.

Serve warm.

NUTRITION

Per 1 cup (250 ml) serving: 178 cal, 13 g pro, 10 g total fat (1 g saturated fat), 12 g carb, 6 g fibre, 0 mg chol, 300 mg sodium

Tip: Swap regular sesame seeds for black sesame seeds, available at major grocery and specialty food stores, for an attractive variation.

Spicy Candied Walnuts

Sweet, salty and spicy—these walnuts have it all! Although this recipe makes an addictive cocktail snack all year 'round, it's also a special treat for holiday parties.

Serves 6

1-1/2 cups (375 ml) walnut halves

1/4 cup (50 ml) shredded unsweetened coconut

2 tbsp (25 ml) honey

1/8 tsp (0.5 ml) cayenne pepper, or to taste

Pinch salt, or to taste

1/3 cup (75 ml) dried cranberries

Preheat oven to 350°F (180°C).

In a medium bowl, combine walnuts, coconut, honey, cayenne pepper and salt.

Spread walnut mixture onto a baking sheet and bake, turning once, for 8 to 10 minutes or until brown and slightly crispy.

Transfer walnut mixture to a bowl to cool. Toss with cranberries. Store in an airtight container.

NUTRITION

Per 1/4 cup (50 ml) serving: 251 cal, 8 g pro, 19 g total fat (2 g saturated fat), 18 g carb, 2 g fibre, 0 mg chol, 59 mg sodium

Tamari Roasted Almonds

These almonds take only minutes to prepare and are a tasty variation on regular toasted almonds. Add lemon zest for extra flavour.

Serves 6

1-1/2 cups (375 ml) raw unsalted almonds

2 tbsp (25 ml) tamari or sodium-reduced soy sauce

2 tbsp (25 ml) freshly squeezed lemon juice

Heat a skillet over medium heat. Add almonds and cook for 3 to 5 minutes, shaking skillet frequently, until nuts become fragrant.

Drizzle tamari and lemon juice over almonds, and as soon as pan begins to dry out remove from heat.

Serve warm, or transfer almonds to a bowl to cool and then store in an airtight container.

NUTRITION
Per 1/4 cup (50 ml) serving: 214 cal, 8 g pro, 18 g total fat (1 g saturated fat), 8 g carb, 4 g fibre, 0 mg chol, 171 mg sodium

Toasted Almond and Coconut Oat Squares

These chewy squares have a delicious nutty flavour and make a perfect mid-afternoon snack. You can use other grains in place of oatmeal, including spelt flakes and rye flakes. These squares also double as a quick grab-and-go breakfast when you're short on time.

Serves 16

2 cups (500 ml) quick cooking oats

1 cup (250 ml) sliced almonds

1/3 cup (75 ml) shredded unsweetened coconut

3/4 cup (175 ml) sweetened applesauce

1/3 cup (75 ml) honey

1/4 cup (50 ml) canola oil

2 egg whites

1 tsp (5 ml) vanilla extract

1/2 cup (125 ml) all-purpose flour

1/2 cup (125 ml) whole wheat flour

2 tsp (10 ml) cinnamon

1/4 tsp (1 ml) nutmeg

1/2 tsp (2 ml) baking soda

1/2 tsp (2 ml) baking powder

1/4 tsp (1 ml) salt

Preheat oven to 350°F (180°C).

Lightly grease and flour a 9 × 9 (2.5 L) metal cake pan.

Combine oats, almonds and coconut on a large baking sheet. Place in oven and toast for 5 to 7 minutes. Remove from heat and place in a large mixing bowl to cool.

In a separate bowl, whisk together applesauce, honey, canola oil, egg whites and vanilla.

When oat mixture is cool, add all-purpose and whole wheat flour, cinnamon, nutmeg, baking soda, baking powder and salt; stir to combine.

Add applesauce and honey mixture to flour and toasted oat mixture; stir to combine.

Empty batter into the prepared cake pan and bake for 22 to 25 minutes, or until squares begin to brown and a knife inserted in the centre comes out clean.

NUTRITION
Per serving: 179 cal, 5 g pro, 8 g total fat (2 g saturated fat), 23 g carb, 3 g fibre, 0 mg chol, 95 mg sodium

White Bean and Garlic Dip

This tangy dip is excellent served with Herbed Pita Chips (page 89) or with fresh vegetables, such as red pepper strips and baby carrots. It also doubles as a sandwich spread—it's excellent on whole-grain bread with arugula and sliced heirloom tomatoes.

Serves 6

1 can (19 oz/540 ml) white kidney or cannellini beans, drained and rinsed well

2 cloves garlic, crushed

1/4 cup (50 ml) chopped parsley

2 tbsp (25 ml) olive oil

2 tbsp (25 ml) freshly squeezed lemon juice

1 tbsp (15 ml) chopped fresh thyme

1/4 tsp (1 ml) sea salt, or to taste

Freshly ground black pepper, to taste

Combine beans, garlic, parsley, oil, lemon juice, thyme, salt and pepper in a food processor; pulse until smooth.

Cover and refrigerate until ready to serve.

NUTRITION
Per 1/4 cup (50 ml) serving: 133 cal, 6 g pro, 5 g total fat (0 g saturated fat), 17 g carb, 0 g fibre, 0 mg chol, 103 mg sodium

Tip: If dip is too thick, add an additional teaspoon (5 ml) of lemon juice.

Zesty Edamame

You'll find bags of edamame, frozen young green soybeans in pods, in the freezer section of most grocery stores and health food stores. They're a nutritious snack and they're quick to prepare—they need only be boiled or steamed for a few minutes and they're ready to enjoy. Best of all, kids love them too!

Serves 4

1 bag (1.1 lb/500 g) frozen edamame

Zest of 1 lemon

1/2 tsp (2 ml) coarse sea salt, or to taste

1/8 tsp (0.5 ml) red pepper flakes

Fill a saucepan with water and bring to a boil. Add edamame and bring water back to a boil. Continue to boil for 3 to 4 minutes; remove from heat and drain.

Place edamame in a serving bowl and toss with lemon zest, salt and red pepper flakes. Serve warm.

NUTRITION
Per 1 cup (250 ml) serving: 138 cal, 13 g pro, 6 g total fat (0 g saturated fat), 11 g carb, 6 g fibre, 0 mg chol, 300 mg sodium

Soups

MEAT/POULTRY SOUPS

Carrot Ginger Soup

This tasty, creamy soup is a staple lunch for me in the fall and winter. I just love the combination of ginger, orange and carrots!

Serves 8

1 tbsp (15 ml) canola oil

1 cup (250 ml) chopped onion

4 cups (1 L) chopped carrot

2 cups (500 ml) diced potato

1 tbsp (15 ml) grated fresh ginger root

4 cups (1 L) water

1 cup (250 ml) orange juice

1 tsp (5 ml) coarse sea salt, or to taste

1/2 tsp (2 ml) nutmeg

1/4 tsp (1 ml) cinnamon

1/4 tsp (1 ml) cumin

1/4 tsp (1 ml) freshly ground black pepper, or to taste

Heat oil in a large saucepan over medium heat. When pan is hot, add onions; reduce heat to medium and sauté for 8 to 10 minutes.

Add carrots, potato, ginger root, water, orange juice, salt, nutmeg, cinnamon, cumin and pepper. Cover and bring to a boil; reduce heat and simmer for 30 minutes.

Remove from heat; purée with a hand blender until carrots and potatoes are broken up but still slightly chunky, or to desired consistency.

NUTRITION
Per 1 cup (250 ml) serving: 94 cal, 2 g pro, 2 g total fat (0 g saturated fat), 18 g carb, 3 g fibre, 0 mg chol, 342 mg sodium

Creamy Cold Berry Soup

This antioxidant-rich soup is a colourful addition to any summer meal as a starter or a dessert. Alternatively, eat it as a snack—or even breakfast. Just about any type of berry can be substituted for the strawberries or blueberries.

Serves 4

2 cups (500 ml) sliced strawberries, washed and trimmed

1 pear, peeled and cored

1/2 cup (125 ml) fresh blueberries

1/2 cup (125 ml) pure pomegranate juice

1-1/2 cups (375 ml) low-fat (1% MF or less) plain yogurt

Fresh mint sprigs, as garnish

In batches, blend strawberries, pear, blueberries, pomegranate juice and yogurt until smooth. Combine blended ingredients in a large bowl. Refrigerate until ready to serve.

Garnish with sprigs of fresh mint.

Serve cold.

NUTRITION
Per 1 cup (250 ml) serving: 127 cal, 5 g pro, 1 g total fat (0 g saturated fat), 26 g carb, 4 g fibre, 2 mg chol, 69 mg sodium

Curried Pumpkin Soup

The combination of orange juice, pumpkin and curry powder gives this soup a rich flavour and creamy consistency. And it's lower in sodium than most commercial soups.

Serves 8

2 tbsp (25 ml) canola oil

2 cups (500 ml) finely chopped onions

2 cloves garlic, crushed

4 cups (1 L) water

1 can (28 oz/796 ml) pure pumpkin purée

1 cup (250 ml) orange juice

1 cup (250 ml) coconut milk

2 tbsp (25 ml) freshly squeezed lime juice

1 tbsp (15 ml) curry powder

1-1/2 tsp (7 ml) coarse sea salt, or to taste

1/8 tsp (0.5 ml) red pepper flakes, or to taste

Freshly ground black pepper, to taste

1/2 cup (125 ml) coarsely chopped fresh cilantro

Heat oil in a large saucepan over medium heat. When pan is hot, add onions and sauté for about 8 to 10 minutes. Add garlic; sauté for another minute.

Add water, pumpkin purée, orange juice, coconut milk, lime juice, curry powder, salt, red pepper flakes and pepper. Cover and bring to a boil; reduce heat and simmer for 30 minutes.

Garnish with fresh cilantro just before serving.

NUTRITION
Per 1 cup (250 ml) serving: 156 cal, 3 g pro, 10 g total fat (6 g saturated fat), 17 g carb, 4 g fibre, 0 mg chol, 452 mg sodium

Fresh Tomato Soup with Garlic and Basil

This light and healthy soup tastes best when made with fresh, locally grown tomatoes, in abundance during the summer months. This recipe clocks in at fewer than 100 calories and about 300 mg of sodium per serving—less than half of the sodium in most store-bought brands.

Serves 4

1 tbsp (15 ml) canola oil

1 cup (250 ml) chopped onions

3 cloves garlic, crushed

6 cups (1.5 L) chopped fresh tomatoes

2 cups (500 ml) water

1/4 cup (50 ml) fresh basil leaves, loosely packed

1/2 tsp (2 ml) coarse sea salt, or to taste

Freshly ground black pepper, to taste

Heat oil in a large saucepan over medium heat. When pan is hot, add onions; sauté for 8 to 10 minutes. Add garlic; sauté for another minute.

Add tomatoes, water, basil, salt and pepper. Cover and bring to a boil; reduce heat and simmer for 30 minutes.

Remove from heat; purée with a hand blender until smooth. Serve hot.

NUTRITION
Per 1-1/2 cup (375 ml) serving: 84 cal, 2 g pro, 4 g total fat (0 g saturated fat), 12 g carb, 3 g fibre, 0 mg chol, 306 mg sodium

Gazpacho

Gazpacho is a cold Spanish-style tomato soup loaded with vitamin C. It's very refreshing and meant for those summer days when it's too hot to cook and fresh, local tomatoes are readily available. This soup gets better the longer it sits, so if you have time, make it the day before you plan to serve it.

Serves 4

4 cups (1 L) chopped tomato

2 cups (500 ml) diced cucumber

1 cup (250 ml) chopped red onion

2 cups (500 ml) chopped red bell pepper

1 tbsp (15 ml) freshly squeezed lime juice

1 tbsp (15 ml) extra-virgin olive oil

3 cloves garlic, crushed

3 tbsp (50 ml) red wine vinegar

1 tbsp (15 ml) finely chopped jalapeno pepper, or to taste

1/2 tsp (2 ml) coarse sea salt, or to taste

Freshly ground black pepper, to taste

In a large mixing bowl, combine all ingredients. Remove and reserve about 2 cups (500 ml) of mixture.

Purée ingredients in a bowl with a hand blender until smooth. Add reserved solid ingredients; stir to combine. Serve chilled.

NUTRITION
Per 1-1/2 cup (375 ml) serving: 137 cal, 4 g pro, 5 g total fat (1 g saturated fat), 25 g carb, 5 g fibre, 0 mg chol, 325 mg sodium

Tip: Serve this soup in chilled soup bowls by placing them in the refrigerator for 30 minutes. Garnish the soup with shredded cucumber.

Roasted Garlic and Butternut Squash Soup

The bright orange colour of this soup is an indicator of its exceptional phytochemical content. Thanks to the butternut squash, it's packed with beta carotene as well as vitamins C and E. The roasted garlic adds a wonderful subtle flavour.

Serves 6

2 bulbs garlic

1 tsp (5 ml) + 2 tbsp (25 ml) canola oil

1 medium butternut squash (about 2 lb/1 kg)

2 cups (500 ml) chopped onions

6 cups (1.5 L) water

1 tsp (5 ml) coarse sea salt, or to taste

Preheat oven to 375°F (190°C).

Gently remove papery skin from garlic cloves and slice off a quarter-inch (0.5 cm) from the top of each. Place garlic on a baking sheet and drizzle with 1/4 tsp (1 ml) of the oil.

Slice squash in half lengthwise and scoop out seeds. Place squash cut side up on the baking sheet with the garlic. Drizzle squash with 3/4 tsp (3 ml) of the oil.

Place baking sheet in oven; bake for 1 hour, or until squash is cooked through and can easily be pierced with a fork.

Meanwhile, heat the last 2 tbsp (25 ml) of the oil in a large saucepan over medium heat. When pan is hot, add onions and sauté until onions begin to brown and caramelize, about 15 to 20 minutes. (Reduce heat if onions begin to burn.) Add water and salt to pan.

Meanwhile, gently scoop out flesh of butternut squash and add to the saucepan. Gently squeeze each clove of roasted garlic out of the skin; add to saucepan with squash.

Cover saucepan and bring to a boil; reduce heat and simmer for 20 minutes.

Remove from heat; purée with a hand blender until smooth.

NUTRITION
Per 1-1/3 cup (325 ml) serving: 134 cal, 2 g pro, 5 g total fat (0 g saturated fat), 22 g carb, 3 g fibre, 0 mg chol, 403 mg sodium

Tip: A bulb of garlic is the large papery cluster that usually contains 10 to 12 individual cloves. While two bulbs of garlic sound like a lot for one recipe, it develops a lovely mellow flavour once it's roasted.

Roasted Parsnip and Pear Soup

Parsnips are a white root vegetable related to carrots. While they lack their cousin's beta carotene, they're a good source of other nutrients, including vitamin C, folate and potassium. This recipe pairs the nutty flavour of parsnips with the sweetness of pears.

Serves 6

1 lb (454 g) parsnips (about 6 medium), cut into 1-inch (2.5 cm) pieces

2 cups (500 ml) chopped onion

2 tbsp (25 ml) canola oil

6 cups (1.5 L) water

2 pears, peeled, cored and diced

1 tsp (5 ml) coarse sea salt, or to taste

Preheat oven to 375°F (190°C).

In a large bowl, toss parsnips, onion, and oil. Place on a baking sheet; bake for 30 minutes or until parsnips are cooked through and beginning to brown.

In a large saucepan, combine water, pears, salt and roasted parsnips and onion.

Cover and bring to a boil over high heat; reduce heat and simmer for 20 to 30 minutes or until pears are soft.

Remove from heat; purée with a hand blender to smooth consistency. Serve warm.

NUTRITION
Per 1-1/3 cup (325 ml) serving: 151 cal, 2 g pro, 5 g total fat (0 g saturated fat), 28 g carb, 5 g fibre, 0 mg chol, 404 mg sodium

Squash and Apple Soup

A simple yet delicious puréed soup perfect for a cool autumn day when locally grown apples are plentiful. I like to garnish this soup with shredded apple or toasted pumpkin seeds.

Serves 8

2 tbsp (25 ml) canola oil

2 cups (500 ml) chopped onion

6 cups (1.5 L) water

4 cups (1 L) cubed butternut squash

2 apples, peeled, cored and chopped

1 tbsp (15 ml) minced fresh ginger root

1 tsp (5 ml) coarse sea salt, or to taste

Heat oil in a large saucepan over medium heat. When pan is hot, add onions and sauté for about 8 to 10 minutes.

Add water, squash, apples, ginger root and salt.

Cover and bring to a boil; reduce heat and simmer for 30 minutes, or until squash is tender.

Purée with a hand blender until smooth, or to desired consistency.

NUTRITION
Per 1 cup (250 ml) serving: 94 cal, 1 g pro, 4 g total fat (0 g saturated fat), 17 g carb, 2 g fibre, 0 mg chol, 300 mg sodium

Sweet Potato Soup with Maple-Glazed Walnuts

This recipe provides a simple and tasty way to get your daily serving of bright orange vegetables. This soup is packed with beta carotene—one serving contains a whopping 13 milligrams! It's also a good source of fibre, vitamin K and potassium.

Serves 6

SOUP

2 tbsp (25 ml) canola oil

1 cup (250 ml) diced onion

1 medium sweet potato, peeled and diced (about 1-1/2 lb/670 g)

2 cups (500 ml) chopped carrot

6 cups (1.5 L) water

1 tsp (5 ml) coarse sea salt, or to taste

1 tsp (5 ml) nutmeg

1 tsp (5 ml) grated fresh ginger root

Freshly ground black pepper, to taste

MAPLE-GLAZED WALNUTS

1/4 cup (50 ml) coarsely chopped walnuts

1 tbsp (15 ml) maple syrup

Heat oil in a large saucepan over medium heat. When pan is hot, add onions and sauté for 8 to 10 minutes.

Add sweet potato, carrots, water, salt, nutmeg, ginger and pepper. Cover and bring to a boil; reduce heat and simmer for 30 to 40 minutes or until sweet potatoes and carrots are tender and can easily be pierced with a fork.

Meanwhile, in a small mixing bowl combine walnuts and maple syrup; toss to coat. Heat a skillet over medium heat; add walnut mixture and toast until fragrant and sticky, about 3 to 4 minutes. Set aside to cool.

Remove soup from heat; purée with a hand blender until smooth.

Garnish soup with glazed walnuts.

NUTRITION
Per 1-1/3 cup (325 ml) soup and 1 tbsp (15 ml) walnuts: 203 cal, 3 g pro, 8 g total fat (1 g saturated fat), 33 g carb, 5 g fibre, 0 mg chol, 488 mg sodium

Curried Lentil Soup

High in fibre and an excellent source of vitamin A and iron, this flavourful soup has a creamy, thick texture after the lentils are puréed. Serve this soup with a piece of fresh whole-grain bread spread with roasted garlic for a quick, healthy meal.

Serves 6

2 tbsp (25 ml) canola oil

1 cup (250 ml) chopped onion

1 cup (250 ml) chopped celery

2 cups (500 ml) chopped carrot

3 cloves garlic, crushed

1 tbsp (15 ml) grated fresh ginger root

6 cups (1.5 L) water

1 cup (250 ml) dried green lentils

1 tbsp (15 ml) freshly squeezed lime juice

2 tsp (10 ml) curry powder

1 tsp (5 ml) coarse sea salt, or to taste

Heat oil in a large saucepan over medium heat. When pan is hot, add onions, celery and carrots and sauté for about 8 to 10 minutes. Add garlic and ginger; sauté for another minute.

Add water, lentils, lime juice, curry powder and salt. Cover and bring to a boil; reduce heat and simmer for 45 minutes or until lentils are soft.

Remove from heat. Purée with a hand blender until lentils are broken up, but still slightly chunky.

NUTRITION
Per 1-1/3 cup (325 ml) serving: 177 cal, 8 g pro, 6 g total fat (0 g saturated fat), 27 g carb, 7 g fibre, 0 mg chol, 442 mg sodium

Hearty Minestrone Soup

Minestrone soup has always been a favourite of mine. To me, it's a meal in a bowl. In this recipe, the combination of wild rice, beans and veggies results in a hearty soup that's low in fat and high in fibre. This soup freezes extremely well—I suggest freezing it in individual portions so it's ready to grab to take to work or school for lunch.

Serves 8

1 tbsp (15 ml) canola oil

2 cups (500 ml) chopped onion

3 cloves garlic, crushed

8 cups (2 L) water

1 tbsp (15 ml) tomato paste

1 cup (250 ml) chopped carrot

1/4 cup (50 ml) uncooked wild rice

1 can (28 oz/796 ml) diced tomatoes

1 can (19 oz/540 ml) chickpeas, drained and rinsed well

1 can (19 oz/540 ml) kidney beans, drained and rinsed well

6 Brussels sprouts, trimmed and halved

1 cup (250 ml) chopped green or yellow zucchini

3 tbsp (50 ml) sodium-reduced soy sauce

1 tsp (5 ml) coarse sea salt, or to taste

Freshly ground black pepper, to taste

2 cups (500 ml) sliced bok choy

2 tbsp (25 ml) chopped fresh basil

Heat oil in a large saucepan over medium heat. When pan is hot, add onions and sauté for about 8 to 10 minutes. Add garlic; sauté for another minute.

Add water, tomato paste, carrots, wild rice, tomatoes, chickpeas, kidney beans, Brussels sprouts, zucchini, soy sauce, salt and pepper.

Cover and bring to a boil; reduce heat and simmer for 50 minutes, or until rice is tender.

Remove from heat and stir in bok choy and basil.

NUTRITION
Per 1-1/2 cup (375 ml) serving: 207 cal, 11 g pro, 3 g total fat (0 g saturated fat), 37 g carb, 8 g fibre, 0 mg chol, 660 mg sodium

Hot and Sour Soup

This delicious soup is so easy to make—it's ready in less than 25 minutes! If you don't have kale, you can add the same amount of spinach just before serving. It also tastes great with sliced bamboo shoots (available canned in most major grocery stores). I often make this soup when someone in the house has a cold—it's nice and spicy and clears the sinuses!

Serves 6

1 tbsp (15 ml) canola oil

1 cup (250 ml) finely chopped onion

1 tbsp (15 ml) grated fresh ginger root

6 cups (1.5 L) water

2 cups (500 ml) kale, stems removed and finely chopped

1 cup (250 ml) sliced button mushrooms

Half pkg (12 oz/350 g) extra firm tofu, cubed

2 tbsp (25 ml) unseasoned or low-sodium seasoned rice vinegar

2 tbsp (25 ml) balsamic vinegar

2 tbsp (25 ml) sodium-reduced soy sauce

1 tsp (5 ml) coarse sea salt, or to taste

1 tsp (5 ml) sesame oil

1 tsp (5 ml) freshly squeezed lime juice

1/8 tsp (0.5 ml) red pepper flakes

Freshly ground black pepper, to taste

2 green onions, chopped

Heat oil in a large saucepan over medium heat. When pan is hot, add onions and sauté for about 8 to 10 minutes. Add ginger; sauté for another minute.

Add water, kale, mushrooms, tofu, rice vinegar, balsamic vinegar, soy sauce, salt, sesame oil, lime juice, red pepper flakes and pepper.

Cover and bring to a boil; reduce heat and simmer for 20 minutes.

Remove from heat; garnish with chopped green onions.

NUTRITION
Per 1-1/4 cup (300 ml) serving: 98 cal, 6 g pro, 5 g total fat (1 g saturated fat), 8 g carb, 1 g fibre, 0 mg chol, 589 mg sodium

Tip: What's the difference between unseasoned and seasoned rice vinegar? Seasoned rice vinegar has added sugar and salt. In fact, some brands of seasoned rice vinegar have up to 530 milligrams of sodium per tablespoon—one-third of a day's worth! This recipe calls for unseasoned rice vinegar—if you can't find it, choose rice vinegar that has 60 milligrams of sodium or less per serving.

Kale and Cannellini Soup

Kale's sturdy leaves hold up well in soups—in fact, it's one of my favourite ways to serve kale. I like to serve this hearty soup in the fall when the temperature begins to drop. Serve a bowl of this soup with a slice of freshly baked Rosemary Beer Bread (page 342) for a satisfying meal.

Serves 6

3 tbsp (50 ml) canola oil

2 cups (500 ml) chopped onion

2 cups (500 ml) chopped carrot

1 cup (250 ml) chopped celery

4 cloves garlic, crushed

6 cups (1.5 L) water

1 can (19 oz/540 ml) cannellini beans, drained and rinsed well

1 large bunch kale, stems removed and finely chopped (about 4 cups/1 L)

1/3 cup (75 ml) white wine

2 tbsp (25 ml) sodium-reduced soy sauce

2 tbsp (25 ml) freshly squeezed lemon juice

1 tsp (5 ml) coarse sea salt, or to taste

1 tsp (5 ml) dried Herbes de Provence

Freshly ground black pepper, to taste

Heat oil in a large saucepan over medium heat. When pan is hot, add onions, carrots and celery, and sauté for about 8 to 10 minutes. Add garlic; sauté for another minute.

Add water, cannellini beans, kale, wine, soy sauce, lemon juice, salt, herbs and pepper. Cover and bring to a boil; reduce heat and simmer for 30 minutes.

NUTRITION
Per 1-1/3 cup (325 ml) serving: 208 cal, 7 g pro, 8 g total fat (1 g saturated fat), 27 g carb, 7 g fibre, 0 mg chol, 662 mg sodium

Tip: You can swap cannellini beans for other mild-tasting beans, such as chickpeas. Likewise, you can use other leafy greens in place of the kale, such as spinach or Swiss chard—but because their leaves are more delicate, add them during the last five minutes of cooking.

Lemon and Spinach Chickpea Soup

This high-fibre soup makes for a satisfying midday meal when combined with a whole-grain roll and side salad, such as Pomegranate Garden Salad with Maple Dressing (page 152). If you don't have chickpeas, white kidney beans are equally good in this recipe.

Serves 6

2 tbsp (25 ml) canola oil

1 cup (250 ml) chopped onion

1 cup (250 ml) finely chopped carrot

3 cloves garlic, crushed

4 cups (1 L) water

1 tbsp (15 ml) white wine

1 tbsp (15 ml) unseasoned rice vinegar

2 tbsp (25 ml) freshly squeezed lemon juice

1 can (19 oz/540 ml) chickpeas, drained and rinsed well

3/4 tsp (4 ml) coarse sea salt, or to taste

1/2 tsp (2 ml) cumin seeds

2 cups (500 ml) finely chopped spinach

Heat oil in a large saucepan over medium heat. When pan is hot, add onions and sauté for 8 to 10 minutes. Add carrots and garlic; sauté for another 2 to 3 minutes.

Add water, wine, rice vinegar, lemon juice, chickpeas, salt and cumin. Cover and bring to a boil; reduce heat and simmer for 30 minutes.

Remove from heat and stir in spinach.

NUTRITION

Per 1 cup (250 ml) serving: 157 cal, 5 g pro, 6 g total fat (0 g saturated fat), 23 g carb, 4 g fibre, 0 mg chol, 560 mg sodium

Moroccan Lentil Soup

This flavourful soup reminds me of my trip to Morocco, where I often enjoyed lentil soup at lunch. The secret to making this soup is puréeing it to the right consistency; the cooked lentils will give it a rich, creamy texture. Adjust cayenne pepper to taste. Keep in mind this soup tends to get slightly spicier after being refrigerated.

Serves 8

1 tbsp (15 ml) canola oil

2 cups (500 ml) chopped onion

2 cloves garlic, crushed

1 tbsp (15 ml) grated fresh ginger root

8 cups (2 L) water

1 cup (250 ml) dried brown or green lentils, rinsed and picked over

1 cup (250 ml) chopped carrot

1 can (28 oz/796 ml) plum tomatoes

3 tbsp (45 ml) freshly squeezed lemon juice

1 tsp (5 ml) coarse sea salt, or to taste

1 tsp (5 ml) turmeric

1/8 tsp (0.5 ml) cayenne pepper, or to taste

1/8 tsp (0.5 ml) cinnamon

Freshly ground black pepper, to taste

Heat oil in a large saucepan over medium heat. When pan is hot, add onions and sauté for 8 to 10 minutes. Add garlic and ginger root; sauté another minute.

Add water, lentils, carrots, tomatoes, lemon juice, salt, turmeric, cayenne pepper, cinnamon and pepper. Cover and bring to a boil, reduce heat and simmer for 45 minutes.

Remove from heat. Purée with a hand blender until carrots and lentils are a uniformly creamy consistency.

NUTRITION

Per 1-1/2 cup (375 ml) serving: 141 cal, 8 g pro, 2 g total fat (0 g saturated fat), 24 g carb, 5 g fibre, 0 mg chol, 458 mg sodium

Red Lentil Soup

Don't be fooled by their red hue—when cooked, red lentils turn pale yellow. And unlike many other dried legumes, which require a long soaking and cooking time, red lentils are very quick and easy to prepare. They're also high in iron and folate and an excellent source of fibre.

Serves 6

2 tbsp (25 ml) canola oil

2 cups (500 ml) chopped onion

2 cloves garlic, crushed

6 cups (1.5 L) water

1 cup (250 ml) raw red lentils

1/4 cup (50 ml) freshly squeezed lemon juice

1 tsp (5 ml) coarse sea salt, or to taste

1/2 tsp (2 ml) ground cumin

1/2 tsp (2 ml) turmeric

Heat oil in a large saucepan over medium heat. When pan is hot, add onions and sauté for about 8 to 10 minutes. Add garlic; sauté for another minute.

Add water, lentils, lemon juice, salt, cumin and turmeric.

Cover and bring to a boil; reduce heat and simmer for 30 minutes, or until lentils are soft.

Remove from heat; purée with a hand blender until smooth.

Serve hot.

NUTRITION
Per 1 cup (250 ml) serving: 178 cal, 9 g pro, 5 g total fat (1 g saturated fat), 26 g carb, 4 g fibre, 0 mg chol, 399 mg sodium

Spicy Black Bean Soup

This easy to prepare, spicy and fibre-rich soup is definitely a crowd pleaser. And you'll like the fact it's lower in sodium than store-bought brands. Serve it with a side salad, such as Spinach and Grapefruit Salad with Citrus Maple Dressing (page 142), for a satisfying meal.

Serves 8

2 tbsp (25 ml) canola oil

1 cup (250 ml) chopped onion

3 cloves garlic, crushed

1 cup (250 ml) chopped carrot

6 cups (1.5 L) water

2 cans (19 oz/540 ml each) black beans, drained and rinsed well

1 can (28 oz/796 ml) diced tomatoes

2 tbsp (25 ml) freshly squeezed lime juice

1 tsp (5 ml) coarse sea salt, or to taste

1 tsp (5 ml) ground cumin

1/4 tsp (1 ml) red pepper flakes, or to taste

1 cup (250 ml) fresh or frozen corn kernels

1/2 cup (125 ml) chopped cilantro

Heat oil in a large saucepan over medium heat. When pan is hot, add onions and sauté for about 8 to 10 minutes or until soft. Add garlic; sauté another minute.

Add carrots, water, beans, tomatoes, lime juice, salt, cumin and red pepper flakes. Cover and bring to a boil; reduce heat and simmer for 30 minutes.

Remove from heat; purée with a hand blender until beans are somewhat blended but still chunky. Add corn. Garnish with cilantro.

NUTRITION
Per 1-1/2 cup (375 ml) serving: 200 cal, 9 g pro, 4 g total fat (0 g saturated fat), 34 g carb, 7 g fibre, 0 mg chol, 444 mg sodium

Chicken Barley Soup

This is definitely a soup that will warm you up on a cold winter's day. I often freeze it in single servings so I can take it to work and enjoy it for lunch during the week.

Serves 8

3 tbsp (50 ml) canola oil

1 cup (250 ml) chopped onion

1 cup (250 ml) diced celery

2 cups (500 ml) diced carrot

12 oz (350 g) cooked chicken breast, cut into 1-inch (2.5 cm) cubes

3 cloves garlic, crushed

8 cups (2 L) water, or Homemade Chicken Stock (page 129)

1/2 cup (125 ml) white wine

1/2 cup (125 ml) pearl barley

2 tbsp (25 ml) sodium-reduced soy sauce

1 tbsp (15 ml) balsamic vinegar

1 tsp (5 ml) coarse sea salt, or to taste

1/2 tsp (2 ml) dried rosemary

1/2 tsp (2 ml) dried basil

Heat 2 tbsp (25 ml) oil in a large saucepan over medium heat. When pan is hot, add onions and sauté for 8 to 10 minutes.

When onions are soft and begin to brown, add 1 tbsp (15 ml) oil, celery, carrots and chicken; continue to sauté until chicken is brown, about 10 to 12 minutes. Add garlic; sauté for another minute.

Add water, wine, barley, soy sauce, vinegar, salt, rosemary and basil. Cover and bring to a boil; reduce heat and simmer for 45 minutes.

NUTRITION

Per 1-1/4 cup (300 ml) serving: 175 cal, 12 g pro, 6 g total fat (1 g saturated fat), 16 g carb, 2 g fibre, 24 mg chol, 487 mg sodium

Tip: If you're using store-bought chicken broth to make this soup, choose a product with no added salt, such as PC Blue Menu Chicken Broth. If you do choose a chicken broth product with added salt, eliminate the sea salt called for in this recipe.

Homemade Chicken Stock

Store-bought chicken stock can pack a lot of sodium—some brands have as much as 900 milligrams of sodium per 1 cup (250 ml) serving. I like to make my own chicken stock by slowly simmering a chicken carcass, veggies and herbs in water for a few hours. The end result is stock rich in flavour without the added sodium. This version of chicken stock has less than 60 milligrams of sodium per serving!

Makes 6 cups

1 chicken carcass (from a 3 lb/1300 g chicken), meat and skin removed

6 cups (1.5 L) water

1 large onion, quartered

3 stalks celery, cut into 2-inch (5 cm) pieces

2 carrots, cut into 1-inch (2.5 cm) pieces

3 cloves garlic

10 peppercorns

2 bay leaves

Combine all ingredients in a large saucepan. Bring to a boil over high heat; reduce heat and simmer for two to three hours.

Remove from heat; sieve stock to remove chicken carcass and vegetables.

NUTRITION
Per 1 cup (250 ml): 13 cal, 2 g pro, 0 g total fat (0 g saturated fat), 1 g carb, 0 g fibre, 0 mg chol, 55 mg sodium

Tip: Use the carcass of a leftover roast chicken for this recipe. If you don't want to make the stock right away after roasting a chicken, freeze the carcass until you're ready to use it.

Italian Wedding Soup

Despite what its name suggests, this soup isn't served at Italian weddings. Originally called *Minestra Maritata* in Italian, its name is a reference to the combination of greens and meat that go so well together. There are endless variations to this soup, like chicken and Swiss chard—so be creative and add whatever you have on hand.

Serves 6

1 tbsp (15 ml) canola oil

2 cups (500 ml) finely diced carrot

1 cup (250 ml) finely chopped onion

1 cup (250 ml) chopped celery

4 cloves garlic, crushed

6 cups (1.5 L) water, or Homemade Chicken Stock (page 129)

1 tsp (5 ml) coarse sea salt, or to taste

2 bay leaves

2 cups (500 ml) coarsely chopped spinach

1 cup (250 ml) cooked pasta, such as farfalle ("bow-tie") or conchiglie (seashell-shaped)

MEATBALLS

0.5 lb (227 g) lean ground beef

1/2 cup (125 ml) finely chopped parsley

3 tbsp (50 ml) whole wheat bread crumbs

1 egg

1/2 tsp (2 ml) dried basil

Freshly ground black pepper, to taste

In a large mixing bowl, combine ground beef, parsley, bread crumbs, egg, basil and pepper. Using the palm of your hand, roll mixture into 1-inch (2.5 cm) balls. Set aside.

In a large saucepan, heat oil over medium heat. When pan is hot, add carrots, onions and celery; sauté for 10 minutes, or until vegetables are soft. Add garlic; sauté for another minute.

Add water, salt and bay leaves; bring to a boil over high heat. Gently add the meatballs to the soup, and continue to boil for 5 minutes without stirring.

Cover, reduce heat, and simmer for 25 minutes. Add spinach and cooked pasta to soup; stir and continue to cook for 5 minutes until spinach is wilted and pasta is heated through.

NUTRITION
Per 1-1/3 cup (325 ml) serving: 172 cal, 12 g pro, 6 g total fat (2 g saturated fat), 17 g carb, 3 g fibre, 48 mg chol, 524 mg sodium

Tip: If you're using store-bought chicken broth instead of water or Homemade Chicken Stock, choose a product with no added salt, such as PC Blue Menu Chicken Broth. If you do choose a chicken broth product with added salt, eliminate the sea salt called for in the recipe.

Thai Coconut Chicken Soup

The wonderful taste of this creamy soup reminds me of my trips to Thailand and Laos, where it's called Tom kha gai. I've modified the recipe to use ingredients that are readily available at most major grocery stores. Feel free to use shrimp or diced firm tofu instead of chicken.

Serves 6

4 cups (1 L) water, or Homemade Chicken
    Stock (page 129)

2 tbsp (25 ml) grated fresh ginger root

1 tsp (5 ml) lemon zest

1/2 tsp (2 ml) coarse sea salt, or to taste

1/2 tsp (2 ml) Thai fish sauce

Pinch red pepper flakes, or to taste

1 cup (250 ml) thinly sliced red pepper
    strips (2 inches/5 cm long)

1 cup (250 ml) snow peas, trimmed

1 cup (250 ml) sliced mushrooms

1 cup (250 ml) coconut milk

2 tbsp (25 ml) freshly squeezed lime juice

1 cup (250 ml) shredded, cooked chicken
    breast (about 5 oz/150 g)

1/2 cup (125 ml) chopped cilantro

In a large saucepan, combine water, ginger, lemon zest, salt, fish sauce and red pepper flakes; bring to a boil over high heat. Reduce heat to medium and add red pepper, snow peas and mushrooms; simmer for 5 minutes.

Reduce heat to low; gradually stir in coconut milk and lime juice. Add chicken breast. Cook just until heated through, about 4 to 5 minutes. Remove from heat, ladle into bowls and garnish with fresh cilantro.

NUTRITION
Per 1-1/3 cup (325 ml) serving: 130 cal, 9 g pro, 9 g total fat (7 g saturated fat), 5 g carb, 1 g fibre, 19 mg chol, 261 mg sodium

Tip: If you're using store-bought chicken broth instead of water or Homemade Chicken Stock, choose a product with no added salt, such as PC Blue Menu Chicken Broth. If you do choose a chicken broth product with added salt, eliminate the sea salt called for in the recipe.

Wild Rice, Mushroom and Beef Soup

This stick-to-your-ribs soup features wild rice, which gives it a nutty flavour. Wild rice is actually the seed of an aquatic grass native to Canada. Traditionally it's found in shallow rivers and streams in Saskatchewan, Manitoba and Northern Ontario. Look for locally grown wild rice at major grocery stores or specialty food stores.

Serves 6

2 tbsp (25 ml) canola oil

2 cups (500 ml) finely chopped onion

4 cups (1 L) sliced brown mushrooms, such as cremini or portobello

1 lb (454 g) topside steak, trimmed of fat and cut into 1-inch (2.5 cm) strips

4 cloves garlic, crushed

6 cups (1.5 L) water, or low-sodium beef stock

1/2 cup (125 ml) white wine

1/3 cup (75 ml) wild rice

1 tsp (5 ml) coarse sea salt, or to taste

1/2 tsp (2 ml) dried rosemary

1/2 tsp (2 ml) dried marjoram

Freshly ground pepper, to taste

Heat oil in a large saucepan over medium heat. When pan is hot, add onions and mushrooms and sauté for 12 to 15 minutes, or until pan begins to dry out.

Increase heat to high and add steak; continue to sauté until steak is brown, about 5 minutes. Add garlic; sauté for another minute.

Add water, wine, rice, salt, rosemary, marjoram and pepper. Cover and bring to a boil; reduce heat and simmer for 55 minutes, or until rice is tender.

NUTRITION
Per 1-1/3 cup (325 ml) serving: 223 cal, 20 g pro, 8 g total fat (2 g saturated fat), 14 g carb, 2 g fibre, 36 mg chol, 443 mg sodium

Salads

ENTRÉE SALADS

Blueberry and Roasted Walnut Spinach Salad with Lemon Walnut Dressing

This salad tastes as good as it sounds—and looks. If you have other types of berries on hand, such as raspberries or strawberries, feel free to add them for extra flavour and colour. Drizzle the salad with dressing just before serving, otherwise the spinach will wilt.

Serves 4

SALAD

1/4 cup (50 ml) walnut halves

8 cups (2 L) spinach

1 cup (250 ml) fresh blueberries

1/4 cup (50 ml) dried cranberries

Zest of 1 lemon

DRESSING

1/4 cup (50 ml) walnut oil

2 tbsp (25 ml) freshly squeezed lemon juice

1 tbsp (15 ml) Dijon mustard

2 tsp (10 ml) honey

Zest of 1 lemon

Preheat oven to 375°F (190°C).

Bake nuts on a baking sheet for 5 to 7 minutes, or until nuts are slightly brown and fragrant. Remove from oven and set aside to cool.

In a small bowl, whisk together walnut oil, lemon juice, mustard, honey and lemon zest until thick and creamy. Cover and refrigerate until ready to serve.

In a large bowl, toss spinach with blueberries, cranberries and the toasted walnuts.

Drizzle with dressing and transfer to individual plates. Garnish each with lemon zest.

NUTRITION

Per 2 cup (500 ml) serving of salad with 2 tbsp (25 ml) Lemon Walnut Dressing: 255 cal, 5 g pro, 19 g total fat (1 g saturated fat), 20 g carb, 5 g fibre, 0 mg chol, 134 mg sodium

Tip: Use unrefined walnut oil in this recipe. Not only does it have more flavour than refined walnut oil, but it also tends to be higher in essential fatty acids, since it's been processed to a lesser extent. Unrefined oils are more prone to the effects of heat, light and air, so be sure to store walnut oil in a cool, dark place or in the refrigerator.

Fig and Roasted Walnut Salad with Honey Balsamic Vinaigrette

Dried figs, red onion and roasted walnuts give this salad plenty of flavour and texture. The walnuts make this salad a great source of an omega-3 fat called alpha-linolenic acid (ALA), while the figs boost its magnesium content.

Serves 6

SALAD

1/4 cup (50 ml) walnut pieces

12 dried figs, cut into eighths

8 cups (2 L) spinach

1/2 cup (125 ml) sliced red onion

1/4 cup (50 ml) crumbled feta cheese

DRESSING

3 tbsp (50 ml) extra-virgin olive oil

3 tbsp (50 ml) balsamic vinegar

1 tbsp (15 ml) honey

1/2 tbsp (7 ml) Dijon mustard

1 clove garlic, crushed

Preheat oven to 350°F (180°C).

Place walnut pieces on a baking sheet and bake for 5 to 7 minutes or until nuts are golden brown and fragrant. Remove from heat and cool.

In a small bowl, whisk together olive oil, vinegar, honey, mustard and garlic.

In a large salad bowl, toss figs, spinach, onion, feta cheese and roasted walnuts. Drizzle with dressing and serve immediately.

NUTRITION

Per 1-1/2 cup (375 ml) serving with 1 tbsp (15 ml) Honey Balsamic Vinaigrette: 205 cal, 5 g pro, 14 g total fat (2 g saturated fat), 18 g carb, 3 g fibre, 6 mg chol, 119 mg sodium

Pomegranate Garden Salad with Maple Dressing

With their signature deep crimson colour, pomegranates are an exceptional source of an antioxidant called polyphenols. This tasty salad combines baby greens, tomatoes and carrots. Pomegranate seeds, technically called arils, add a crunchy texture to this salad.

Serves 4

SALAD

4 cups (1 L) mixed baby greens, such as mesclun mix

1 cup (250 ml) halved cherry tomatoes

1/2 cup (125 ml) shredded carrot

1/2 cup (125 ml) pomegranate seeds

2 tbsp (25 ml) sunflower seeds

DRESSING

1/4 cup (50 ml) pure pomegranate juice, such as POM

2 tbsp (25 ml) apple cider vinegar

2 tbsp (25 ml) flaxseed oil

2 tsp (10 ml) Dijon mustard

2 tsp (10 ml) freshly squeezed lemon juice

1 tsp (5 ml) maple syrup

In a large bowl, combine greens, tomatoes, carrots, pomegranate seeds and sunflower seeds.

In a small bowl, whisk together pomegranate juice, vinegar, flaxseed oil, mustard, lemon juice and maple syrup.

Toss salad with dressing and serve immediately.

NUTRITION

Per 1-1/2 cup (375 ml) serving of salad with 2 tbsp (25 ml) Maple Dressing: 161 cal, 3 g pro, 10 g total fat (1 g saturated fat), 19 g carb, 3 g fibre, 0 mg chol, 69 mg sodium

Tip: Unopened pomegranates can last up to one month on the counter, or up to two months when refrigerated. Pomegranate seeds, or arils, can last up to two weeks in the refrigerator once removed from the inside of a pomegranate.

Red Grape, Arugula and Toasted Walnut Salad

Walnut oil may be more expensive than olive and canola oil, but it's well worth the extra cost thanks to its exceptional ALA content (an omega-3 fat) and rich nutty flavour. Walnut oil can vary widely in flavour; for the best-tasting oil, look for a product that's unrefined.

Serves 6

SALAD

1/2 cup (125 ml) coarsely chopped walnut halves

4 cups (1 L) tightly packed arugula

2 cups (500 ml) red grapes, halved

DRESSING

4 tbsp (60 ml) walnut oil

2 tbsp (25 ml) freshly squeezed lemon juice

2 tsp (10 ml) honey

1 tsp (5 ml) whole-grain mustard

Preheat oven to 350°F (180°C).

Arrange walnuts on a baking sheet and place in the oven for 5 to 7 minutes, or until fragrant; remove from heat and cool.

In a large mixing bowl, toss together arugula, grapes and toasted walnuts; set aside.

In a small mixing bowl, whisk together walnut oil, lemon juice, honey and mustard. Drizzle dressing over salad; serve immediately.

NUTRITION
Per 1 cup (250 ml) salad and 1 tbsp (15 ml) dressing: 182 cal, 2 g pro, 15 g total fat (1 g saturated fat), 13 g carb, 1 g fibre, 0 mg chol, 15 mg sodium

Tip: Walnut oil is susceptible to damage from heat and light and has a limited shelf life. Store it in the refrigerator for up to six months.

Spinach and Grapefruit Salad with Citrus Maple Dressing

This is a refreshing combination of three disease-fighting foods: spinach, grapefruit and walnuts. For extra colour, toss in a handful of fresh berries. If you prefer, you can serve this salad warm by sautéing the mushrooms with onions in balsamic vinegar before tossing with spinach.

Serves 4

SALAD

1/4 cup (50 ml) walnut halves

4 cups (1 L) spinach

1 grapefruit, peeled and sectioned

1 small red onion, thinly sliced

1 cup (250 ml) sliced mushrooms

1/2 cup (125 ml) low-fat goat cheese

DRESSING

1/4 cup (50 ml) freshly squeezed grapefruit juice

1 tbsp (15 ml) freshly squeezed lemon juice

1 tbsp (15 ml) maple syrup

1 tbsp (15 ml) extra-virgin olive oil

1/2 tbsp (7 ml) Dijon mustard

1/2 tsp (2 ml) minced fresh ginger root

1 clove garlic, crushed

Preheat oven to 350°F (180°C).

Bake walnuts on a baking sheet for 5 to 7 minutes, until lightly brown and fragrant. Remove from oven; set aside to cool.

In a large bowl, toss spinach with grapefruit, onion, mushrooms, goat cheese and toasted walnuts.

In a small bowl, whisk together grapefruit juice, lemon juice, maple syrup, olive oil, mustard, ginger root and garlic.

Drizzle salad with dressing; serve immediately.

NUTRITION

Per 1-3/4 cup (425 ml) serving of salad with 2 tbsp (25 ml) Citrus Maple Dressing: 208 cal, 8 g pro, 14 g total fat (1 g saturated fat), 16 g carb, 3 g fibre, 0 mg chol, 168 mg sodium

Spinach Salad with Strawberries, Pine Nuts and Champagne Vinaigrette

This is such an easy salad to prepare and it's sure to impress your dinner guests. Other toasted nuts can be substituted for the pine nuts, such as sliced almonds and shelled pistachios. For variety, use half spinach leaves and half arugula for a peppery version.

Serves 4

1/4 cup (50 ml) pine nuts

8 cups (2 L) baby spinach

2 cups (500 ml) sliced strawberries

1/4 cup (50 ml) thinly sliced red onion

2 tbsp (25 ml) extra-virgin olive oil

2 tbsp (25 ml) champagne vinegar

4 tsp (20 ml) honey

1/2 tsp (2 ml) grainy Dijon mustard

Preheat oven to 350°F (180°C).

Arrange pine nuts on a baking sheet; bake for 5 to 7 minutes, or until pine nuts are light golden brown and fragrant. Remove from heat; set aside to cool.

In a large salad bowl, toss together spinach, strawberries and red onion.

In a small mixing bowl, whisk together olive oil, vinegar, honey and Dijon.

Sprinkle toasted pine nuts over salad; drizzle with vinaigrette. Serve immediately.

NUTRITION

Per 1-1/2 cups (325 ml) salad and 1-1/2 tbsp (22 ml) dressing: 110 cal, 2.4 g pro, 8 g total fat (0 g saturated fat), 10 g carb, 1.2 g fibre, 0 mg chol, 97 mg sodium

Tip: Champagne vinegar is a light and mild vinegar that works well when paired with fresh fruit. If you don't have champagne vinegar, substitute an equal amount of white wine vinegar or apple cider vinegar.

Warm Spinach and Mushroom Salad with Goat Cheese

Low in sodium and saturated fat and packed with potassium, this decadent-tasting salad is ready in less than 20 minutes. The recipe suggests serving it warm, but it tastes just as good cold, so consider making extra for the next day's lunch.

Serves 4

2 tsp (10 ml) olive oil

1 cup (250 ml) sliced red onion

4 cups (1 L) sliced button mushrooms

1 clove garlic, crushed

1 tbsp (15 ml) balsamic vinegar

8 cups (2 L) spinach

1/2 cup (125 ml) crumbled goat cheese

Freshly ground black pepper, to taste

Heat oil in a skillet over medium heat. When pan is hot, add onion and sauté about 5 to 6 minutes or until soft. Add mushrooms; sauté about 8 to 10 minutes or until soft and the pan begins to dry out. Add garlic; sauté for another minute.

Remove from heat. Add balsamic vinegar and gently scrape the bottom of the skillet to remove any brown bits of mushroom or onions.

Meanwhile, place spinach in a large bowl. Spoon warm mushroom and onion mixture over spinach; toss to combine.

Sprinkle with goat cheese, season with pepper and serve immediately.

NUTRITION
Per 2 cup (500 ml) serving: 87 cal, 5 g pro, 5 g total fat (2 g saturated fat), 7 g carb, 2 g fibre, 6 mg chol, 91 mg sodium

Cabbage and Carrot Coleslaw

This colourful slaw delivers plenty of cruciferous phytochemicals that guard against cancer, heart disease and stroke. And you can make it any time—cabbage is available year-round and is one of the least expensive vegetables.

Serves 6

1/4 cup (50 ml) seasoned rice vinegar

2 tbsp (25 ml) olive oil

1 tbsp (15 ml) granulated sugar

2 cups (500 ml) shredded red or purple cabbage

2 cups (500 ml) shredded green cabbage

2 cups (500 ml) shredded carrot

1/4 tsp (1 ml) coarse sea salt, or to taste

Freshly ground black pepper, to taste

In a large mixing bowl, combine rice vinegar, olive oil and sugar. Whisk together until sugar is dissolved.

Add cabbage and carrot and toss until they are evenly coated with dressing. Season with salt and pepper.

Cover and refrigerate for at least 2 hours before serving.

NUTRITION
Per 1 cup (250 ml) serving: 76 cal, 1 g pro, 5 g total fat (1 g saturated fat), 9 g carb, 2 g fibre, 0 mg chol, 134 mg sodium

Greek Salad

One of my favourite summertime salads! Greek salad tastes best when made with fresh, locally grown tomatoes, cucumbers and bell peppers. Despite all the vegetables in a Greek salad, it's traditionally high in sodium thanks to the olives and feta cheese. Here both are used in moderation to keep the sodium content down.

Serves 8

4 large tomatoes, each cut into 8 to 10 wedges

1 medium cucumber, cut in half lengthwise and sliced

1/4 cup (50 ml) thinly sliced red onion

16 medium kalamata olives

1 cup (250 ml) green pepper slices (about 1 pepper)

1/2 cup (125 ml) feta cheese, crumbled

3 tbsp (50 ml) extra-virgin olive oil

2 tbsp (25 ml) freshly squeezed lemon juice

1 clove garlic, crushed

1/2 tsp (2 ml) dried oregano

In a large bowl, toss together tomato wedges, cucumber slices, red onion, olives, green pepper and feta cheese.

In a separate bowl, whisk together olive oil, lemon juice, garlic and oregano; drizzle over salad. Serve immediately.

NUTRITION
Per 1 cup (250 ml) serving: 108 cal, 3 g pro, 8 g total fat (3 g saturated fat), 5 g carb, 1 g fibre, 9 mg chol, 230 mg sodium

Tip: For an eye-catching variation of this salad, use four large heirloom tomatoes that range in colour from orange to yellow to purple.

Hot Apple and Cabbage Salad

Though often used in cold salads like coleslaw, cabbage makes the perfect ingredient for a warm salad, thanks to its hardy leaves. Serve this colourful salad with grilled pork chops or chicken breast.

Serves 6

1 cup (250 ml) water

1/2 medium red or purple cabbage, shredded

2 apples, peeled, cored and grated

1/4 cup (50 ml) large-flake rolled oats

2 tbsp (25 ml) brown sugar

1 tbsp (15 ml) apple cider vinegar

1/4 tsp (1 ml) ground cloves

In a large saucepan, combine water, cabbage, apples, oats, sugar, vinegar and cloves, and bring to a boil. Reduce heat and simmer for 40 to 45 minutes or until cabbage is tender.

Serve hot or cold.

NUTRITION

Per 3/4 cup (175 ml) serving: 79 cal, 2 g pro, 1 g total fat (0 g saturated fat), 18 g carb, 3 g fibre, 0 mg chol, 12 mg sodium

Mango Cashew Salad

This refreshing salad, packed with beta carotene, requires no oil at all! Be sure to use mangos that are slightly firm so they hold their shape when you mix the salad.

Serves 4

2 mangos, peeled and cubed

1/2 cup (125 ml) thinly sliced red onion

1/4 cup (50 ml) thinly sliced red bell pepper

16 cashews

1/2 cup (125 ml) chopped cilantro

2 tbsp (25 ml) freshly squeezed lime juice

1/8 tsp (0.5 ml) red pepper flakes, or to taste

In a large bowl, toss mango, red onion, bell pepper, cashews and cilantro.

Add lime juice and pepper flakes; toss to coat.

NUTRITION
Per 3/4 cup (175 ml) serving: 166 cal, 3 g pro, 7 g total fat (1 g saturated fat), 26 g carb, 3 g fibre, 0 mg chol, 6 mg sodium

Mixed Berry Salad with Candied Lemon Zest

Candied lemon zest turns ordinary fruit into extraordinary fruit. This simple yet elegant dish makes a refreshing salad in the summer. It can also stand in as a light and delicious dessert when served with a square of dark chocolate.

Serves 4

SALAD

2 cups (500 ml) mixed fresh berries (such as strawberries, blackberries, raspberries and blueberries)

2 tbsp (25 ml) finely chopped fresh mint

CANDIED LEMON ZEST

Zest of 1 lemon

1 tbsp (15 ml) granulated sugar

In a large bowl, gently toss berries with mint.

To prepare candied lemon zest, combine lemon zest and sugar in a small bowl. Set aside for 30 minutes, until zest and sugar begin to crystallize.

Just before serving, top berries with crystallized zest. Serve cold.

NUTRITION

Per 1/2 cup (125 ml) serving: 45 cal, 1 g pro, 0 g total fat (0 g saturated fat), 11 g carb, 2 g fibre, 0 mg chol, 3 mg sodium

Roasted Beet Salad

Beets are an excellent source of anthocyanins, antioxidants that are thought to ward off heart disease. This colourful salad takes a little longer to prepare than most of the salad recipes in this book, but the end result is well worth the time and effort.

Serves 4

4 medium-sized beets

1/2 cup (125 ml) chopped red onion

2 tbsp (25 ml) seasoned rice vinegar

1/2 tbsp (7 ml) Dijon mustard

1 tsp (5 ml) extra-virgin olive oil

2 green onions, finely sliced

1 tsp (5 ml) orange zest

Preheat oven to 375°F (190°C).

Trim beets and cut into quarters.

Place beets in a glass baking dish; cover with 1/2 cup (125 ml) water. Cover baking dish with foil; bake for 50 to 60 minutes or until beets are tender. (Keep an eye on the beets while they are baking; if the bottom of the dish dries out, add another 1/2 cup/125 ml of water.)

Remove from heat and cool. When beets are cool enough to handle, peel and dice them.

In a large bowl, combine diced beets, red onion, rice vinegar, mustard, olive oil, green onions and orange zest. Toss to coat.

NUTRITION

Per 3/4 cup (175 ml) serving: 60 cal, 2 pro, 1 g total fat (0 g saturated fat), 11 g carb, 2 g fibre, 0 mg chol, 121 mg sodium

Sesame Coleslaw

The sesame oil and rice vinegar in this recipe turn regular coleslaw into a very flavourful, Asian-inspired salad. This salad tastes better the longer it is allowed to sit. I suggest making it a day in advance to let the cabbage marinate and soften in the dressing.

Serves 6

6 cups (1.5 L) shredded green or Savoy cabbage (about 1/2 medium head of cabbage)

1-1/2 cups (375 ml) shredded carrot

2 green onions, thinly sliced

1/4 cup (50 ml) seasoned rice wine vinegar

2 tbsp (25 ml) sesame oil

1 tsp (5 ml) granulated sugar

1 tsp (5 ml) mustard seeds

In a large bowl, combine cabbage, carrot and green onion.

In a small bowl, whisk together rice vinegar, sesame oil, sugar and mustard seeds. Drizzle over cabbage mixture. Toss to mix thoroughly.

Cover and refrigerate for at least 3 hours before serving.

NUTRITION
Per 1-1/4 cup (300 ml) serving: 89 cal, 2 g pro, 5 g total fat (1 g saturated fat), 11 g carb, 4 g fibre, 0 mg chol, 39 mg sodium

Barley Salad with Lemon, Capers and Black Olives

Barley is a versatile grain with a rich nutty flavour and chewy, pasta-like texture. It's an excellent source of fibre and selenium, a powerful antioxidant. Hulled barley (sometimes called dehulled barley) is the whole-grain version. If you don't have a bottle of wine open, you can easily substitute the same amount of orange juice for a vitamin C boost.

Serves 6

2-1/2 cups (625 ml) water

1/2 cup (125 ml) dry white wine

1 cup (250 ml) pearl barley

2 tbsp (25 ml) extra-virgin olive oil

2 tbsp (25 ml) white wine vinegar

1 tbsp (15 ml) freshly squeezed lemon juice

1 tsp (5 ml) Dijon mustard

1/2 tsp (2 ml) coarse sea salt, or to taste

2 carrots, shredded

1/4 cup (50 ml) sliced pitted black olives

2 tbsp (25 ml) capers

2 green onions, finely sliced

In a medium saucepan, bring water and wine to a boil. Add barley; cover and simmer for 1 hour or until barley is tender. Remove from heat, drain any excess liquid, and set aside to cool.

In a small bowl, whisk together olive oil, vinegar, lemon juice, mustard and salt.

Combine barley with carrots, olives, capers and onions. Drizzle with the vinaigrette, tossing to combine. Cover and refrigerate for 2 hours before serving.

Serve cold or at room temperature.

NUTRITION
Per 3/4 cup (175 ml) serving: 192 cal, 4 g pro, 6 g total fat (1 g saturated fat), 30 g carb, 4 g fibre, 0 mg chol, 444 mg sodium

Kasha, Walnut and Apple Salad with Fresh Mint

This flavourful whole-grain salad is as nice to look at as it is to eat. Ideally, make this salad a day or two in advance of serving to allow the flavours to blend. If you don't have seasoned rice vinegar, apple cider vinegar makes for a tasty alternative.

Serves 6

2 cups (500 ml) water

1 cup (250 ml) kasha

1 apple, diced

2 cups (500 ml) shredded carrot

1/4 cup (50 ml) dried cranberries

1/4 cup (50 ml) walnuts, chopped

1/4 cup (50 ml) finely chopped fresh mint

2 green onions, chopped

2 tbsp (25 ml) seasoned rice vinegar

2 tbsp (25 ml) freshly squeezed lemon juice

1 tbsp (15 ml) Dijon mustard

1 tbsp (15 ml) extra-virgin olive oil

1 tsp (5 ml) honey

In a large saucepan, heat water to a boil. Add kasha; cover and simmer for 10 to 12 minutes or until most of the liquid has been absorbed. Rinse kasha with cold water and set aside to cool.

Meanwhile, in a large bowl, combine apple, carrots, cranberries, walnuts, mint and green onions.

In a small bowl, whisk together rice vinegar, lemon juice, mustard, olive oil and honey.

Toss kasha with apple mixture. Drizzle with dressing. Cover and refrigerate until ready to serve.

NUTRITION

Per 3/4 cup (175 ml) serving: 190 cal, 5 g pro, 6 g total fat (1 g saturated fat), 32 g carb, 4 g fibre, 0 mg chol, 39 mg sodium

Mediterranean Pasta Salad

This is one of my favourite salads to make when hosting a barbecue. It's loaded with flavour and it can be made the day before. It's a guaranteed crowd pleaser among my cottage guests.

Serves 8

2 cups (500 ml) cooked whole wheat farfalle ("bow-tie") pasta, or other small pasta

2 cups (500 ml) grilled and shredded chicken breast

2 cups (500 ml) halved cherry tomatoes

1/3 cup (75 ml) tightly packed fresh basil

1/3 cup (75 ml) black olives

1/4 cup (50 ml) sliced green onions

3 tbsp (50 ml) extra-virgin olive oil

2 tbsp (25 ml) freshly squeezed lemon juice

1/4 tsp (1 ml) coarse sea salt, or to taste

Freshly ground black pepper, to taste

In a large mixing bowl, toss together cooked pasta, shredded chicken breast, cherry tomatoes, basil, olives and green onions.

Drizzle with olive oil and lemon juice; sprinkle with salt and pepper. Serve cold.

NUTRITION
Per 3/4 cup (175 ml) serving: 158 cal, 14 g pro, 7 g total fat (1 g saturated fat), 12 g carb, 2 g fibre, 29 mg chol, 150 mg sodium

Quinoa Tabbouleh

Tabbouleh is a Middle Eastern salad traditionally made with bulgur, a cracked wheat. I've changed things up and substituted quinoa, a whole grain that's also a source of protein, calcium and iron.

Serves 6

4 cups (1 L) cooked quinoa

1-1/2 cups (375 ml) diced cucumber

1 cup (250 ml) finely chopped parsley

1/4 cup (50 ml) chopped mint

1 cup (250 ml) chopped tomato

2 green onions, chopped

1/4 cup (50 ml) freshly squeezed lemon juice

1 tbsp (15 ml) extra-virgin olive oil

3 cloves garlic, crushed

1/2 tsp (2 ml) coarse sea salt, or to taste

In a large bowl, toss quinoa, cucumber, parsley, mint, tomato, green onion, lemon juice, olive oil, garlic and salt.

Cover and refrigerate for at least 2 hours before serving.

NUTRITION

Per 1 cup (250 ml) serving: 191 cal, 6 g pro, 5 g total fat (0 g saturated fat), 32 g carb, 5 g fibre, 0 mg chol, 200 mg sodium

Wheat Berry and Pomegranate Salad with Maple Dijon Dressing

Taste-testers loved this salad! The pomegranate seeds add a touch of sweetness, while the arugula lends a peppery taste. And the wheat berries, a whole grain, provide a nutty flavour and make this salad an excellent source of fibre.

Serves 8

SALAD

3 cups (750 ml) water

1-1/2 cups (375 ml) wheat berries, rinsed

1-1/3 cups (325 ml) diced Red Delicious apple, with skin on (about 1 large)

1 cup (250 ml) pomegranate seeds (about 2 medium)

1/4 cup (50 ml) sliced green onions

1-1/2 cups (375 ml) coarsely chopped arugula

DRESSING

3 tbsp (50 ml) olive oil

1/3 cup (75 ml) apple cider vinegar

2 tbsp (25 ml) maple syrup

1 tbsp (15 ml) grainy Dijon mustard

4 tbsp (60 ml) unsweetened apple juice

1/4 tsp (1 ml) coarse sea salt, or to taste

Freshly ground black pepper, to taste

In a medium saucepan, bring water to a boil over high heat. Add wheat berries, stir, cover and simmer over low heat until wheat berries are tender but still chewy, about 30 to 40 minutes. Remove from heat and drain any excess water. Rinse wheat berries under cold water.

In a large mixing bowl, combine cooked wheat berries, apple, pomegranate seeds, green onions and arugula.

In a small mixing bowl, whisk together olive oil, apple cider vinegar, maple syrup, mustard, apple juice, salt and pepper.

Pour dressing over wheat berry salad; toss to coat.

Cover and refrigerate for at least 2 hours before serving.

NUTRITION
Per 1 cup (250 ml) serving: 215 cal, 5 g pro, 6 g total fat (1 g saturated fat), 38 g carb, 6 g fibre, 0 mg chol, 103 mg sodium

Tip: Removing the seeds from a pomegranate can be a messy job. The best way to seed a pomegranate is to slice it into quarters. Using your hands, gently split open the fruit and use your fingers to gently pry the seeds away from the peel and white membrane. An easy way to separate the seeds from the membrane is to drop the seeds into a bowl of cold water—the seeds will sink to the bottom and the membrane will float to the top.

Black Bean and Avocado Salad with Toasted Cumin Dressing

Black beans and avocados team up to add fibre, folate, potassium and heart-healthy monounsaturated fat to this salad. Purchase avocados a few days before to give them time to ripen. You may also quicken the ripening process by putting them in a paper bag with a banana or an apple.

Serves 8

SALAD

2 cans (19 oz/540 ml each) black beans, drained and rinsed well

1 cup (250 ml) finely chopped red pepper (about 1 medium pepper)

1/2 cup (125 ml) finely chopped cilantro

1/4 cup (50 ml) chopped green onion (about 1 onion)

2 avocados, diced

DRESSING

1 tbsp (15 ml) cumin seeds

1/3 cup (75 ml) freshly squeezed lime juice

2 tbsp (25 ml) olive oil

2 cloves garlic, crushed

1/2 tsp (2 ml) red pepper flakes

1/2 tsp (2 ml) coarse sea salt

Freshly ground black pepper, to taste

In a large mixing bowl combine black beans, red pepper, cilantro, green onions and avocados; gently toss to combine. Set aside.

Heat a skillet over high heat; add cumin seeds and toast until fragrant, about 2 minutes. Remove from heat and cool.

In a small mixing bowl, whisk together toasted cumin seeds, lime juice, olive oil, garlic, red pepper flakes, salt and pepper.

Pour dressing over black bean mixture; toss to coat.

NUTRITION

Per 3/4 cup (175 ml) serving: 207 cal, 9 g protein, 10 g total fat (2 g saturated fat), 25 g carb, 9 g fibre, 0 mg chol, 80 mg sodium

Easy Lentil Salad

This is a simple salad to make, and it's loaded with flavour, fibre and the B vitamin folate. It tastes best when made a day or two in advance, so make it on the weekend and enjoy it as a vegetarian lunch during the week.

Serves 8

1/3 cup (75 ml) red wine vinegar

2 tbsp (25 ml) olive oil

2 tsp (10 ml) Dijon mustard

1/2 tsp (2 ml) coarse sea salt

2 cans (19 oz/540 ml each) lentils, drained and rinsed well

1-1/2 cups (375 ml) chopped red bell pepper

1-1/2 cups (375 ml) diced cucumber

1/4 cup (50 ml) finely sliced green onion

In a small bowl, whisk together vinegar, olive oil, mustard and salt.

In a large serving bowl, combine lentils, bell pepper, cucumber and green onion.

Drizzle with dressing; stir to combine.

Cover and refrigerate for at least 2 hours before serving. Serve cold.

NUTRITION
Per 3/4 cup (175 ml) serving: 153 cal, 9 g pro, 4 g total fat (1 g saturated fat), 22 g carb, 5 g fibre, 0 mg chol, 168 mg sodium

Lentil Salad with Citrus Yogurt Dressing

Lentils may be small in size but they pack a powerful punch when it comes to nutrition. A member of the legume family, lentils are loaded with folate, iron, potassium, thiamine and fibre. Here they're combined with antioxidant-rich orange segments, orange bell pepper and cilantro for a colourful, healthy and tasty salad.

Serves 10

SALAD

3 cups (750 ml) water

1/4 cup (50 ml) freshly squeezed lemon juice

1-1/2 cups (375 ml) dried green lentils, rinsed

2 cups (500 ml) diced orange segments

1-1/2 cups (375 ml) finely chopped orange bell pepper

1-1/2 cups (375 ml) diced cucumber

1 cup (250 ml) finely chopped cilantro

3 tbsp (50 ml) freshly squeezed lemon juice

1/2 tsp (2 ml) salt

1/4 tsp (1 ml) cayenne pepper, or to taste

DRESSING

1/2 cup (125 ml) low-fat (1% MF or less) plain yogurt

1/4 cup (50 ml) freshly squeezed orange juice

1 tbsp (15 ml) honey

Heat water and lemon juice in a saucepan over high heat; bring to a boil. Add lentils; stir and bring back to a boil. Cover with a lid and reduce heat to low. Simmer until lentils are cooked but still tender, about 20 to 22 minutes. Drain any excess liquid. Set aside to cool.

In a large mixing bowl, combine cooked lentils with orange segments, bell peppers, cucumber, cilantro, lemon juice, salt and cayenne pepper. Toss to combine.

In a small mixing bowl, whisk together yogurt, orange juice and honey.

Drizzle honey mixture over lentil salad. Toss to combine. Serve cold.

NUTRITION
Per 3/4 cup (175 ml) serving: 135 cal, 7 g pro, 1 g total fat (0 g saturated fat), 27 g carb, 6 g fibre, 0 mg chol, 132 mg sodium

Spicy Black Bean and Pepper Salad with Chili Dressing

Black beans are one of my favourite legumes and they're great in salads. Consider doubling this recipe—not only is it a hit at picnics and barbecues, but its flavour gets even better after chilling in the refrigerator for a few days. If you like your food spicy, save the jalapeno seeds.

Serves 6.

1 can (19 oz/540 ml) black beans, drained and rinsed well

1-1/2 cups (375 ml) chopped red bell pepper (about 1 large)

1-1/2 cups (375 ml) chopped green bell pepper (about 1 large)

1 small jalapeno, seeded and diced

1/4 cup (50 ml) finely diced red onion

2 cups (500 ml) diced fresh tomato (about 2 small)

1/2 cup (125 ml) chopped cilantro

1/4 cup (50 ml) freshly squeezed lemon juice

1 tbsp (15 ml) extra-virgin olive oil

3 cloves garlic, crushed

1/4 tsp (1 ml) coarse sea salt

Freshly ground black pepper, to taste

In a large bowl, combine beans, bell peppers, jalapeno, onion, tomatoes and cilantro.

In a small bowl, whisk together lemon juice, olive oil, garlic, salt and black pepper.

Toss bean mixture with dressing. Cover and refrigerate for at least 1 hour before serving, stirring occasionally. Serve cold.

NUTRITION
Per 3/4 cup (175 ml) serving: 129 cal, 6 g pro, 3 g total fat (0 g saturated fat), 21 g carb, 6 g fibre, 0 mg chol, 105 mg sodium

Three Bean Salad with Cilantro Lime Dressing

The cilantro—a favourite herb of mine—and the lime juice make this fibre-rich bean salad taste delicious! I serve it as a side dish with dinner and take it for a vegetarian lunch during the week.

Serves 10

1 can (19 oz/540 ml) black beans, drained and rinsed well

1 can (19 oz/540 ml) kidney beans, drained and rinsed well

1 can (19 oz/540 ml) chickpeas, drained and rinsed well

2 large tomatoes, chopped

3/4 cup (175 ml) loosely packed chopped cilantro

4 green onions, finely chopped

DRESSING

1/2 cup (125 ml) freshly squeezed lime juice

3 cloves garlic, crushed

1 tbsp (15 ml) olive oil

1/2 tsp (2 ml) red pepper flakes, or to taste

1/4 tsp (1 ml) coarse sea salt

In a large bowl, mix together black beans, kidney beans, chickpeas, tomatoes, cilantro and green onions.

In a separate bowl, whisk together lime juice, garlic, oil, red pepper flakes and salt. Drizzle over beans and tomatoes and toss to combine.

Cover and refrigerate the salad for at least 2 hours before serving.

NUTRITION

Per 3/4 cup (175 ml) serving: 194 cal, 11 g pro, 3 g total fat (0 g saturated fat), 33 g carb, 8 g fibre, 0 mg chol, 69 mg sodium

Chicken Caesar Salad with Homemade Croutons

This lighter version of Caesar salad uses low-fat yogurt and skips the raw egg yolks. Paired with grilled chicken and homemade croutons, this entrée salad clocks in at only 345 calories, less than half the calories and a third of the fat found in most restaurant Caesar salads. For a more colourful variation, swap the romaine lettuce with baby spinach. If you don't have anchovy fillets, substitute 1 tsp (5 ml) anchovy paste instead. (I always have a tube of anchovy paste in my fridge.)

Serves 4

CROUTONS

4 cups (1 L) cubed (1-inch/2.5 cm) whole-grain bread (about 4 thick slices)

2 tbsp (25 ml) extra-virgin olive oil

1 tsp (5 ml) dried herbs, such as basil, oregano or rosemary

SALAD

8 cups (2 L) torn romaine lettuce

12 oz (340 g) grilled, sliced skinless chicken breast

2 tbsp (25 ml) grated Parmesan cheese

DRESSING

1/2 cup (125 ml) low-fat (1% MF or less) plain yogurt

2 tbsp (25 ml) freshly squeezed lemon juice

1 tbsp (15 ml) extra-virgin olive oil

1 tsp (5 ml) Worcestershire sauce

2 anchovy fillets, canned in oil, finely chopped

1/2 tsp (2 ml) grainy Dijon mustard

2 cloves garlic, crushed

Few drops Tabasco sauce, or to taste

Preheat oven to 300°F (150°C).

In a large bowl, toss cubed bread with olive oil and dried herbs until bread is evenly coated.

Arrange bread in a single layer on a large baking sheet. Bake for 10 to 20 minutes; 10 minutes will give crispy croutons with a soft centre, 20 minutes will give very crunchy croutons. Set aside to cool.

In a small bowl, whisk together yogurt, lemon juice, olive oil, Worcestershire sauce, anchovy fillets, mustard, garlic and Tabasco.

In a large bowl, combine lettuce with sliced chicken breast and croutons. Drizzle with dressing and toss to coat. Sprinkle with Parmesan cheese. Serve immediately.

NUTRITION
Per 3 cups (750 ml) salad and 2-1/2 tbsp (32 ml) dressing: 345 cal, 35 g pro, 14 g total fat (3 g saturated fat), 20 g carb, 4 g fibre, 78 mg chol, 362 mg sodium

Tip: These rustic croutons taste delicious on just about any salad and are a great way to use up day-old and stale bread.

Grilled Steak Salad

I love to whip up this salad when I want a satisfying meal, but am not in the mood to cook on a hot summer night. The salad tastes and looks great with spinach, cherry tomatoes and cucumber, but it also tastes great with shredded carrot, leftover Roasted Beets with Honey Balsamic Glaze (page 306) and sliced mushrooms. This is a great salad to make if you have leftover grilled steak.

Serves 4

1 lb (454 g) grilling steak, such as tenderloin or strip loin (New York strip)

Freshly ground black pepper, to taste

8 cups (2 L) baby spinach

2 cups (500 ml) halved cherry tomatoes

2 cups (500 ml) sliced cucumber

2 tbsp (25 ml) extra-virgin olive oil

2 tbsp (25 ml) freshly squeezed lemon juice

1 tsp (5 ml) honey

1/2 tsp (2 ml) Worcestershire sauce

1/2 tsp (2 ml) grainy Dijon mustard

1/4 tsp (1 ml) coarse sea salt, or to taste

Preheat grill over medium-high heat.

Season steak with pepper; place on grill and cook to desired degree of doneness. Use a meat thermometer to gauge doneness: cook to 145°F (63°C) for medium-rare, 160°F (71°C) for medium and 170°F (77°C) for well done. Let steak rest for at least five minutes. Cut the steak against the grain into 1/2-inch (1 cm) strips.

In a large salad bowl, toss together spinach, cherry tomatoes, cucumber and grilled steak.

In a small bowl, whisk together olive oil, lemon juice, honey, Worcestershire sauce and mustard. Drizzle over salad; season with sea salt. Serve immediately.

NUTRITION

Per 3 cups (750 ml) salad and 1 tbsp (15 ml) dressing: 258 cal, 28 g pro, 12 g total fat (3 g saturated fat), 10 g carb, 3 g fibre, 53 mg chol, 384 mg sodium

Tip: For a different version, swap half the spinach for arugula—it has a peppery taste that works well with steak.

Salmon Quinoa Salad with Spicy Ginger Dressing

This simple salad is big on taste and packed with nutrients. One serving contains more than a day's worth of vitamins A, B12, C and K and a whopping 7 grams of fibre. Dress the salad just prior to serving to prevent it from going soggy.

Serves 4

SALAD

1 cup (250 ml) water

1/2 cup (125 ml) quinoa

8 cups (2 L) spinach

2 cans (7-1/2 oz/213 g each) salmon, drained

2 cups (500 ml) sliced red pepper

2 cups (500 ml) grated carrot

DRESSING

4 tbsp (60 ml) rice vinegar

2 tbsp (25 ml) honey

1 tbsp (15 ml) grated fresh ginger root

1 tbsp (15 ml) olive oil

In a small saucepan, bring water to a boil over high heat. Add quinoa, stir and then cover and simmer over low heat until quinoa is cooked and all of the moisture is absorbed, about 12 to 15 minutes. Remove lid, fluff quinoa with a fork; set aside to cool.

In a large mixing bowl, toss cooled quinoa, spinach, salmon, red pepper and carrot.

In a small mixing bowl, whisk together rice vinegar, honey, ginger and olive oil.

Drizzle salad with dressing; toss to coat. Serve immediately.

NUTRITION

Per 3 cups (750 ml) salad and 2 tbsp (25 ml) dressing: 364 cal, 30 g pro, 11 g total fat (2 g saturated fat), 37 g carb, 7 g fibre, 42 mg chol, 218 mg sodium

Tip: Look for quinoa, an ancient grain, in natural food stores and large supermarkets. It's usually sold next to the rice.

Seared Tofu Salad

Pressing the excess water out of the tofu and then searing it in a hot skillet yields tofu that is incredibly delicious and crispy. If you have time, I recommend marinating the tofu for at least two hours, or overnight if you can, for the most flavour. Use tofu that is extra firm so it holds its shape.

Serves 4

1 pkg (12 oz/350 g) extra firm tofu

2 tbsp (25 ml) freshly squeezed lime juice

1 tbsp (15 ml) sodium-reduced soy sauce

2 tsp (10 ml) sesame oil

1 tsp (5 ml) granulated sugar

8 cups (2 L) mixed salad greens

2 cups (500 ml) halved cherry tomatoes

2 cups (500 ml) cucumber slices

1 cup (250 ml) sliced red pepper

DRESSING

2 tbsp (25 ml) unseasoned rice vinegar

2 tbsp (25 ml) extra-virgin olive oil

1 tbsp (15 ml) brown sugar

1 tsp (5 ml) sesame oil

1 clove garlic, crushed

Pinch sea salt, or to taste

Slice tofu width-wise into 6 pieces (about 3/4 inch/2 cm thick).

Place a layer of paper towel, or a clean tea towel, on a cutting board. Arrange tofu in a single layer; cover with another layer of paper towel (or tea towel), and firmly press on tofu to remove excess moisture. Repeat two more times with dry towels.

Cut tofu into cubes. Set aside.

In a small bowl, whisk together lime juice, soy sauce, sesame oil and sugar. Place tofu cubes in a resealable container; drizzle with marinade and toss to coat. Put in the fridge to marinate for at least 2 hours.

In a large salad bowl, toss together salad greens, cherry tomatoes, cucumber and red pepper slices.

In a small bowl, whisk together rice vinegar, extra-virgin olive oil, brown sugar, sesame oil, garlic and salt.

Preheat a skillet over medium-high heat. Remove tofu from marinade. When pan is hot, add tofu and sear for 5 to 6 minutes, flipping frequently, or until tofu begins to brown on all sides. Set aside to cool.

Add tofu to salad; drizzle with dressing. Serve immediately.

NUTRITION

Per 3 cups (750 ml) salad and 4 tsp (20 ml) dressing: 255 cal, 15 g pro, 16 g total fat (2 g saturated fat), 16 g carb, 3 g fibre, 0 mg chol, 154 mg sodium

Shrimp, Mango and Avocado Salad

If you avoid eating avocados because they're high in fat content, think again. Avocados are an exceptional source of heart-healthy monounsaturated fat. What's more, they're also an excellent source of folate and potassium. This delicious salad will make you want to eat more than one!

Serves 4

2 avocados, peeled and diced

2 mangos, peeled and diced

1/3 cup (75 ml) freshly squeezed lime juice

1 tbsp (15 ml) olive oil

1/8 tsp (0.5 ml) red pepper flakes, or to taste

1/4 tsp (1 ml) coarse sea salt, or to taste

1 lb (454 g) large cooked shrimp

2 tbsp (25 ml) sliced green onion

2 tbsp (25 ml) finely chopped mint

1/2 cup (125 ml) finely chopped cilantro

In a large mixing bowl combine avocado, mango, lime juice, olive oil, red pepper flakes, salt and shrimp. Gently toss to combine.

Sprinkle shrimp mixture with green onions, mint and cilantro. Serve cold.

NUTRITION
Per 1-1/2 cup (375 ml) serving: 330 cal, 26 g pro, 15 g total fat (2 g saturated fat), 26 g carb, 7 g fibre, 221 mg chol, 410 mg sodium

Soba Noodle Salad with Tofu and Toasted Sesame Seeds

Soba noodles are traditional Japanese noodles made from buckwheat flour and wheat flour. They're thinner than udon noodles, another traditional Japanese noodle made with wheat flour. Look for dried soba noodles in major grocery stores or Asian markets. This salad tastes best after the noodles have marinated in the dressing overnight—if you have time, make it a day before you plan to serve it. Top with cilantro, mint and toasted sesame seeds just before serving.

Serves 6

4 cups (1 L) cooked soba noodles (about 250 g dry)

2 tbsp (25 ml) sesame oil

1/3 cup (75 ml) freshly squeezed lime juice

3 tbsp (50 ml) sodium-reduced soy sauce

2 tbsp (25 ml) brown sugar

1 pkg (12 oz/350 g) extra firm tofu, cut into 1/2-inch (1 cm) cubes

3 tbsp (50 ml) sesame seeds

2 cups (500 ml) grated carrot

2 cups (500 ml) diced cucumber

1 cup (250 ml) finely diced red bell pepper

1/2 cup (125 ml) chopped cilantro

1/2 cup (125 ml) chopped mint

Pinch red pepper flakes, or to taste

Cook noodles according to package directions. Drain and toss with 1 tbsp (15 ml) sesame oil. Set aside to cool.

In a small bowl, whisk together lime juice, soy sauce, brown sugar and 1 tbsp (15 ml) sesame oil. Place tofu in a large shallow dish; pour marinade over tofu and set aside to marinate.

Preheat oven to 350°F (180°C). Place sesame seeds on a baking sheet; put in oven to toast for 5 to 7 minutes, or until seeds begin to brown. Set aside to cool.

In a large mixing bowl, toss together carrot, cucumber, red pepper, cilantro, mint and red pepper flakes. Add cooled noodles, tofu and marinade; toss to combine. Sprinkle with toasted sesame seeds. Serve cold.

NUTRITION
Per 1-1/2 cup (375 ml) serving: 269 cal, 14 g pro, 11 g total fat (2 g saturated fat), 31 g carb, 3 g fibre, 0 mg chol, 352 mg sodium

Vegetarian Mains

BEANS & LENTILS

SOY, TOFU & TEMPEH

OTHER MEATLESS MAINS

Chana Masala

Chana masala, a classic North Indian vegetarian dish, is a delicious way to boost your intake of protein- and fibre-rich chickpeas. This recipe, cooked in a flavourful broth of tomatoes, onions and traditional Indian spices, will be a hit with vegetarians and meat eaters! Serve it with a small piece of naan bread or steamed brown rice.

Serves 4

1 tbsp (15 ml) ghee or canola oil

1/4 tsp (1 ml) cardamom seeds, removed from pods

1 cup (250 ml) finely diced onions

2 cloves garlic, crushed

2 tsp (10 ml) grated fresh ginger root

2 cups (500 ml) diced fresh tomatoes

1 can (19 oz/540 ml) chickpeas, drained and rinsed well

1/4 tsp (1 ml) red pepper flakes, or to taste

1/2 tsp (2 ml) ground cumin

1/2 tsp (2 ml) ground cardamom

1/2 tsp (2 ml) turmeric

1 small cinnamon stick

1/2 cup (125 ml) chopped cilantro

Heat ghee or oil in a skillet over medium heat. When pan is hot, add cardamom seeds and sauté for 1 to 2 minutes or until fragrant. Add onion; sauté for another 8 to 10 minutes. Add garlic and ginger; continue to sauté for another minute.

Add tomatoes, chickpeas, red pepper flakes, cumin, cardamom, turmeric and cinnamon stick; stir to combine. Cover and bring to a boil; reduce heat and simmer for 20 minutes. If pan begins to dry out, add 1/4 cup (50 ml) water.

Remove the cinnamon stick and garnish with cilantro. Serve hot.

NUTRITION
Per 3/4 cup (175 ml) serving: 188 cal, 6 g pro, 5 g total fat (0 g saturated fat), 31 g carb, 6 g fibre, 0 mg chol, 323 mg sodium

Tip: Ghee, also known as clarified butter, is a staple in South Asian cooking that gives a rich flavour to dishes, including curries. Look for it in ethnic or major grocery stores. If you don't have ghee on hand, substitute an equal amount of canola oil.

Chickpea Curry

Serve this rich, fragrant curry with steamed basmati rice or a piece of naan bread. There are endless variations to this recipe. Substitute any protein-rich food for the chickpeas, such as lentils, tofu or chicken breast.

Serves 6

1 tbsp (15 ml) ghee or canola oil

6 black peppercorns

6 cloves

2 cups (500 ml) chopped onion

3 cloves garlic, crushed

1 tbsp (15 ml) grated fresh ginger root

2 cans (19 oz/540 ml each) chickpeas, drained and rinsed well

1 cup (250 ml) crushed tomatoes

1 cup (250 ml) water

2 tsp (10 ml) coriander

2 tsp (10 ml) cumin

1/2 tsp (2 ml) turmeric

1/4 tsp (1 ml) salt

1/8 tsp (0.5 ml) cayenne pepper, or to taste

1/4 cup (50 ml) chopped cilantro

Heat ghee or oil in a medium saucepan over high heat. When pan is hot, add peppercorns and cloves and reduce heat to medium; sauté for 20 seconds, or until fragrant. Add onion; sauté for 8 to 10 minutes. Add garlic and ginger; sauté for another minute.

Add chickpeas, tomatoes, water, coriander, cumin, turmeric, salt and cayenne pepper. Stir to combine. Cover and simmer for 20 minutes. Sprinkle with cilantro before serving.

NUTRITION

Per 1 cup (250 ml) serving: 235 cal, 11 g pro, 6 g total fat (2 g saturated fat), 38 g carb, 7 g fibre, 7 mg chol, 163 mg sodium

Chipotle Chili

This recipe uses dried chipotle chili pepper powder, which gives it a rich, smoky flavour I really enjoy. You can find it in the spice section of your local grocery store or gourmet food shop. Be sure to save some of this chili for leftovers—it's even tastier after chilling in the fridge overnight.

Serves 8

1 tbsp (15 ml) canola oil

1 cup (250 ml) chopped onion

3 cloves garlic, crushed

1-1/2 cups (375 ml) chopped green pepper (about 1 large)

1 can (28 oz/796 ml) diced tomatoes

1 can (19 oz/540 ml) kidney beans, drained and rinsed well

1 can (19 oz/540 ml) chickpeas, drained and rinsed well

1 can (14 oz/398 ml) baked beans in tomato sauce

1-1/2 cups (375 ml) fresh or frozen corn kernels

2 tbsp (25 ml) molasses

2 tbsp (25 ml) white vinegar

1 tbsp (15 ml) cocoa powder

1/4 tsp (1 ml) dried chipotle chili pepper powder

Heat oil in a large saucepan over medium heat. When pan is hot, add onions and sauté about 8 to 10 minutes. Add garlic and green pepper; sauté another minute.

Add tomatoes, kidney beans, chickpeas, baked beans, corn, molasses, vinegar, cocoa powder and chipotle chili pepper. Cover and bring to a gentle boil over high heat; reduce and simmer for 30 minutes.

NUTRITION
Per 1 cup (250 ml) serving: 275 cal, 12 g pro, 4 g total fat (1 g saturated fat), 54 g carb, 10 g fibre, 0 mg chol, 434 mg sodium

Falafel Wrap with Lemon Tahini Sauce

Falafels, a staple in Middle Eastern cuisine, are patties made of ground chickpeas. While sometimes eaten on their own, they're usually stuffed in a pita with pickled vegetables and a creamy sauce made from tahini (sesame seed paste). Falafels are usually deep-fried, which gives them a lovely crunchy texture but bumps up the calories. This version uses just a tablespoon of oil for pan-frying, which results in a crispy texture without the extra fat.

Serves 6

1 can (19 oz/540 ml) chickpeas, drained and rinsed well

3/4 cup (175 ml) coarsely chopped parsley

1/2 cup (125 ml) coarsely chopped onion

1/2 cup (125 ml) coarsely chopped cilantro

1/2 cup (125 ml) whole wheat bread crumbs

1 medium egg

2 cloves garlic

1 tsp (5 ml) ground cumin

1/4 tsp (1 ml) coarse sea salt

Pinch red pepper flakes, or to taste

1 tbsp (15 ml) canola oil

1/4 cup (50 ml) tahini

2 tsp (10 ml) freshly squeezed lemon juice

2 tbsp (25 ml) water

3 whole wheat or multigrain pitas (6 inches/15 cm each), cut in half and opened to form a pocket

2 cups (500 ml) coarsely chopped spinach

1 large tomato, sliced

In a food processor, combine chickpeas, parsley, onion, cilantro, bread crumbs, egg, garlic, cumin, salt and red pepper flakes; pulse until ingredients are well blended.

Using clean hands, form the falafel dough into 12 uniform-sized balls. Gently press on each falafel to flatten it until it's about 2 inches (5 cm) across. Place falafel balls on a plate and set aside.

Heat oil in a large skillet over medium heat. When pan is hot, add falafel balls and cook for 4 minutes per side, or until falafels are golden brown.

In a small bowl, whisk together tahini, lemon juice and water; mix until just combined and runny (add an extra tablespoon of water if tahini thickens too much).

Stuff each pita half with two falafel balls, spinach and tomato; drizzle with 1 tbsp (15 ml) lemon tahini sauce; serve immediately.

NUTRITION
Per falafel: 312 cal, 12 g pro, 11 g total fat (2 g saturated fat), 44 g carb, 7 g fibre, 27 mg chol, 389 mg sodium

Garlic, White Bean and Arugula Wrap

White kidney beans, also known as cannellini beans, are a staple of the Mediterranean diet. They're well known for their creamy texture and sweet taste. Here, they're teamed with garlic, lemon and peppery arugula, a combination that makes a delicious wrap that's high in fibre and vitamin K.

Serves 4

1 can (19 oz/540 ml) white kidney beans, drained and rinsed well

1 tbsp (15 ml) olive oil

2 tbsp (25 ml) freshly squeezed lemon juice

2 tbsp (25 ml) chopped chives

1 clove garlic, crushed

Freshly ground pepper, to taste

4 7-inch (18 cm) whole-grain tortilla wraps

2 cups (500 ml) loosely packed arugula, washed and rinsed

1 cup (250 ml) sliced tomato (about 1 medium tomato)

In a small mixing bowl, combine kidney beans, olive oil, lemon juice, chives, garlic and pepper. Use the back of a fork to mash ingredients together until beans are smooth. Alternatively, use a food processor to purée ingredients until smooth.

Arrange wraps on a clean work surface. Evenly spread bean mixture on the top third of each wrap. Evenly divide the arugula and tomato among the wraps.

To wrap tortillas, gently fold the bottom of the wrap over the filling, then fold one side up over the filling and roll tightly. Serve immediately.

NUTRITION
Per wrap: 237 cal, 12 g pro, 6 g total fat (1 g saturated fat), 37 g carb, 7 g fibre, 0 mg chol, 574 mg sodium

Moroccan Chickpea Stew

This tasty stew shows up regularly on my fall and winter menus. I love its blend of savoury and sweet ingredients. Reminds me of the wonderful meals I enjoyed in Morocco.

Serves 6

1 tbsp (15 ml) canola oil

1 cup (250 ml) chopped onion

2 cloves garlic, crushed

2 cups (500 ml) cubed sweet potatoes

1 cup (250 ml) sliced carrots

1/2 cup (125 ml) chopped celery

1 can (19 oz/540 ml) chickpeas, drained and rinsed well

1 can (28 oz/796 ml) diced tomatoes

1/4 cup (50 ml) dried apricots, coarsely chopped

1/4 cup (50 ml) raisins

1 tsp (5 ml) cinnamon

1/2 tsp (2 ml) each ground ginger, turmeric and nutmeg

1 bay leaf

In a large saucepan, heat oil over medium heat. When pan is hot, add onion and sauté for 8 to 10 minutes. Add garlic; sauté another minute.

Add sweet potatoes, carrots, celery, chickpeas, tomatoes, apricots, raisins, cinnamon, ginger, turmeric, nutmeg and bay leaf. Cover and bring to a boil; reduce heat and simmer for 45 minutes. Serve warm.

NUTRITION

Per 1-1/3 cup (325 ml) serving: 236 cal, 8 g pro, 4 g total fat (0 g saturated fat), 46 g carb, 7 g fibre, 0 mg chol, 368 mg sodium

Mushroom Lentil Patties

These patties taste great on their own or served on a whole-grain bun with horseradish, fresh spinach leaves, sliced avocado and tomato slices. I usually use white button mushrooms, but cremini or shiitake mushrooms also work well in this recipe.

Serves 4

1 tbsp (15 ml) canola oil

1 cup (250 ml) chopped onion

4 cups (1 L) thinly sliced mushrooms

2 tbsp (15 ml) balsamic vinegar

2 cups (500 ml) shredded carrot

1-1/2 cups (375 ml) cooked or canned (drained and rinsed well) brown lentils

1/2 cup (125 ml) whole wheat bread crumbs

1/2 cup (125 ml) large-flake rolled oats

1/4 cup (50 ml) ground flaxseed

1/4 cup (50 ml) slivered almonds, coarsely chopped

2 eggs, beaten

1 tbsp (15 ml) Dijon mustard

1/2 tsp (2 ml) coarse sea salt, or to taste

1/8 tsp (0.5 ml) cayenne pepper, or to taste

Freshly ground black pepper, to taste

Heat oil in a skillet over medium heat. Add onions and sauté for 8 to 10 minutes. Add mushrooms; sauté for another 8 to 10 minutes or until all the moisture from the mushrooms has evaporated and the pan begins to dry out. Transfer mushrooms and onions to a large mixing bowl.

Deglaze the skillet by pouring in the balsamic vinegar and scraping the bottom to lift up any onion or mushroom bits. Pour the vinegar mixture over the mushrooms.

Preheat oven to 350°F (180°C).

Add the carrots, lentils, bread crumbs, oats, flaxseed, almonds, eggs, mustard, sea salt and cayenne pepper to the bowl. Stir until well combined with the mushrooms and onions. Season with black pepper.

Spray a baking sheet with cooking spray. With your hands, form mushroom and lentil mixture into 8 patties. Place on baking sheet; bake for 20 to 25 minutes, or until they are cooked through and begin to brown.

NUTRITION
Per 2 patties: 206 cal, 10 g pro, 8 g total fat (1 g saturated fat), 27 g carb, 6 g fibre, 37 mg chol, 260 mg sodium

Red Rice and Leek Casserole with White Wine and Lemon

Leeks don't often get the attention they deserve as a healthy food. Not only are they low in calories, they're also high in vitamin C and iron. A distant relative of the onion, leeks belong to the allium family of vegetables, which have been shown to play a role in cancer and heart disease prevention.

Serves 4

1 tbsp (15 ml) canola oil

1 cup (250 ml) sliced leeks

3 cloves garlic, crushed

1-1/2 cups (375 ml) water

1/2 cup (125 ml) white wine

1/2 cup (125 ml) red rice, rinsed

1/2 cup (125 ml) red lentils, rinsed

1/2 cup (125 ml) freshly squeezed lemon juice

2 bay leaves

1/2 tsp (2 ml) coarse sea salt

Freshly ground black pepper, to taste

Preheat oven to 350°F (180°C).

Heat oil in a skillet over medium heat. Add leeks; sauté for 5 to 6 minutes. Add garlic; sauté for another minute. Remove from heat.

In a 13 × 9 inch (3.5 L) glass baking dish, combine water, white wine, rice, lentils, lemon juice, bay leaves, salt, pepper and leek mixture. Stir together all ingredients.

Cover and bake for 60 to 70 minutes, or until most of the liquid is absorbed and rice is cooked through. Serve warm.

NUTRITION

Per 1 cup (250 ml) serving: 229 cal, 10 g pro, 4 g total fat (0 g saturated fat), 36 g carb, 5 g fibre, 0 mg chol, 304 mg sodium

Refried Bean Baked Tortilla

Any Mexican dish is a huge hit in my house, especially if it's spicy! These high-fibre, baked tortillas are delicious and a cinch to make. I suggest baking the tortillas until the edges start to brown and get crispy, but be careful not to burn them. These make great leftovers too!

Serves 2

2 10-inch (25 cm) whole-grain tortilla shells

1 cup (250 ml) refried beans

1/2 cup (125 ml) sliced red bell pepper

1/2 jalapeno, finely chopped (or to taste)

1/4 cup (50 ml) sliced green onions

1/4 cup (50 ml) chopped cilantro

1 tsp (5 ml) freshly squeezed lime juice

1/2 cup (125 ml) low-fat (4% MF or less) shredded cheddar cheese

Preheat oven to 350°F (180°C).

Lay tortilla shells flat on a baking sheet.

Divide refried beans over each shell. Top with bell pepper, jalapeno, green onions, cilantro, lime juice and cheese.

Bake for 10 to 12 minutes or until cheese begins to melt and the tortilla is heated through. Place under broiler for an additional minute to brown cheese. Remove from oven and serve immediately.

NUTRITION
Per tortilla: 348 cal, 15 g pro, 8 g total fat (2 g saturated fat), 56 g carb, 12 g fibre, 10 mg chol, 880 mg sodium

Three Bean Garden Chili

This hearty meal is packed with fibre-rich legumes, providing 13 grams of fibre per serving! Cocoa and cinnamon give the chili a unique, subtle flavour that will leave your guests guessing what secret ingredient makes it taste so good. This chili is a breeze to make and freezes well.

Serves 8

1 tbsp (15 ml) canola oil

2 cups (500 ml) chopped onion

3 cloves garlic, crushed

1-1/2 cups (375 ml) diced red bell pepper

1-1/2 cups (375 ml) diced green bell pepper

2 cans (28 oz/796 ml each) diced tomatoes

1 can (19 oz/540 ml) kidney beans, drained and rinsed well

1 can (19 oz/540 ml) black beans, drained and rinsed well

1 can (19 oz/540 ml) chickpeas, drained and rinsed well

1 cup (25 ml) chopped carrot

1/2 cup (125 ml) corn kernels, fresh or frozen

2–3 tbsp (25–50 ml) chili powder

2 tbsp (25 ml) unsweetened cocoa

1/2 tsp (2 ml) cinnamon

1/4 tsp (1 ml) cayenne pepper, or to taste

2 tbsp (25 ml) tomato paste

Freshly ground black pepper, to taste

Heat oil in a large saucepan over medium heat. When pan is hot, add onions and sauté for 8 to 10 minutes. Add garlic and bell peppers; sauté for 2 to 3 minutes.

Add tomatoes, kidney beans, black beans, chickpeas, carrots, corn, chili powder, cocoa, cinnamon, cayenne pepper and tomato paste. Stir to combine. Season with black pepper. Cover and bring to a boil; reduce heat and simmer for 35 minutes.

NUTRITION
Per 1-1/2 cup (375 ml) serving: 280 cal, 14 g pro, 4 g total fat (1 g saturated fat), 51 g carb, 13 g fibre, 0 mg chol, 375 mg sodium

Whole-Grain Lentil Casserole

I've been making this casserole for years and still love it. It's also become a huge hit with my clients—even kids like it! I usually serve it with steamed broccoli for a vegetarian meal but you can also serve it as a side dish instead of plain rice.

Serves 4

1-1/2 cups (375 ml) sodium-reduced chicken or vegetable stock

1/2 cup (125 ml) dried green lentils

1/2 cup (125 ml) uncooked brown rice

1 cup (250 ml) stewed tomatoes

1/2 cup (125 ml) dry white wine or freshly squeezed lemon juice

1 cup (250 ml) chopped onion

1 clove garlic, crushed

1/4 tsp (1 ml) dried thyme

1/4 tsp (1 ml) dried basil

1 bay leaf

Freshly ground black pepper, to taste

1/2 cup (125 ml) reduced-fat shredded cheese, such as cheddar or mozzarella

Preheat oven to 350°F (180°C).

In a 6 cup (1.5 L) casserole dish, combine stock, lentils, rice, tomatoes, wine, onion, garlic, thyme, basil, bay leaf and pepper.

Cover with foil and bake for 1-1/2 hours, stirring two or three times. Sprinkle cheese on top and bake for another 5 minutes.

NUTRITION
Per 1-1/2 cup (375 ml) serving: 288 cal, 15 g pro, 5 g total fat (2 g saturated fat), 43 g carb, 5 g fibre, 11 mg chol, 491 mg sodium

Balsamic-Glazed Mushroom and Soy Burgers

These meat-free burgers contain textured vegetable protein, a dehydrated meat alternative made from soybeans. Bob's Red Mill carries it in their line of dried goods and it's also available in the bulk section of most health food stores. The combination of sweet balsamic-glazed mushrooms and nutty ground flaxseed makes a delicious and healthy alternative to beef burgers. Taste-testers, including meat-lovers, couldn't get enough of these! Serve these burgers in whole-grain pita pockets with spinach leaves, tomato and red onion slices and mashed avocado.

Serves 10

2 cups (500 ml) dry textured vegetable protein granules, such as Bob's Red Mill

2 cups (500 ml) sodium-reduced vegetable or chicken stock

2 tbsp (25 ml) canola oil

2 cups (500 ml) chopped onions

3 cups (750 ml) sliced brown mushrooms, such as portobello or cremini

4 cloves garlic, crushed

2 tbsp (25 ml) balsamic vinegar

1 egg white

1/2 cup (125 ml) ground flaxseed

1/4 cup (50 ml) quick cooking oats

1/4 cup (50 ml) whole wheat bread crumbs

1/2 tsp (2 ml) red pepper flakes, or to taste

1/2 tsp (2 ml) coarse sea salt, or to taste

Freshly ground black pepper, to taste

1 tsp (5 ml) canola oil

Place textured vegetable protein in a large mixing bowl.

In a saucepan, bring stock to a boil. Remove from heat and pour over textured vegetable protein. Stir together until all of the liquid is absorbed. Set aside.

Heat oil in a skillet over medium heat; add onions and mushrooms and sauté for 15 to 18 minutes, or until pan begins to dry out. Add garlic; sauté for another minute.

Remove skillet from heat; drizzle with balsamic vinegar.

Add warm mushroom-balsamic mixture to textured vegetable protein and set aside to cool.

When textured vegetable protein and mushroom mixture is cool, add egg white, ground flaxseed, oats, bread crumbs, red pepper flakes, salt and pepper. Stir ingredients together until mixed well and mixture begins to hold its shape.

Use a 1/3-cup (75 ml) measuring cup to scoop out mixture to form each burger. Firmly press ingredients together using your hands. Set formed burgers aside.

Heat oil in a skillet over medium heat. Add burgers and cook until brown and slightly crispy on the outside, about 5 to 6 minutes per side.

NUTRITION
Per burger: 174 cal, 14 g pro, 6 g total fat (1 g saturated fat), 16 g carb, 6 g fibre, 0 mg chol, 163 mg sodium

Tip: To bake burgers instead, preheat oven to 375°F (190°C). Place burgers on lightly oiled baking sheet and bake for 40 to 45 minutes, turning once, until they are cooked through.

Grilled Tofu with Sautéed Greens

My vegetarian dinner guests love this dish and so do I! Feel free to use other greens in place of the spinach, such as bok choy or Swiss chard. If you don't have black sesame seeds, regular white sesame seeds work just as well.

Serves 2

GRILLED TOFU

1 pkg (12 oz/350 g) extra firm tofu

2 tsp (10 ml) sesame oil

2 tbsp (25 ml) unseasoned rice vinegar

1 tbsp (15 ml) brown sugar

1 clove garlic, crushed

SAUTÉED GREENS

1 tsp (5 ml) canola oil

1 clove garlic, crushed

8 cups (2 L) baby spinach leaves

Pinch red pepper flakes, or to taste

Freshly ground black pepper, to taste

Pinch coarse sea salt, or to taste

1/4 tsp (1 ml) black sesame seeds

Slice tofu width-wise into 6 pieces (each slice about 3/4 inch/2 cm thick).

Place a layer of paper towel, or clean tea towel, on a cutting board. Arrange tofu in a single layer; cover with another layer of paper towel (or tea towel), and firmly press on tofu to remove excess moisture. Repeat two more times with dry towels.

In a shallow dish, whisk together sesame oil, rice vinegar, brown sugar and garlic. Add tofu; marinate for at least 30 minutes, turning once.

Preheat grill over medium heat.

Meanwhile, heat canola oil in a skillet over medium heat. When pan is hot, add garlic and sauté for 30 seconds. Add spinach and sauté for 2 minutes, or until most of the spinach is wilted, but some leaves still retain their shape. Season with red pepper flakes and pepper; remove from heat, and cover to keep warm.

Place tofu on preheated grill and reduce heat to medium-low. Grill for 4 to 5 minutes per side, turning once or twice, or until tofu turns golden brown and has visible grill marks.

Divide sautéed greens between two plates; sprinkle with sea salt and black sesame seeds. Gently place three pieces of tofu over sautéed greens. Serve immediately.

NUTRITION
Per serving: 345 cal, 28 g pro, 20 g total fat (2 g saturated fat), 17 g carb, 0 g fibre, 0 mg chol, 442 mg sodium

Sesame-Crusted Tofu

The tofu in this recipe needs marinating for only one hour, but it's even more flavourful when marinated overnight. Enjoy these tofu cutlets on their own, in a burrito or as a sandwich filling. I like to eat them in a sandwich with avocado slices and Lemon Hummus (page 92), fresh basil, coarse sea salt and freshly ground black pepper.

Serves 2

2 tbsp (25 ml) sodium-reduced soy sauce

2 tbsp (25 ml) freshly squeezed lime juice

1 tsp (5 ml) sesame oil

2 cloves garlic, crushed

1 pkg (12 oz/350 g) extra firm tofu, cut into 8 slices

1/4 cup (50 ml) sesame seeds

1 tbsp (15 ml) canola oil

In a small bowl, whisk together soy sauce, lime juice, sesame oil and garlic.

Lay tofu in a single layer in a glass baking dish. Pour soy sauce mixture over tofu and refrigerate for at least 1 hour.

Spread sesame seeds on a plate. Remove tofu from marinade one piece at a time and dredge in sesame seeds.

Heat oil in a skillet over high heat. Add tofu and reduce heat to medium-high; fry for 6 to 8 minutes per side or until tofu begins to brown and gets crispy.

NUTRITION
Per 4 slices: 421 cal, 29 g pro, 31 g total fat (4 g saturated fat), 12 g carb, 2 g fibre, 0 mg chol, 564 mg sodium

Sesame Ginger Stir-Fried Tofu with Bok Choy and Brown Rice

This high-fibre vegetarian dish is packed with flavour—and nutrients. It's an excellent source of vitamin C, folate, vitamin K, calcium, iron, magnesium, potassium and beta carotene! Brown rice takes 40 to 45 minutes to cook, so get it started before you begin to prep the vegetables.

Serves 4

1 tbsp (15 ml) canola oil

4 cloves garlic, crushed

2 tbsp (25 ml) grated fresh ginger root

1 tsp (5 ml) lemon zest

8 cups (2 L) sliced bok choy, loosely packed

2 tbsp (25 ml) oyster sauce

2 tbsp (25 ml) water

4 tsp (20 ml) sodium-reduced soy sauce

2 tsp (10 ml) freshly squeezed lemon juice

1 pkg (1 lb/454 g) medium firm tofu, cut into 1-inch (2.5 cm) cubes

1 tsp (5 ml) sesame seeds, toasted

3 cups (750 ml) cooked brown rice

Heat oil in a skillet over medium heat. When pan is hot, add garlic, ginger and lemon zest; sauté for 2 minutes.

Add bok choy, oyster sauce, water, soy sauce and lemon juice; stir-fry until bok choy begins to wilt, about 1 minute.

Add tofu, continue to stir-fry until tofu is heated through, about 3 to 4 minutes. Remove from heat; sprinkle with sesame seeds. Serve over brown rice.

NUTRITION
Per 3/4 cup (175 ml) brown rice and 1-1/4 cup (300 ml) bok choy mixture: 333 cal, 19 g pro, 11 g total fat (1 g saturated fat), 44 g carb, 6 g fibre, 0 mg chol, 526 mg sodium

Spicy Baked Tofu

These spicy tofu bites are excellent served with Spicy Sweet Potato Wedges (page 314) and Garlic Sautéed Spinach (page 296). They also make a great high-protein snack that even kids will enjoy!

Serves 2

3 tbsp (50 ml) sodium-reduced soy sauce

3 tbsp (50 ml) unseasoned rice vinegar

1 tbsp (15 ml) honey

2 cloves garlic, crushed

1 tsp (5 ml) sesame oil

1/4 tsp (1 ml) red pepper flakes

1 pkg (12 oz/350 g) extra firm tofu, cut into 1-inch (2.5 cm) cubes

In a shallow dish, combine soy sauce, vinegar, honey, garlic, sesame oil and red pepper flakes. Add tofu; cover and marinate in the fridge for a couple of hours or overnight.

Preheat oven to 350°F (180°C).

Remove tofu from marinade and place on a baking sheet.

Bake for 15 to 20 minutes or until tofu begins to brown. Serve warm.

NUTRITION

Per serving: 257 cal, 26 g pro, 14 g total fat (2 g saturated fat), 10 g carb, 0 g fibre, 0 mg chol, 429 mg sodium

Tempeh Vegetable Summer Rolls

Like tofu, tempeh is extremely versatile, taking on the flavour of whatever it's cooked with. There are different types of tempeh, including those made from quinoa and kasha. Any type can be used in this recipe. This recipe tastes great with other fresh ingredients, such as sliced mango, steamed shrimp and basil leaves—so be creative.

Serves 6

SUMMER ROLLS

1 block (8-1/2 oz/240 g) tempeh

1/2 pkg (8 oz/250 g) vermicelli noodles

1 tsp (5 ml) canola oil

2 cloves garlic, crushed

1 tbsp (15 ml) minced fresh ginger root

1 tbsp (15 ml) sodium-reduced soy sauce

12 pieces (9 inches/23 cm each) rice paper

2 cups (500 ml) baby spinach leaves

1 cup (250 ml) shredded carrot

1 cup (250 ml) chopped cilantro

1-1/2 cups (375 ml) thinly sliced red pepper strips

1/2 cup (125 ml) coarsely chopped mint leaves

HOISIN DIPPING SAUCE

1/2 cup (125 ml) hoisin sauce

2 tbsp (25 ml) sweet chili sauce

Cut tempeh into strips 1/4 inch (0.5 cm) thick; set aside.

Fill a large saucepan with water and bring to a boil. When water begins to boil, remove from heat. Soak noodles in the water for 2 to 3 minutes, until noodles become soft; drain immediately and run under cold water.

Meanwhile, heat oil in a skillet over medium heat. Add garlic and ginger root; sauté for 1 minute. Add tempeh and soy sauce; cook until tempeh is slightly crispy. Remove from heat and set aside.

Fill a large mixing bowl with lukewarm water. Add one piece of rice paper and gently move it around with your fingers until the paper is soft and flexible (about 30 seconds); immediately remove from water, gently shaking off any excess moisture. Lay the rice paper on a plate.

In the middle of the rice paper, arrange a small handful (about 1/4 cup/50 ml) of noodles and a sixth of the remaining ingredients, including tempeh, spinach, shredded carrots, cilantro, red peppers strips and mint leaves. Gently fold the bottom of the rice paper over the filling. Holding it firmly in place, fold both sides of the wrapper toward the middle. Then, pressing firmly down to hold the folds in place, roll the entire pile up to close the top. Seal any loose seams with a dab of water.

Place finished rolls on a clean plate; cover with a damp, clean tea towel or damp paper towels. Repeat process with remaining ingredients.

In a small bowl, combine hoisin sauce and sweet chili sauce. Serve immediately.

NUTRITION
Per 2 rolls: 275 cal, 10 g pro, 5 g total fat (1 g saturated fat), 48 g carb, 5 g fibre, 1 mg chol, 393 mg sodium
Per 2 rolls with 1-1/2 tbsp (22 ml) hoisin dipping sauce: 325 cal, 11 g pro, 6 g fat (1 g saturated fat), 58 g carb, 6 g fibre, 2 mg chol, 757 mg sodium

Vegetarian Chili with Soy

My vegetarian clients really like this chili. It's packed with protein, fibre and vitamin C and it tastes great! Sometimes I will add a can of chickpeas to this recipe too.

Serves 6

1 tbsp (15 ml) canola oil

1 cup (250 ml) chopped onions

1/2 cup (125 ml) chopped celery

2 cloves garlic, crushed

1 pkg (12 oz/340 g) ground meat substitute, such as Yves Ground Round

1 can (28 oz/796 ml) diced tomatoes

1 can (19 oz/540 ml) kidney beans, drained and rinsed well

1 can (19 oz/540 ml) black beans, drained and rinsed well

3 tbsp (50 ml) chili powder, or to taste

1 tsp (5 ml) ground cumin

1/4 tsp (1 ml) cayenne pepper, or to taste

In a large saucepan, heat oil over medium heat. When pan is hot, add onions and celery and sauté for 8 to 10 minutes. Add garlic; sauté another minute.

Add meat substitute, tomatoes, kidney beans, black beans, chili powder, cumin and cayenne. Cover and bring to a gentle boil; reduce heat and simmer for 30 minutes. Serve warm.

NUTRITION
Per 1-1/2 cup (375 ml) serving: 289 cal, 22 g pro, 4 g total fat (0 g saturated fat), 45 g carb, 13 g fibre, 0 mg chol, 644 mg sodium

Garden Vegetable Thin Crust Pizza

I love loading up this pizza with a variety of fresh, sliced vegetables. Here, zucchini, mushrooms and red bell pepper work well together, but I also like to add sliced heirloom tomatoes, a handful of arugula, or Garlic Roasted Cauliflower (page 295). Feel free to use whatever fresh vegetables you have on hand. I usually double the recipe when I make it—I like to eat the leftovers for lunch the next day.

Serves 2

1 tsp (5 ml) active dry yeast

1/2 tsp (2 ml) granulated sugar

1/2 cup (125 ml) lukewarm water

3/4 cup (175 ml) all-purpose flour

1/2 cup (125 ml) whole wheat flour

1 tbsp (15 ml) extra-virgin olive oil

1/4 tsp (1 ml) coarse sea salt

1/4 cup (50 ml) pizza sauce

1/2 cup (125 ml) thinly sliced zucchini (about one-third of a large zucchini)

1/2 cup (125 ml) thinly sliced brown mushrooms, such as cremini

1/4 cup (50 ml) finely diced red bell pepper

Pinch red pepper flakes, or to taste

1/2 cup (125 ml) reduced-fat mozzarella

Preheat oven to 450°F (230°C).

Lightly grease a large baking sheet.

In a large mixing bowl, whisk together yeast, sugar and water. Set aside for 10 minutes.

Add all-purpose and whole wheat flour, olive oil and salt; stir to combine. When most of the flour is combined into the dough, empty dough onto a lightly floured surface. Knead dough for 8 minutes, adding extra flour as necessary to prevent it from sticking. Dough should be smooth and slightly damp, but not sticky.

Place dough back in bowl and cover with a warm, damp tea towel. Set aside to rest for 30 minutes.

Place dough on lightly floured surface and use a rolling pin to gently roll out dough to about 12 inches (30 cm) square. Place onto prepared baking sheet and spread with pizza sauce; arrange zucchini, mushrooms and red bell peppers on pizza; sprinkle with red pepper flakes and mozzarella cheese. Bake for 18 to 22 minutes, or until crust is golden brown and slightly crispy.

NUTRITION
Per 1/2 pizza: 445 cal, 19 g pro, 13 g total fat (4 g saturated fat), 66 g carb, 7 g fibre, 17 mg chol, 496 mg sodium

Tip: Use a pizza stone instead of a baking sheet for a crisper crust.

Nasi Goreng

A trip to the beaches of Bali inspired this variation on a traditional Indonesian fried rice dish. This version uses a small amount of heart-healthy canola oil and egg whites to keep the calories and saturated fat down. I've also used brown rice instead of white rice to boost fibre and antioxidants.

Serves 5

2 tbsp (25 ml) canola oil

6 shallots, finely chopped

1 cup (250 ml) chopped leek (about 1 leek)

4 cups (1 L) shredded green cabbage

3 cups (750 ml) cooked brown basmati rice

1-1/2 tbsp (22 ml) oyster sauce

1-1/2 tbsp (22 ml) kecap manis (sweet soy sauce)

1/4 tsp (1 ml) red pepper flakes

2 egg whites, whisked

Heat oil in a skillet over medium heat. Add shallots; sauté for 12 to 15 minutes, or until brown and slightly crispy. Add the chopped leek; sauté for another 4 to 5 minutes.

Add cabbage and rice to skillet; continue to stir until heated through.

Add oyster sauce, kecap manis and red pepper flakes; mix ingredients together. Continue to cook over medium-high heat, stirring frequently, until rice begins to get brown and crispy.

Add egg white; quickly mix ingredients together until egg white is absorbed and forms long strands. Serve hot.

NUTRITION
Per 1 cup (250 ml) serving: 237 cal, 7 g pro, 7 g total fat (1 g saturated fat), 39 g carb, 3 g fibre, 0 mg chol, 351 mg sodium

Tip: To yield 3 cups (750 ml) of cooked rice, bring 2 cups (500 ml) of water to a boil in a saucepan. Add 1 cup (250 ml) of brown rice. Cover and cook for 12 minutes or until all of the water is absorbed. Remove from heat and fluff with a fork.

Tip: Kecap manis is a type of Indonesian sweet soy sauce that resembles molasses. Look for it in the Asian section of grocery and specialty food stores.

Quinoa Stuffed Red Bell Peppers

Pale yellow quinoa is the most widely available variety of this whole grain, though some natural food stores carry a dark reddish-brown variety. Both are prepared the same way. If you want a more colourful dish, use equal parts yellow and red quinoa.

Serves 6

6 small red bell peppers

2 cups (500 ml) cooked quinoa

1/2 cup (125 ml) chopped onion

3 cloves garlic, crushed

1 cup (250 ml) shredded carrot

2 tbsp (25 ml) chopped chives

1 tbsp (15 ml) chopped fresh basil

1 tbsp (15 ml) freshly squeezed lemon juice

Preheat oven to 375°F (190°C).

Cut off and reserve the tops of the bell peppers. Scoop out and discard the seeds.

In a large bowl, combine quinoa, onion, garlic, carrots, chives, basil and lemon juice. Stuff each pepper with the quinoa mixture, evenly distributing the mixture among the peppers. Place a reserved top on each of the peppers.

Gently place the peppers in a glass baking dish. Bake for 30 minutes. If the peppers begin to burn on the bottom, add about 2 tbsp (25 ml) water to the baking dish.

NUTRITION
Per stuffed pepper: 276 cal, 10 g pro, 4 g total fat (0 g saturated fat), 54 g carb, 7 g fibre, 0 mg chol, 21 mg sodium

Thin Crust Pizza with Portobello Mushrooms and Goat Cheese

Making homemade pizzas is a great way to get the kids involved in preparing a healthy dinner. Let them help roll out the dough and arrange the toppings on the pizza. If you don't have portobello mushrooms, which add a lot of flavour to this pizza, use white button or cremini mushrooms.

Serves 2

1 tsp (5 ml) active dry yeast

1/2 tsp (2 ml) granulated sugar

1/2 cup (125 ml) lukewarm water (slightly warmer than room temperature)

3/4 cup (175 ml) all-purpose flour

1/2 cup (125 ml) whole wheat flour

1 tbsp (15 ml) extra-virgin olive oil

1/4 tsp (1 ml) coarse sea salt

1/4 cup (50 ml) pizza sauce

1 small tomato, thinly sliced

1 portobello mushroom, thinly sliced

1/2 cup (125 ml) coarsely chopped fresh basil

1/3 cup (75 ml) crumbled goat cheese

Preheat oven to 450°F (230°C).

Lightly grease a large baking sheet.

In a large mixing bowl, whisk together yeast, sugar and water. Set aside for 10 minutes.

Add all-purpose and whole wheat flour, olive oil and salt; stir to combine. When most of the flour is combined into the dough, empty dough onto a lightly floured surface. Knead dough for 8 minutes, adding extra flour as necessary to prevent it from sticking. Dough should be smooth and slightly damp but not sticky.

Place dough back in bowl and cover with a warm, damp tea towel. Set aside to rest for 30 minutes.

Place dough on lightly floured surface and use a rolling pin to gently roll out dough to about 12 inches (30 cm) square. Place onto prepared baking sheet and spread with pizza sauce; arrange tomato slices, mushroom and basil on pizza and sprinkle with crumbled goat cheese. Bake for 18 to 22 minutes, or until crust is golden brown and slightly crispy.

NUTRITION
Per 1/2 pizza: 453 cal, 17 g pro, 14 g total fat (5 g saturated fat), 67 g carb, 8 g fibre, 12 mg chol, 453 mg sodium

Tip: Use a pizza stone instead of a baking sheet for a crisper crust.

Fish & Seafood

Citrus Soy Salmon

Salmon is my go-to fish. I love its flavour and, of course, its high omega-3 fatty acid content. This recipe is very tasty and a cinch to make any busy weeknight!

Serves 4

1/4 cup (50 ml) freshly squeezed orange juice

1 tbsp (15 ml) sodium-reduced soy sauce

1 tsp (5 ml) honey

1 clove garlic, crushed

1 tsp (5 ml) grated fresh ginger root

1 tsp (5 ml) olive oil

4 4-oz (120 g) salmon fillets

In a small bowl, whisk together orange juice, soy sauce, honey, garlic, ginger and oil.

Place salmon fillets in a shallow dish, drizzle with orange garlic sauce and set aside to marinate for 20 minutes.

Heat a skillet over high heat. When pan is hot, add salmon fillets with orange garlic sauce and reduce heat to medium; cover and cook for 4 to 6 minutes per side, or until fish is cooked through and flakes easily when tested with a fork.

Drizzle salmon with any remaining sauce in pan; serve hot.

NUTRITION
Per serving: 222 cal, 23 g pro, 12 g total fat (2 g saturated fat), 4 g carb, 0 g fibre, 65 mg chol, 184 mg sodium

Easy Fish Tacos with Tomato and Avocado Salsa

Tacos de pescado, a.k.a. fish tacos, originated in Baja California. They typically consist of grilled or fried fish, shredded cabbage and fresh salsa served in a corn or flour tortilla. This version is made with fresh, flavourful ingredients, including cherry tomatoes, cilantro and mint. Use your imagination and add whatever vegetables you have on hand. I also like to add Guacamole (page 88) or Sesame Coleslaw (page 152) to these fish tacos. I prefer corn tortillas but they're hard to find in Toronto. (My in-laws who live in California bring me bags of them, which I throw in the freezer.) Not only do they taste better, but they're half the calories of wheat tortillas.

Serves 4

SALSA

2 cups (500 ml) halved cherry tomatoes

1 large avocado, diced

1/2 cup (125 ml) finely chopped cilantro

1 tbsp (15 ml) finely chopped mint

Pinch red pepper flakes, or to taste

FISH

2 tsp (10 ml) canola oil

2 cloves garlic, crushed

2 tsp (10 ml) grated fresh ginger root

1 lb (454 g) firm white fish (such as halibut or haddock) cut into 1-1/2-inch (4 cm) cubes

2 tbsp (25 ml) freshly squeezed lime juice

1/8 tsp (0.5 ml) coarse sea salt

4 7-inch (18 cm) whole wheat tortillas

In a small bowl, combine cherry tomatoes, avocado, cilantro, mint and red pepper flakes. Set aside.

Heat oil in a skillet over medium heat. When pan is hot, add garlic and ginger; sauté for 30 seconds. Add fish and sauté for 10 to 12 minutes, or until fish is cooked through and flakes easily when tested with a fork. Remove from heat and sprinkle with lime juice and salt.

Meanwhile, in a separate skillet, heat tortillas over low heat until soft.

Arrange each warmed tortilla on a plate. Evenly distribute fish among four tortillas; top each with one-quarter of the salsa mixture. Fold up bottom of tortilla and wrap sides around fish mixture. Serve immediately.

NUTRITION
Per taco: 380 cal, 29 g pro, 14 g total fat (2 g saturated fat), 35 g carb, 5 g fibre, 36 mg chol, 362 mg sodium

Halibut with Sesame and Cilantro

I serve fish a few times every week and this recipe has become a staple for any white fish. It's so easy and quick to make.

Serves 4

3 tbsp (50 ml) finely chopped cilantro

1/4 cup (50 ml) freshly squeezed lime juice

2 tsp (10 ml) sesame oil

1 clove garlic, crushed

Freshly ground black pepper, to taste

4 4-oz (120 g) halibut fillets

In a shallow dish, combine cilantro, lime juice, sesame oil, garlic and pepper. Add halibut; marinate for 20 minutes.

Preheat oven to 375°F (190°C).

Arrange halibut on a baking sheet lined with parchment paper; drizzle with marinade. Bake, uncovered, for 12 to 16 minutes, or until fish is cooked through and flakes easily when tested with a fork.

NUTRITION
Per serving: 145 cal, 24 g pro, 4 g total fat (1 g saturated fat), 1 g carb, 0 g fibre, 42 mg chol, 68 mg sodium

Honey Ginger Tilapia

Tilapia is a lean white fish that's available year-round. This recipe gives its mild flavour a big boost.

Serves 4

1/4 cup (50 ml) freshly squeezed lime juice

1 tbsp (15 ml) grated fresh ginger root

1 tbsp (15 ml) honey

1 tsp (5 ml) grainy Dijon mustard

1 tsp (5 ml) olive oil

4 4-oz (120 g) tilapia fillets

In a small bowl, whisk together lime juice, ginger, honey, mustard and oil.

Place tilapia fillets in a shallow dish; drizzle with honey ginger sauce and set aside to marinate for 20 minutes.

Heat a skillet over high heat. When pan is hot, add tilapia fillets with honey ginger sauce and reduce heat to medium; cover and cook for 4 to 6 minutes per side, or until fish is cooked through and flakes easily when tested with a fork.

Drizzle tilapia with any remaining sauce in pan; serve hot.

NUTRITION
Per serving: 149 cal, 24 g pro, 2 g total fat (1 g saturated fat), 7 g carb, 0 g fibre, 45 mg chol, 31 mg sodium

Lemon Dill Salmon

Dill and lemon are my standby ingredients for heart-healthy salmon. If you don't have fresh dill, substitute 2 teaspoons (10 ml) of dried dill. For extra flavour, garnish each fillet with freshly grated lemon zest before serving.

Serves 4

4 4-oz (120 g) salmon fillets

2 cloves garlic, crushed

2 tbsp (25 ml) finely chopped fresh dill

1/4 tsp (1 ml) coarse sea salt

Freshly ground black pepper, to taste

4 lemon slices

Zest of 1/2 lemon to garnish, optional

Preheat oven to 400°F (200°C).

Arrange fillets, skin side down, on a baking sheet lined with parchment paper.

Evenly sprinkle the fillets with the garlic, dill, sea salt and pepper. Place a lemon slice on top of each fillet.

Bake for 10 to 14 minutes or until fish is cooked through and flakes easily when tested with a fork.

Garnish with lemon zest if desired.

NUTRITION

Per serving: 165 cal, 23 g pro, 7 g total fat (1 g saturated fat), 1 g carb, 0 g fibre, 63 mg chol, 201 mg sodium

Lemon Linguine with Shrimp

This dish is a crowd pleaser and it's so easy to make! If you don't have fresh shrimp, frozen shrimp works just as well. To save time, consider cooking pasta in advance and freezing it. When you want pasta in a hurry, simply run boiling water over it in a colander and voila—you've got pasta in less than a minute!

Serves 4

1 tbsp (15 ml) extra-virgin olive oil

1 pound (454 g) fresh shrimp, shelled and deveined

3 cloves garlic, crushed

4 cups (1 L) cooked whole wheat pasta, such as linguine

4 tbsp (60 ml) freshly squeezed lemon juice

3 tbsp (50 ml) extra-virgin olive oil

1 cup (250 ml) fresh basil, coarsely chopped

1/4 tsp (1 ml) coarse sea salt, or to taste

Freshly ground black pepper, to taste

Heat oil in a large skillet over medium heat; when pan is hot add shrimp and sauté until cooked through and bright pink, about 4 to 5 minutes (or longer for large shrimp). Add garlic; sauté for another minute.

Add pasta to skillet, toss with shrimp. Drizzle with lemon juice and olive oil. Sauté until heated through. Remove from heat and toss pasta with basil; season with salt and pepper. Serve warm.

NUTRITION
Per 1-1/2 cup (375 ml) serving: 423 cal, 31 g pro, 16 g total fat (2 g saturated fat), 41 g carb, 5 g fibre, 172 mg chol, 320 mg sodium

Tip: If you don't like the taste of whole wheat pasta, use white pasta with added fibre, such as Catelli Smart Pasta.

Lemon Thyme Trout

Trout is a great alternative to salmon. It's just as flavourful and an excellent source of heart-healthy omega-3 fatty acids. Rainbow and lake trout both work well for this recipe. If you eat fish at least twice per week, consider growing your own lemon thyme, a citrus-flavoured variety that's especially good with fish and seafood.

Serves 4

1/4 cup (50 ml) fresh thyme

2 tbsp (25 ml) lemon juice

1 tsp (5 ml) honey

4 4-oz (120 g) trout fillets

4 slices lemon

In a small bowl, whisk together thyme, lemon juice and honey.

Place trout fillets in a shallow dish; drizzle with lemon honey mixture and set aside to marinate for 20 minutes.

Heat a skillet over high heat. When pan is hot, add trout fillets with lemon honey mixture and reduce heat to medium; cover and cook for 4 to 6 minutes per side, or until fish is cooked through and flakes easily when tested with a fork.

Drizzle trout with any remaining sauce in pan and top each piece of fish with a slice of lemon; serve hot.

NUTRITION
Per serving: 142 cal, 23 g pro, 4 g total fat (1 g saturated fat), 3 g carb, 0 g fibre, 64 mg chol, 31 mg sodium

Lime Cilantro Halibut

There's a reason halibut is a favourite among fish lovers—it has firm white meat and a slightly sweet flavour. It also gets two thumbs up from a nutrition standpoint. Not only is it a lean source of protein with less than 3 grams of fat per 120 gram serving, but it's also an excellent source of vitamin D.

Serves 4

1 tbsp (15 ml) canola oil

1/4 cup (50 ml) sliced green onions

1 tbsp (15 ml) grated fresh ginger root

4 4-oz (120 g) halibut fillets

1/4 cup (50 ml) freshly squeezed lime juice

1/2 tsp (2 ml) sesame oil

1/2 cup (125 ml) chopped cilantro

Heat canola oil in a skillet over medium heat. When pan is hot, add onions and ginger and sauté for 2 minutes.

Add fish to skillet, skin side up. Drizzle with lime juice, then cover and continue to cook for 4 to 6 minutes per side until fish is cooked through and flakes easily when tested with a fork.

Remove from heat. Drizzle the fillets with sesame oil and sprinkle with cilantro. Serve immediately.

NUTRITION
Per serving: 167 cal, 24 g pro, 7 g total fat (1 g saturated fat), 2 g carb, 0 g fibre, 36 mg chol, 64 mg sodium

Maple-Glazed Salmon

I don't think you can have too many quick recipes for salmon. This one teams up soy sauce, maple syrup, mustard and ginger for a very flavourful meal.

Serves 4

2 tbsp (25 ml) sodium-reduced soy sauce

1 tbsp (15 ml) maple syrup

2 tsp (10 ml) grainy Dijon mustard

1 tsp (5 ml) grated fresh ginger root

4 4-oz (120 g) salmon fillets

In a small bowl, whisk together soy sauce, maple syrup, mustard and ginger.

Place salmon fillets in a shallow dish; drizzle with maple mustard mixture and set aside to marinate for 20 minutes.

Preheat oven to 375°F (190°C).

Arrange fish on a baking sheet lined with parchment paper and bake for 12 to 16 minutes, or until fish is cooked through and flakes easily when tested with a fork.

Serve hot.

Note: Do not bake the fish without parchment paper—otherwise the marinade will burn. If you don't have parchment paper, be sure to cover the baking sheet with foil.

NUTRITION
Per serving: 215 cal, 24 g pro, 11 g total fat (2 g saturated fat), 4 g carb, 0 g fibre, 65 mg chol, 338 mg sodium

Mediterranean Fish Stew

This recipe is inspired by bouillabaisse, a traditional Provençal fish stew originating in Marseille. Bouillabaisse is typically prepared with four to seven types of seafood. This easy version uses only one type of fish and takes less than an hour to prepare. I like to serve it with a fresh, crusty whole-grain baguette for dipping in the stew.

Serves 4

2 tbsp (25 ml) canola oil

1 cup (250 ml) finely chopped onion

1 cup (250 ml) thinly sliced fennel (about 2 small bulbs)

1 cup (250 ml) diced celery

1 cup (250 ml) thinly sliced leek, white part only

2 cloves garlic, crushed

1 can (12 oz/369 ml) diced tomatoes

1 cup (250 ml) white wine

1 tsp (5 ml) grated orange zest

2 tbsp (25 ml) freshly squeezed orange juice

1/4 tsp (1 ml) coarse sea salt, or to taste

1 lb (454 g) firm white fish, such as halibut or haddock, cut into 2-inch (5 cm) cubes

1/2 cup (125 ml) coarsely chopped parsley

Heat oil in a large saucepan over high heat; when pan is hot, add onions, fennel, celery and leek. Reduce heat to medium-high and sauté until soft and fragrant, about 8 minutes. Add garlic; sauté for another minute.

Add tomatoes, wine, orange zest, orange juice and salt. Bring to a boil, reduce heat, cover and simmer for 30 minutes. Place fish in pan; gently cover with tomato mixture. Cover and continue to simmer for 15 minutes or until fish is cooked through and flakes easily when tested with a fork.

Remove from heat; sprinkle with parsley and serve immediately.

NUTRITION
Per 1-1/4 cup (300 ml) stew: 298 cal, 27 g pro, 10 g total fat (1 g saturated fat), 16 g carb, 4 g fibre, 36 mg chol, 448 mg sodium

Miso-Glazed Trout

Trout, an excellent source of omega-3 fatty acids, has become a favourite of mine. I serve it as an alternative to salmon. If you don't want the hassle of peeling and grating fresh ginger root, use puréed ginger (sold in jars)—it works really well in this recipe, giving the sauce a thick and creamy texture.

Serves 4

4 4-oz (120 g) rainbow trout fillets

4 tsp (20 ml) grated fresh ginger root

4 tsp (20 ml) frozen orange juice concentrate

2 tsp (10 ml) miso

1 tbsp (15 ml) chopped fresh chives

Preheat oven to 400°F (200°C).

Arrange fillets on a baking sheet lined with parchment paper and bake for 10 to 14 minutes or until fish is cooked through and flakes easily when tested with a fork.

Meanwhile, in a small bowl, whisk together ginger root, orange juice concentrate and miso. Pour sauce over cooked fillets; sprinkle with chives.

NUTRITION
Per serving: 151 cal, 24 g pro, 4 g total fat (1 g saturated fat), 3 g carb, 0 g fibre, 65 mg chol, 135 mg sodium

Tip: The miso sauce can double as a salad dressing.

Mussels in White Wine Herb Sauce

It takes no time at all to cook mussels! However, properly preparing them can be time consuming. Clean the mussels well and discard any that are chipped, broken or cracked, as well as those that don't close when you're rinsing them (read the Tip on the next page for more details).

Serves 4

2 tsp (10 ml) canola oil

1/2 cup (125 ml) onion, finely chopped

1 clove garlic, crushed

1 cup (250 ml) dry white wine

1/4 cup (50 ml) finely chopped parsley

2 lb (900 g) mussels, scrubbed and de-bearded

Heat oil in a large saucepan over high heat. When pan is hot, add onions and reduce heat to medium; sauté for 4 to 5 minutes. Add garlic; sauté for another minute.

Add wine and parsley and bring to a boil over high heat. Reduce heat and simmer over medium-low heat.

Add mussels; cover and steam for 4 to 5 minutes or until all of the mussels have opened up. Remove from heat and serve immediately.

NUTRITION
Per serving: 265 cal, 27 g pro, 7 g total fat (1 g saturated fat), 11 g carb, 0 g fibre, 64 mg chol, 653 mg sodium

Tip: Serve these mussels with a fresh loaf of whole-grain crusty bread for dipping in the broth.

Tip: To ensure you are serving mussels that are safe and free of sand, follow these simple steps:
1. Buy mussels from a reputable fishmonger and avoid mussels that are chipped, broken or cracked. Ask for a bag of ice from the fish counter so you can keep them cool until you can get them home and in the fridge.
2. To clean mussels, dump them in a large bowl or sink of cold water. Some mussels will have a fibrous web of vegetation, called a "beard." This can be removed with a firm tug. Scrub the mussels and remove any barnacles. Tap any mussels that are open; if they do not close, they are dead and should be discarded.
3. Rinse mussels a few times before cooking to ensure all sand and grit is removed.
4. Any mussels that are closed after cooking should be thrown away.

Pasta with Sautéed Prawns, Garlic and Tomatoes

Ever wonder what the difference is between shrimp and prawns? In many cases, the words are used interchangeably. In North America, small and medium-sized shrimp are often called shrimp, while large shrimp are usually called prawns. Biologically, there is a slight difference between the two, but for practical purposes the terms usually refer to size. Look for fairly large prawns for this recipe.

Serves 4

3 tbsp (50 ml) extra-virgin olive oil

12 large fresh prawns or shrimp, peeled and deveined (about 1 lb/454 g)

12 cloves garlic, crushed

4 large tomatoes, diced

1/2 tsp (2 ml) coarse sea salt

Freshly ground black pepper, to taste

Pinch red pepper flakes, or to taste

4 cups (1 L) loosely packed spinach, coarsely chopped

4 cups (1 L) cooked whole-grain pasta, such as linguine

1/3 cup (75 ml) tightly packed fresh basil

Heat 1 tbsp (15 ml) olive oil in a skillet over medium heat. When pan is hot, add prawns and sauté until they turn pink and are cooked through, about 5 minutes. Add 2 tbsp (25 ml) of olive oil and garlic to skillet; sauté for 1 to 2 minutes until garlic is fragrant.

Add tomatoes, salt, pepper and red pepper flakes to skillet; cook for 7 to 8 minutes, or until tomatoes soften and begin to release their juices. Add spinach; cook for another few minutes, or until spinach is wilted. Add cooked pasta to skillet; toss ingredients and cook until heated through.

Remove from heat and toss with fresh basil.

NUTRITION
Per 1 cup (250 ml) pasta and 1 cup (250 ml) sauce: 438 cal, 34 g pro, 13 g total fat (2 g saturated fat), 50 g carb, 7 g fibre, 172 mg chol, 548 mg sodium

Tip: Ask your fishmonger to peel and devein the prawns for you. If you don't have fresh, frozen pre-cooked prawns or shrimp can be substituted.

Pepper-Crusted Salmon

Salmon, packed with omega-3 fatty acids, helps guard against heart disease and possibly Alzheimer's disease. Include it in your menu at least once per week. Use a good quality pepper mill to coarsely grind the fresh pepper for this recipe—doing so will make a big difference.

Serves 4

2 tbsp (25 ml) maple syrup

2 tbsp (25 ml) sodium-reduced soy sauce

2 cloves garlic, crushed

4 4-oz (120 g) salmon fillets

1/4 cup (50 ml) fresh coarsely ground pepper

2 tsp (10 ml) canola oil

In a shallow dish, combine maple syrup, soy sauce and garlic. Place salmon fillets, skin side up, in marinade. Cover and refrigerate for at least 2 hours.

Place ground pepper on a large plate. Remove salmon from marinade and firmly press each fillet (skin side up) into pepper.

Meanwhile, heat oil in a skillet over high heat. When pan is hot, place salmon in the skillet, skin side up; reduce heat to medium and continue to cook for 4 to 6 minutes per side, or until fish is cooked through and flakes easily when tested with a fork.

NUTRITION
Per serving: 217 cal, 23 g pro, 10 g total fat (1 g saturated fat), 9 g carb, 2 g fibre, 62 mg chol, 320 mg sodium

Rainbow Trout with Citrus Mustard Sauce

Trout is a great stand-in for salmon. While this recipe calls for frying the fish (in no oil!), you can also bake it or grill it.

Serves 4

1/4 cup (50 ml) freshly squeezed lemon juice

1 tbsp (15 ml) honey

1 tsp (5 ml) grainy Dijon mustard

1 tsp (5 ml) olive oil

Freshly ground black pepper, to taste

4 4-oz (120 g) rainbow trout fillets

In a small bowl, whisk together lemon juice, honey, mustard, oil and pepper.

Place trout fillets in a shallow dish; drizzle with honey mustard sauce and set aside to marinate for 20 minutes.

Heat a skillet over high heat. When pan is hot, add trout fillets with honey mustard sauce and reduce heat to medium; cover and cook for 4 to 6 minutes per side, or until fish is cooked through and flakes easily when tested with a fork.

Drizzle trout with any remaining sauce in pan; serve hot.

NUTRITION
Per serving: 134 cal, 18 g pro, 4 g total fat (1 g saturated fat), 7 g carb, 0 g fibre, 49 mg chol, 40 mg sodium

Salmon Burgers

These tasty burgers are a very healthy alternative to beef burgers. The recipe calls for tinned salmon but I'll also use leftover cooked salmon. Don't forget the horseradish—it goes so well with these salmon burgers.

Serves 4

1 medium egg

1/2 cup (125 ml) whole wheat bread crumbs

1 tbsp (15 ml) ground flaxseed

2 cans (7-1/2 oz/213 g each) salmon, drained

1/4 cup (50 ml) finely chopped onions

2 tbsp (25 ml) chopped fresh dill

2 tbsp (25 ml) lemon juice

1/4 tsp (1 ml) coarse sea salt, or to taste

Freshly ground black pepper, to taste

1 tbsp (15 ml) canola oil

2 6-inch (15 cm) whole wheat pita pockets, toasted and cut in half

2 tsp (10 ml) horseradish

1 cup (250 ml) baby spinach leaves

1 medium tomato, sliced

In a large mixing bowl, combine egg, bread crumbs, flaxseed, salmon, onions, dill, lemon juice, salt and pepper. Using clean hands, thoroughly mix ingredients together and form into 4 patties.

Heat oil in a skillet over high heat; when pan is hot, add salmon patties and reduce heat to medium. Cook patties for about 3 to 4 minutes per side, or until golden brown.

Remove from heat and serve each patty in half a pita pocket, topped with horseradish, spinach and tomato.

NUTRITION

Per burger with pita, horseradish, spinach and tomato: 271 cal, 22 g pro, 15 g total fat (3 g saturated fat), 12 g carb, 1 g fibre, 73 mg chol, 198 mg sodium

Salmon with White Wine, Lemon and Garlic

The Heart and Stroke Foundation of Canada recommends that adults consume fish, especially fatty fish such as salmon, at least twice a week. Salmon not only is packed with heart-healthy omega-3 fatty acids, but also is a great source of vitamin D.

Serves 4

2 cloves garlic, crushed

1/4 cup (50 ml) white wine

1/4 cup (50 ml) freshly squeezed lemon juice

4 4-oz (120 g) salmon fillets

2 tsp (10 ml) canola oil

Lemon wedges, as garnish

In a shallow dish, combine garlic, white wine and lemon juice. Place salmon, skin side up, in dish. Set aside to marinate for 20 minutes.

Heat oil in a skillet over high heat. Add salmon, skin side up, and marinade to the skillet. Cover, and reduce heat to medium. Cook for 4 to 6 minutes per side, or until fish is cooked through and flakes easily when tested with a fork.

Remove from heat.

Drizzle salmon with any remaining sauce in pan; serve hot. Garnish with a lemon wedge if desired.

NUTRITION
Per serving: 244 cal, 23 g pro, 15 g total fat (3 g saturated fat), 2 g carb, 0 g fibre, 67 mg chol, 68 mg sodium

Tip: The natural oils from the salmon will release as the salmon cooks, coating the pan. If the pan begins to dry out, add a tablespoon or two (15–30 ml) of white wine or water to keep the fish from sticking.

Sautéed Prawns with Ginger and Lime

Shrimp is a healthy protein alternative to meat because it's low in calories and saturated fat. This mouth-watering combination of shrimp, fresh ginger, lime juice and cilantro is a must-try. My taste-testers couldn't get enough.

Serves 4

1 tbsp (15 ml) olive oil

2 tbsp (25 ml) sliced green onions

3 cloves garlic, finely crushed

1 tbsp (15 ml) grated fresh ginger root

1 lb (454 g) large pre-cooked prawns or large shrimp, fresh or frozen

2 tbsp (25 ml) freshly squeezed lime juice

1/4 cup (50 ml) finely chopped cilantro

Heat oil in a skillet over medium heat. Add green onions, garlic and ginger; sauté for 2 minutes.

Add shrimp and continue to sauté for 3 to 4 minutes, or until shrimp is heated through.

Remove from heat; toss with lime juice and cilantro. Serve immediately.

NUTRITION
Per serving: 150 cal, 24 g pro, 5 g total fat (1 g saturated fat), 2 g carb, 0 g fibre, 221 mg chol, 256 mg sodium

Sesame Ginger Salmon

This Asian-inspired salmon recipe is a favourite in my house. It also works well if you bake this salmon in a 400°F (200°C) oven for 10 to 14 minutes, or until salmon flakes with a fork.

Serves 4

1/4 cup (50 ml) freshly squeezed lemon juice

1 tbsp (15 ml) sodium-reduced soy sauce

2 tsp (10 ml) sesame oil

1 tsp (5 ml) lemon zest

1 tsp (5 ml) grated fresh ginger root

1 tsp (5 ml) honey

1 clove garlic, crushed

4 4-oz (120 g) salmon fillets

In a small bowl, whisk together lemon juice, soy sauce, sesame oil, lemon zest, ginger, honey and garlic.

Place salmon fillets in a shallow dish; drizzle with sesame ginger mixture and set aside to marinate for 20 minutes.

Heat a skillet over high heat. When pan is hot, add salmon fillets with sesame ginger mixture and reduce heat to medium; cover and cook for 4 to 6 minutes per side, or until fish is cooked through and flakes easily when tested with a fork.

Drizzle salmon with any remaining sauce in pan; serve hot.

NUTRITION
Per serving: 229 cal, 23 g pro, 14 g total fat (2 g saturated fat), 4 g carb, 0 g fibre, 65 mg chol, 184 mg sodium

Sesame Salmon Wrap

Salmon is one of the few food sources naturally high in vitamin D, the "sunshine" vitamin. But this wrap isn't just an excellent source of vitamin D—it's also very high in vitamin C, folate, vitamin K, calcium and potassium.

Serves 4

2 cans (7-1/2 oz/213 g each) salmon, drained

2 tbsp (25 ml) sodium-reduced soy sauce

2 tbsp (25 ml) rice vinegar

2 tbsp (25 ml) freshly squeezed lime juice

1/2 tsp (2 ml) wasabi paste, or to taste

1/2 tsp (2 ml) sesame oil

4 whole-grain tortilla wraps (10 inches/ 25 cm each)

2 cups (500 ml) spinach, loosely packed

2 cups (500 ml) cucumber strips, thinly sliced

2 cups (500 ml) red pepper strips, thinly sliced

1/2 cup (125 ml) sliced green onions

In a small bowl, combine salmon, soy sauce, rice vinegar, lime juice, wasabi paste and sesame oil. Use the back of a fork to mash ingredients together.

On a clean work surface, lay out the four wraps. Gently arrange a layer of spinach on each wrap. Evenly distribute the salmon mixture, cucumber, red pepper strips and green onions among the four wraps.

To wrap tortillas, gently fold the bottom of the wrap over the filling, then fold one side over the filling and roll tightly. Serve immediately.

NUTRITION

Per wrap: 380 cal, 31 g pro, 12 g total fat (5 g saturated fat), 36 g carb, 6 g fibre, 42 mg chol, 788 mg sodium

Tip: If you're brown bagging these wraps for lunch, pack the salmon mixture, wrap and vegetables separately to prevent them from getting soggy.

Sesame Soy Trout

This trout has a slight teriyaki flavour, without the added sugar found in most teriyaki sauces. Read labels when buying rice vinegar: choose a brand with less than 60 mg of sodium per tablespoon (15 ml).

Serves 4

2 tbsp (25 ml) sodium-reduced soy sauce

1 tbsp (15 ml) rice vinegar

1 tsp (5 ml) grated fresh ginger root

1 tsp (5 ml) sesame oil

4 4-oz (120 g) trout fillets

In a small bowl, whisk together soy sauce, vinegar, ginger and oil.

Place trout fillets in a shallow dish; drizzle with soy sauce mixture and set aside to marinate for 20 minutes.

Heat a skillet over high heat. When pan is hot, add trout fillets with soy sauce mixture and reduce heat to medium; cover and cook for 4 to 6 minutes per side, or until fish is cooked through and flakes easily when tested with a fork.

Drizzle trout with any remaining sauce in pan; serve hot.

NUTRITION
Per serving: 149 cal, 24 g pro, 5 g total fat (1 g saturated fat), 1 g carb, 0 g fibre, 66 mg chol, 274 mg sodium

Shrimp Curry with Cardamom Scented Basmati Rice

This authentic curry is truly bursting with flavour. If you want a change from shrimp, this sauce also works well with chicken, tofu or firm white fish. White, fluffy basmati rice is the perfect accompaniment to this aromatic curry, but you can also serve it with brown rice or a piece of naan bread.

Serves 4

SHRIMP CURRY

1 tbsp (15 ml) ghee or canola oil

1 cup (250 ml) finely chopped onion

1 small cinnamon stick, 2 inches (5 cm) long

4 cardamom pods, split open and seeds removed

1 tsp (5 ml) cumin seeds

2 cloves garlic, crushed

1 tsp (5 ml) grated fresh ginger root

4 cups (1 L) diced tomatoes

1/2 cup (125 ml) water, or Homemade Chicken Stock (page 129)

1 lb (454 g) raw shrimp, peeled and deveined

1-1/2 tsp (7 ml) garam masala

1/2 tsp (2 ml) ground cardamom

1/4 tsp (1 ml) coarse sea salt

1/8 tsp (0.5 ml) turmeric

Pinch red pepper flakes, or to taste

CARDAMOM SCENTED BASMATI RICE

1-1/2 cups (375 ml) water

3/4 cup (175 ml) basmati rice

4 cardamom pods, split open

Heat oil in a large skillet over medium heat; when pan is hot, add onions and sauté for 8 to 10 minutes. When onions are soft and golden brown, add cinnamon stick, seeds from cardamom pods, cumin seeds, garlic and ginger; sauté for another 2 minutes, or until spices are fragrant.

Add tomatoes, water, shrimp, garam masala, cardamom, salt, turmeric and red pepper flakes. Cover and simmer for 15 minutes, or until shrimp are bright pink and cooked through (add more water if sauce becomes too thick).

Meanwhile, bring water to a boil in a small saucepan. When water is boiling, add basmati rice and cardamom pods; bring back to a boil. Reduce heat, cover and simmer for 12 minutes, or until all of the water is absorbed. Remove from heat and fluff with a fork.

Remove cinnamon stick and cardamom pods before serving. Serve shrimp curry over steamed rice.

NUTRITION
Per serving: 331 cal, 28 g pro, 6 g total fat (3 g saturated fat), 41 g carb, 3 g fibre, 182 mg chol, 329 mg sodium

Tip: Ghee, also known as clarified butter, is a staple in South Asian cooking that adds a rich flavour to dishes, including curries. Look for it in ethnic stores or major supermarkets. If you don't have ghee on hand, substitute an equal amount of canola oil.

Snapper with Cajun Rub

These seasoned snapper fillets are very flavourful. They're also low in fat and sodium.

Serves 4

1 tsp (5 ml) each dried thyme, paprika and garlic powder

1/4 tsp (1 ml) each cayenne and crushed black pepper

4 4-oz (120 g) snapper fillets

Preheat oven to 400°F (200°C).

In a small bowl, mix together thyme, paprika, garlic powder, cayenne pepper and black pepper.

Sprinkle Cajun spice mixture on a large dinner plate. Firmly press each fillet in spice mixture to coat snapper.

Place fillets on a baking sheet lined with parchment paper and bake for 10 to 14 minutes or until fish is cooked through and flakes easily when tested with a fork.

NUTRITION

Per serving: 121 cal, 24 g pro, 1 g total fat (0 g saturated fat), 1 g carb, 0 g fibre, 43 mg chol, 74 mg sodium

Thai Roasted Trout with Fresh Lime

Rainbow trout, with its silvery, speckled flesh and pink meat, is as attractive as it is nutritious. Like other cold-water fatty fish, including salmon, it's an excellent source of omega-3 fatty acids that protect your heart and your brain.

Serves 4

1/4 cup (50 ml) freshly squeezed lime juice

1 tbsp (15 ml) rice vinegar

1 tbsp (15 ml) sodium-reduced soy sauce

1 tbsp (15 ml) brown sugar

1 tsp (5 ml) grated fresh ginger root

1/4 tsp (1 ml) sesame oil

4 4-oz (120 g) rainbow trout fillets

Preheat oven to 375°F (190°C).

In a small mixing bowl, whisk together lime juice, rice vinegar, soy sauce, brown sugar, ginger and sesame oil.

In a shallow glass baking dish, arrange trout fillets. Pour the lime juice marinade over the fillets.

Cover and bake for 25 to 30 minutes, or until fish is cooked through and flakes easily when tested with a fork.

Remove from heat. Drizzle trout with any remaining sauce; serve hot.

NUTRITION
Per serving: 178 cal, 24 g pro, 6 g total fat (2 g saturated fat), 5 g carb, 0 g fibre, 67 mg chol, 174 mg sodium

Tilapia in a Tomato Fennel Sauce

Tilapia is an extremely versatile white fish that has a delicate taste and tends to take on the flavour of the ingredients it's cooked with. This recipe is low in saturated fat and sodium. Serve the fish with steamed brown rice or whole wheat couscous.

Serves 4

1 tsp (5 ml) canola oil

2 cloves garlic, crushed

1 cup (250 ml) crushed tomatoes

2 tbsp (25 ml) freshly squeezed lemon juice

1 tbsp (15 ml) lemon zest

1 tbsp (15 ml) capers

1/4 cup (50 ml) chopped parsley

1 tsp (5 ml) fennel seeds

4 4-oz (120 g) tilapia fillets

Heat oil in a skillet over high heat. When pan is hot, add garlic and reduce heat to medium; sauté for 1 minute. Add tomatoes, lemon juice, lemon zest, capers, parsley and fennel seeds. Bring to a simmer.

Gently lay tilapia fillets in tomato sauce. Cover and continue to simmer for 8 to 10 minutes or until fish is cooked through and flakes easily when tested with a fork.

NUTRITION
Per serving: 145 cal, 24 g pro, 3 g total fat (1 g saturated fat), 6 g carb, 2 g fibre, 56 mg chol, 142 mg sodium

Wasabi and Ginger Baked Salmon

Wild or farmed? Pacific or Atlantic? The health benefits of salmon are well known, but there's a lot of confusion around which type of salmon to choose. According to Sea Choice, Canada's sustainable seafood program and partner with the David Suzuki Foundation, wild Pacific salmon is the most environmentally friendly choice. When it's in season, I always buy wild salmon.

Serves 4

2 tsp (10 ml) wasabi paste

1 tbsp (15 ml) water

1 tbsp (15 ml) rice vinegar

1 tbsp (15 ml) sodium-reduced soy sauce

1 tbsp (15 ml) brown sugar

2 tbsp (25 ml) freshly squeezed lime juice

1 tbsp (15 ml) grated fresh ginger root

4 4-oz (120 g) salmon fillets

Preheat oven to 375°F (190°C).

In a small mixing bowl, whisk together wasabi, water, rice vinegar, soy sauce, brown sugar, lime juice and ginger root.

Place salmon, skin side down, in a glass baking dish. Cover with wasabi ginger mixture.

Cover and bake for 25 to 35 minutes, or until fish is cooked through and flakes easily when tested with a fork.

Remove from heat, serve immediately.

NUTRITION
Per serving: 226 cal, 23 g pro, 12 g total fat (3 g saturated fat), 5 g carb, 0 g fibre, 67 mg chol, 202 mg sodium

Meat

Balsamic Maple Pork Tenderloin

Called "the other white meat," pork tenderloin is very lean—only 1 gram of saturated fat per 4 ounce (120 g) serving. While I don't eat meat often, I do enjoy serving this tasty pork tenderloin.

Serves 4

1/4 cup (50 ml) balsamic vinegar

2 tbsp (25 ml) maple syrup

1 tbsp (15 ml) canola oil

1 clove garlic, crushed

1/4 tsp (1 ml) salt

Freshly ground black pepper, to taste

1 lb (454 g) pork tenderloin

In a shallow dish, combine vinegar, maple syrup, oil, garlic, salt and pepper. Add pork; marinate for 20 to 30 minutes.

Meanwhile, preheat grill to medium.

Transfer pork to the grill; cook for 20 to 22 minutes, or until cooked through.

Remove pork from grill, cover with foil and set aside to rest for 5 minutes before serving.

NUTRITION

Per serving: 197 cal, 27 g pro, 6 g total fat (1 g saturated fat), 8 g carb, 0 g fibre, 67 mg chol, 210 mg sodium

Beef Stroganoff

This recipe is a bit nostalgic for me. Growing up, my mother would often prepare a delicious beef stroganoff she served over egg noodles. This version is just as creamy as I remember and uses low-fat sour cream and whole wheat fettuccine.

Serves 6

1 tbsp (15 ml) canola oil

2 cups (500 ml) chopped onions

4 cups (1 L) sliced button mushrooms

18 oz (510 g) lean stewing beef, cut into 1-inch (2.5 cm) pieces

2 tbsp (25 ml) all-purpose flour

1 can (28 oz/796 ml) diced tomatoes

1/8 tsp (0.5 ml) freshly ground black pepper, or to taste

1 tsp (5 ml) Worcestershire sauce

4 cups (1 L) cooked whole wheat pasta, such as fettuccine

1/2 cup (125 ml) reduced-fat sour cream

Heat oil in a skillet over medium heat. When skillet is hot, add onions and sauté for 8 to 10 minutes.

Add mushrooms; continue to sauté about 8 to 10 minutes, or until most of the moisture is out of the mushrooms. Empty onion and mushroom mixture from skillet into a large saucepan.

Place the same skillet over medium-high heat. Dredge beef in flour and add to the skillet; cook about 6 to 8 minutes, or until beef begins to brown. Place browned beef into saucepan with mushrooms and onions.

Add tomatoes, pepper, and Worcestershire sauce to the saucepan. Cover and simmer for about 1-1/2 to 2 hours or until beef is cooked through and begins to fall apart.

Toss cooked sauce with pasta. Serve warm; garnish with a dollop of sour cream.

NUTRITION
Per serving: 417 cal, 26 g pro, 17 g total fat (6 g saturated fat), 44 g carb, 6 g fibre, 63 mg chol, 412 mg sodium

Tip: The sauce for this pasta can easily be prepared in a slow cooker. Brown the onions, mushrooms and beef as called for in the recipe, but simmer the sauce in a slow cooker on low for three to four hours or until the beef is cooked through and falls apart when pierced with a fork.

Cumin Scented Grilled Pork Tenderloin

This very flavourful pork tenderloin is a favourite of mine. To maximize the flavours, I'll often marinate it overnight in a resealable plastic bag. Feel free to bake this pork tenderloin in a 375°F (190°C) oven if you don't want to grill it.

Serves 4

1/4 cup (50 ml) freshly squeezed lime juice

1 tsp (5 ml) honey

2 cloves garlic, crushed

1 tsp (5 ml) grated fresh ginger root

1 tsp (5 ml) each ground cumin and ground coriander

1 tsp (5 ml) canola oil

1 lb (454 g) pork tenderloin

In a shallow dish, combine lime juice, honey, garlic, ginger, cumin, coriander and oil. Add pork; marinate for 20 minutes, turning once or twice.

Meanwhile, preheat grill to medium.

Transfer pork to the grill; cook for 20 to 22 minutes, or until cooked through.

Remove pork from grill. Cover with foil and set aside to rest for 5 minutes before serving.

NUTRITION
Per serving: 164 cal, 28 g pro, 4 g total fat (1 g saturated fat), 4 g carb, 0 g fibre, 67 mg chol, 60 mg sodium

Ginger Beef Stir-Fry

This colourful, flavourful stir-fry takes less than 20 minutes to prepare, making it perfect for weeknights when you're short on time. If you don't have time to cook brown rice, as the recipe suggests, serve the stir-fry over whole wheat couscous or soba noodles. Alternatively, I like to cook a pot of brown rice on the weekend and freeze individual portions. When I need a serving of brown rice during the week, I just take it out of the freezer, put it in a colander and pour boiling water over it until it's heated through.

Serves 4

3/4 cup (175 ml) orange juice

1 tbsp (15 ml) sodium-reduced soy sauce

1 tbsp (15 ml) unseasoned rice vinegar

1 tbsp (15 ml) honey

1 tsp (5 ml) sesame oil

2-1/2 tsp (12 ml) cornstarch

2 tsp (10 ml) canola oil

1 lb (454 g) sirloin steak, fat removed and sliced into 1/2-inch (1 cm) strips

4 cups (1 L) broccoli florets

1 large red bell pepper, cut into thin strips

1-1/2 tbsp (22 ml) grated fresh ginger root

2 cloves garlic, crushed

4 cups (1 L) cooked brown rice

1 tsp (5 ml) sesame seeds

In a small bowl, whisk together orange juice, soy sauce, rice vinegar, honey, sesame oil and cornstarch. Set aside.

Heat 1 tsp (5 ml) canola oil in a large skillet over high heat. When pan is hot, add steak and sauté until brown, about 8 minutes. Transfer steak to a plate; set aside.

Add remaining 1 tsp (5 ml) of canola oil to the skillet; heat over medium-high heat. When pan is hot, add broccoli and red pepper. Sauté until tender-crisp, about 6 to 8 minutes. Add ginger and garlic; sauté for another minute.

Add cooked steak and orange juice mixture to the skillet; increase heat to high. Cook until heated through and sauce begins to boil and thicken, about 2 to 3 minutes. Remove from heat. Serve on a bed of rice; sprinkle with sesame seeds.

NUTRITION
Per serving: 486 cal, 34 g pro, 10 g total fat (3 g saturated fat), 65 g carb, 6 g fibre, 60 mg chol, 241 mg sodium

Tip: This recipe uses unseasoned rice vinegar, which has no added sugar or salt. If you can't find unseasoned vinegar, choose a brand of seasoned rice vinegar that has less than 60 mg of sodium per tablespoon (15 ml).

Herbed Pork Tenderloin

Pork tenderloin is a perfect meat to marinate—its mild taste lets you really enjoy the flavour of the marinade. I often add grated orange zest to this marinade for a stronger citrus flavour.

Serves 4

1/4 cup (50 ml) freshly squeezed orange juice

2 tbsp (25 ml) canola oil

2 cloves garlic, crushed

1 tbsp (15 ml) chopped fresh rosemary

1 tbsp (15 ml) chopped fresh thyme

Freshly ground black pepper, to taste

1 lb (454 g) pork tenderloin

In a shallow dish, combine orange juice, oil, garlic, rosemary, thyme and pepper. Add pork; marinate for 20 minutes, turning once or twice.

Meanwhile, preheat grill to medium.

Transfer pork to the grill; cook for 20 to 22 minutes, or until cooked through.

Remove pork from grill, cover with foil and set aside to rest for 5 minutes before serving.

NUTRITION
Per serving: 209 cal, 28 g pro, 9 g total fat (1 g saturated fat), 2 g carb, 0 g fibre, 67 mg chol, 59 mg sodium

Honey-Glazed Pork Tenderloin

There's nothing not to like about this Asian-inspired pork tenderloin. The combination of hoisin sauce (a staple in my fridge!), soy sauce, ginger root and sesame oil is so delicious. You can also marinate the pork overnight in a resealable plastic bag.

Serves 4

2 tbsp (25 ml) hoisin sauce

2 tbsp (25 ml) sodium-reduced soy sauce

1 tbsp (15 ml) minced fresh ginger root

1 tbsp (15 ml) apple cider vinegar

1 tbsp (15 ml) honey

2 tsp (10 ml) sesame oil

1/4 tsp (1 ml) black pepper

1 lb (454 g) pork tenderloin

In a shallow dish, combine hoisin sauce, soy sauce, ginger, vinegar, honey, oil and pepper. Add pork; marinate for 20 to 30 minutes.

Meanwhile, preheat grill to medium. Transfer pork to the grill; cook for 20 to 22 minutes, or until cooked through.

Remove pork from grill, cover and set aside to rest for 5 minutes before serving.

NUTRITION
Per serving: 204 cal, 28 g pro, 5 g total fat (1 g saturated fat), 10 g carb, 0 g fibre, 67 mg chol, 427 mg sodium

Hungarian Beef Goulash

When I visited Budapest goulash became a favourite dish of mine. In fact, I brought back jars of hot paprika so I could make a spicy version of my own. Goulash is not quite a soup or a stew—it's somewhere in between. Serve it on its own, over brown rice or with a slice of fresh whole-grain bread. When I serve this dish, I like to add a dollop of low-fat sour cream and chopped fresh chives.

Serves 6

1 tbsp (15 ml) canola oil

21 oz (600 g) stewing beef, cut into 1-inch (2.5 cm) cubes, trimmed of fat

2 cups (500 ml) finely chopped onions

2 cloves garlic, crushed

1/2 cup (125 ml) canned crushed tomatoes

2 cups (500 ml) water

3 large potatoes, cut into 1-inch (2.5 cm) cubes

2 tbsp (25 ml) red wine vinegar

2 tbsp (25 ml) paprika

1 tsp (5 ml) Worcestershire sauce

3/4 tsp (4 ml) coarse sea salt, or to taste

Freshly ground black pepper, to taste

Heat oil in a large saucepan over high heat. Add beef, stirring constantly, until beef is brown on all sides, about 6 to 8 minutes (reduce heat to medium-high if beef begins to burn).

Add onions; sauté until onions are soft, about 6 minutes. Add garlic; sauté for another minute.

Add crushed tomatoes, water, potatoes, red wine vinegar, paprika, Worcestershire sauce, salt and pepper. Bring to a boil over high heat; reduce heat, cover and simmer until beef is tender and begins to fall apart, about 1-1/2 to 2 hours.

NUTRITION

Per 1 cup (250 ml) serving: 350 cal, 24 g pro, 11 g total fat (3 g saturated fat), 38 g carb, 5 g fibre, 65 mg chol, 421 mg sodium

Mushroom and Garlic Beef Burgers

Homemade burger patties are a cinch to make and cost a fraction of store-bought burgers. Sautéed mushrooms, onions and garlic add plenty of flavour and keep the burgers very moist. Any type of mushroom works well in these burgers, including cremini or portobello.

Serves 4

1 tbsp (15 ml) canola oil

1 cup (250 ml) finely chopped onion

2 cups (500 ml) sliced mushrooms

2 cloves garlic, crushed

1 lb (454 g) lean ground beef

1 egg white

1/4 cup (50 ml) quick cooking oats

1/4 cup (50 ml) finely chopped parsley

1/2 tsp (2 ml) Worcestershire sauce

Pinch red pepper flakes, or to taste

Freshly ground black pepper, to taste

Preheat grill over medium heat.

Heat oil in a skillet over medium heat. When pan is hot, add onions and mushrooms and sauté for 10 minutes, or until pan begins to dry out. Add garlic; sauté another minute. Remove from heat, and set aside to cool.

In a large mixing bowl, combine cooled mushroom and onion mixture, ground beef, egg white, oats, parsley, Worcestershire sauce, red pepper flakes and pepper. Using clean hands, mix ingredients together until well combined. Evenly divide mixture into four; firmly press each portion into a patty.

Place on grill and cook for 16 minutes, flipping every 4 minutes, or until beef burgers are cooked through.

NUTRITION

Per burger: 264 cal, 27 g pro, 13 g total fat (4 g saturated fat), 10 g carb, 2 g fibre, 62 mg chol, 98 mg sodium

Pasta with Brown Mushroom Garlic Sauce

Mushrooms add a delicious earthy flavour and meaty texture to this pasta without many calories. Here they're paired with lean ground beef, lots of garlic and fresh tomatoes for a simple, tasty pasta sauce. Cremini mushrooms, also called Italian brown mushrooms, are darker in colour and tend to be more flavourful than white button mushrooms. Portobello mushrooms are actually large cremini mushrooms with a rich, earthy flavour. Either one works well in this dish.

Serves 4

2 tbsp (25 ml) canola oil

1/2 cup (125 ml) chopped onion

1 lb (454 g) lean ground beef

2 cups (500 ml) chopped brown mushrooms, such as cremini or portobello

8 cloves garlic, crushed

1/2 tsp (2 ml) dried oregano

1/2 tsp (2 ml) dried rosemary

4 cups (1 L) freshly diced tomato

1/4 tsp (1 ml) coarse sea salt

Freshly ground black pepper

4 cups (1 L) cooked whole wheat pasta, such as linguine

4 cups (1 L) coarsely chopped spinach

1/2 cup (125 ml) coarsely chopped fresh basil

Heat oil in a skillet over medium heat. When pan is hot add onions and sauté until soft, about 8 to 10 minutes. Increase heat to medium-high; add ground beef and mushrooms and sauté until beef is cooked through and mushrooms begin to dry out, about 10 to 12 minutes.

Add garlic, oregano and rosemary; sauté for another minute.

Add tomato, salt and pepper to skillet; stir to combine. Cover and simmer for 20 minutes or until tomatoes have released most of their juices.

In a large serving bowl, toss together cooked pasta and spinach. Top with cooked tomato mixture, toss to coat. Garnish with fresh basil. Serve warm.

NUTRITION
Per 1 cup (250 ml) pasta and 1 cup (250 ml) sauce: 502 cal, 37 g pro, 17 g total fat (5 g saturated fat), 55 g carb, 8 g fibre, 62 mg chol, 313 mg sodium

Tip: For a vegetarian version of this dish, swap the ground beef with a 12 oz/ 340 g package of soy ground round.

Pork Loin Chops
with Apple Chutney

Many people think pork chops are a high-fat meat. Not so! This recipe derives fewer than 30% of its calories from fat and fewer than 10% from saturated fat. And it tastes great, too. The apple chutney adds just the right touch of spice to the pork chops, making it simply delicious.

Serves 6

4 apples, peeled and grated

1 tbsp (15 ml) apple cider vinegar

1/8 tsp (0.5 ml) cayenne pepper, or to taste

1/2 tsp (2 ml) ground cloves

1 tsp (5 ml) cinnamon

1 tsp (5 ml) cumin seeds

1/2 tbsp (7 ml) olive oil

1 tsp (5 ml) ground cumin

6 4-oz (120 g) boneless centre-cut loin chops

In a small saucepan, combine apples, vinegar, cayenne pepper, cloves, cinnamon and cumin seeds. Cover and simmer for 15 to 20 minutes or until apple is soft and chutney is fragrant.

Meanwhile, preheat broiler over medium heat.

In a small bowl, combine olive oil and cumin. Rub over loin chops and place on a baking sheet.

Place under broiler; cook for 3 to 4 minutes per side or until chops are cooked through. Remove from heat. Serve with warm apple chutney.

NUTRITION
Per serving: 200 cal, 26 g pro, 6 g total fat (2 g saturated fat), 12 g carb, 1 g fibre, 77 mg chol, 76 mg sodium

Shepherd's Pie with Sweet Potatoes

Shepherd's pie is the ultimate comfort food, especially during our long, dark Canadian winters. This version swaps regular potatoes with sweet potatoes, so it's got a vibrant orange colour and is packed with beta carotene. Any kind of ground meat can be used in place of the beef, including chicken, turkey or lamb.

Serves 8

2 medium sweet potatoes, peeled and diced into 1-inch (2.5 cm) cubes (about 1-1/2 lb/700 g)

1 tbsp (15 ml) non-hydrogenated margarine

1 tbsp (15 ml) canola oil

2 cups (500 ml) finely diced onion

2 cups (500 ml) sliced mushrooms

2 lb (900 g) lean ground beef

6 cloves garlic, crushed

1 cup (250 ml) sodium-reduced beef stock

1 tbsp (15 ml) flour

1 tsp (5 ml) Worcestershire sauce

1/2 tsp (2 ml) coarse sea salt, or to taste

Freshly ground black pepper, to taste

Pinch red pepper flakes, or to taste

1-1/2 cups (375 ml) corn kernels, fresh, frozen or canned (no added sugar or salt)

Preheat oven to 375°F (190°C).

Fill a large saucepan with 4 inches (10 cm) of water. Bring to a boil. Add sweet potatoes and continue to boil until sweet potatoes are tender and can easily be pierced with a fork, about 15 minutes.

Drain sweet potatoes and place them in a large mixing bowl. Using a potato masher, mash sweet potatoes with margarine until smooth. Set aside.

Heat oil in a large skillet over medium heat; when pan is hot, add onions and mushrooms; sauté for 15 minutes, or until onions and mushrooms begin to brown.

Increase heat to medium-high and add beef. Using a spatula, break up beef; continue to sauté until beef is cooked through and begins to brown, about 15 minutes.

Add garlic; sauté for another minute.

In a small bowl, whisk together stock and flour; add to skillet with beef. Add Worcestershire sauce, salt, pepper and red pepper flakes to skillet; continue to sauté until stock and flour begin to thicken, about 2 minutes. Remove from heat.

Empty beef mixture into a 13 × 9 (3.5 L) glass casserole dish; spread evenly so it covers bottom of dish. Evenly spread corn over beef mixture. Using a spatula, evenly spread sweet potatoes on top so they cover corn and beef mixture. Place in oven and bake, uncovered, for 30 minutes.

NUTRITION
Per serving: 347 cal, 28 g pro, 12 g total fat (4 g saturated fat), 32 g carb, 4 g fibre, 62 mg chol, 356 mg sodium

Slow Cooker Beef and Root Vegetable Stew

I love using my slow cooker on winter weekends. It's nice to let dinner cook while I go cross-country skiing or snowshoeing during the day. This stick-to-your ribs stew is low in fat and a good source of fibre. It freezes well, so be sure to make extra for a quick weekday meal or brown bag lunch.

Serves 8

1 tbsp (15 ml) canola oil

1 lb (454 g) lean stewing beef, cut into 1-inch (2.5 cm) pieces

1-1/2 cups (375 ml) chopped onions

4 cloves garlic, crushed

2 tbsp (25 ml) flour

3 cups (750 ml) sodium-reduced beef stock

2 cups (500 ml) chopped carrot

1 cup (250 ml) chopped parsnip

2 cups (500 ml) chopped celery

2 cups (500 ml) diced potato

1 cup (250 ml) diced sweet potato

1 cup (250 ml) diced eggplant

1/2 tsp (2 ml) coarse sea salt, or to taste

1/2 cup (125 ml) dry red wine

2 bay leaves

Freshly ground black pepper, to taste

Heat oil in a large skillet over high heat. Add stewing beef and reduce heat to medium; sauté about 5 to 7 minutes or until the meat begins to brown.

Add onions to the frying pan with the beef; continue to sauté for 4 to 5 minutes or until onions are soft. Add garlic; sauté for another minute. Sprinkle skillet with flour; sauté for another 30 seconds. Remove from heat.

Add 1 cup of stock to the skillet, scraping the bottom of the pan with a spatula to loosen any brown bits. Pour beef, onion, garlic, flour and stock mixture into a slow cooker.

Add carrot, parsnip, celery, potato, sweet potato, eggplant, salt, red wine, remainder of stock and bay leaves to the slow cooker. Season to taste with black pepper.

Cover slow cooker and simmer on low for 4 to 6 hours or until beef is tender and shreds easily when pierced with a fork. Serve warm.

NUTRITION
Per serving: 222 cal, 15 g pro, 6 g total fat (2 g saturated fat), 24 g carb, 4 g fibre, 35 mg chol, 416 mg sodium

Tip: If you don't have a slow cooker, simmer all the ingredients in a large saucepan on the stovetop for two to three hours or until beef is tender.

Stir-Fried Pork Tenderloin with Peppers and Asparagus

Pork tenderloin not only is low in fat and calories but also cooks quickly, making it perfect for easy meals like this one. Here it's paired with fresh bell peppers, baby asparagus and a tangy sweet and sour sauce for a healthy meal that's as colourful as it is delicious. Use baby asparagus, since large, tough asparagus will take too long to cook. Serve this stir-fry on its own, or with brown rice or rice noodles.

Serves 4

1/3 cup (75 ml) pineapple juice

1 tbsp (15 ml) sodium-reduced soy sauce

1 tbsp (15 ml) unseasoned rice vinegar

2 tsp (10 ml) cornstarch

Pinch red pepper flakes

1 tbsp (15 ml) canola oil

1 lb (454 g) pork tenderloin, cut lengthwise into 1-1/2 inch (4 cm) strips

3 cloves garlic, crushed

2 tsp (10 ml) grated fresh ginger root

1 red pepper, cut into 1-1/2 inch (4 cm) strips

1 green pepper, cut into 1-1/2 inch (4 cm) strips

1 yellow pepper, cut into 1-1/2 inch (4 cm) strips

1 orange pepper, cut into 1-1/2 inch (4 cm) strips

2-1/2 cups (625 ml) baby asparagus, cut into 2-inch (5 cm) pieces (about 1/2 lb/250 g)

In a small bowl, whisk together pineapple juice, soy sauce, rice vinegar, cornstarch and red pepper flakes. Set aside.

Heat oil in a large skillet over high heat. When pan is hot, add pork and sauté until browned and no longer pink, about 7 minutes. Add garlic and ginger; sauté for another minute.

Add peppers and asparagus; continue to sauté until vegetables are heated through, but still crisp, about 5 minutes. Add pineapple mixture to skillet. As soon as sauce thickens, remove skillet from heat. Serve warm.

NUTRITION
Per serving: 224 cal, 29 g pro, 5 g total fat (1 g saturated fat), 16 g carb, 4 g fibre, 63 mg chol, 201 mg sodium

Tip: I like to use the pineapple juice from a can of crushed pineapple for this recipe, although any pineapple juice will do as long as it has no added sugar.

Teriyaki Beef Kebabs

Kebabs are the perfect grilled meal in the summertime. This recipe calls for lean steak, but you can also use pork tenderloin or chicken breast if you prefer.

Serves 4

12 bamboo skewers

3 tbsp (50 ml) brown sugar

3 tbsp (50 ml) sherry

2 tsp (10 ml) water

2 tsp (10 ml) sodium-reduced soy sauce

2 tsp (10 ml) canola oil

1 clove garlic, minced

2 tsp (10 ml) grated fresh ginger root

1 lb (454 g) top sirloin boneless steak, cut into 1-inch (2.5 cm) cubes

2 cups (500 ml) red bell peppers, cut into 1-inch (2.5 cm) chunks

1 cup (250 ml) zucchini, cut into 1-inch (2.5 cm) chunks

1 cup (250 ml) white button mushrooms

Soak bamboo skewers in water for 20 to 30 minutes.

Combine brown sugar, sherry, water, soy sauce, oil, garlic and ginger to make a marinade.

Thread the beef alternately with the bell peppers, zucchini and mushrooms onto the skewers. Arrange in a shallow baking dish, cover with marinade and refrigerate for 1 hour, turning occasionally.

Preheat grill to medium. Arrange skewers on grill and cook, turning often, for 10 to 12 minutes, or until meat is cooked through.

NUTRITION
Per 3 kebabs: 362 cal, 36 g pro, 13 g total fat (4 g saturated fat), 25 g carb, 4 g fibre, 74 mg chol, 161 mg sodium

Poultry

Baked Pita Pizza with Chicken, Spinach and Fresh Basil

Compared with store-bought pizza that can run upwards of 400 calories and 7 grams of saturated fat per serving, these personal-sized pizzas are much easier on the waistline and the arteries. Be creative and add your own combination of fresh vegetables, such as arugula instead of spinach or orange bell peppers instead of red peppers. Leftover Roasted Broccoli (page 307) is another great topping!

Serves 4

4 6-inch (15 cm) whole-grain pitas

1/4 cup (50 ml) pizza sauce

2 cloves garlic, crushed

2 cups (500 ml) baby spinach, loosely packed

1 cup (250 ml) thinly sliced red pepper strips (about 1/2 large pepper)

8 oz (226 g) cooked skinless, boneless chicken breast, shredded

1/2 cup (125 ml) coarsely chopped fresh basil

1/2 cup (125 ml) sliced mushrooms

1/4 tsp (1 ml) red pepper flakes, or to taste

1 cup (250 ml) shredded low-fat cheese, such as mozzarella

Preheat oven to 375°F (190°C).

Place pitas on a large baking sheet.

Evenly divide the sauce, garlic, spinach, red pepper strips, chicken, basil, mushrooms, red pepper flakes and cheese among the pitas.

Place pitas in the oven and bake until cheese melts and edges begin to brown, about 10 to 12 minutes.

Remove from heat and serve hot.

NUTRITION
Per pita pizza: 349 cal, 36 g pro, 5 g total fat (2 g saturated fat), 42 g carb, 6 g fibre, 60 mg chol, 536 mg sodium

Chicken and Arugula Sandwich with Lemon Chive Mayonnaise

So simple, yet so delicious! Taste-testers asked for seconds of this mouth-watering sandwich. Arugula, also known as rocket, is a delicious addition to salads and sandwiches. Like most salad greens, it's high in beta carotene, lutein (for healthy eyes) and vitamin C, and very low in calories—half a cup of arugula contains less than 3 calories!

Serves 4

LEMON CHIVE MAYONNAISE

1/4 cup (50 ml) low-fat mayonnaise

1/4 tsp (1 ml) lemon zest

1 tbsp (15 ml) finely chopped chives

1/4 tsp (1 ml) coarse sea salt

Freshly ground black pepper, to taste

SANDWICH

8 thin slices dark rye bread

12 oz (350 g) cooked boneless, skinless chicken breast, sliced

1 tomato, sliced

2 cups (500 ml) loosely packed arugula

In a small bowl, combine mayonnaise, lemon zest, chives, salt and pepper.

Lightly toast rye bread. Lay bread on a clean work surface. Evenly distribute chicken, tomato, arugula and Lemon Chive Mayonnaise among 4 slices of bread. Top with remaining pieces of bread. Serve warm.

NUTRITION

Per sandwich: 288 cal, 32 g pro, 6 g total fat (1 g saturated fat), 25 g carb, 3 g fibre, 76 mg chol, 579 mg sodium

Chicken Mango Wrap
with Cilantro and Mint

Fresh mango, cilantro and mint taste great in this low-fat chicken wrap. I always prefer to use leftover cooked chicken breast for sandwiches, rather than processed chicken slices. Look for whole-grain tortillas with at least 4 grams of fibre per serving.

Serves 4

4 10-inch (25 cm) whole-grain tortilla wraps

8 oz (226 g) roasted skinless, boneless chicken breast, shredded

1 cup (250 ml) thinly sliced red pepper strips (about 1 large pepper)

1 cup (250 ml) sliced fresh mango (about 1 medium mango)

1 cup (250 ml) loosely packed cilantro, coarsely chopped

16 fresh mint leaves, washed and dried

1/4 cup (50 ml) low-fat (1% MF or less) plain yogurt

1/8 tsp (0.5 ml) coarse sea salt, or to taste

Freshly ground pepper, to taste

Lay wraps flat on a clean work surface.

On the top third of each wrap, evenly distribute chicken, red pepper strips, mango, cilantro and mint. Top with a dollop of yogurt; season with salt and pepper.

To wrap tortillas, gently fold the bottom of the wrap over the filling, then fold one side over the filling and roll tightly. Serve immediately.

NUTRITION
Per wrap: 318 cal, 26 g pro, 6 g total fat (4 g saturated fat), 38 g carb, 6 g fibre, 49 mg chol, 528 mg sodium

Chicken Mango Stir-Fry

Fresh mango and strips of red pepper add colour to this tasty stir-fry, not to mention a considerable amount of vitamin C, potassium and beta carotene.

Serves 4

1 tbsp (15 ml) sesame oil

12 oz (350 g) skinless boneless chicken breast, cut into 1-inch (2.5 cm) strips

3 cloves garlic, crushed

1 tbsp (15 ml) minced fresh ginger root

2 cups (500 ml) broccoli florets

1-1/2 cups (375 ml) red pepper strips

1 mango, peeled and diced

2 tbsp (25 ml) freshly squeezed orange juice

1/8 tsp (0.5 ml) red pepper flakes, or to taste

2 tbsp (25 ml) cashews

2 cups (500 ml) cooked brown rice

Heat sesame oil in a skillet over medium heat. Add chicken; sauté until chicken begins to brown and is cooked through, about 12 to 15 minutes.

Add garlic and ginger root; continue to sauté for another minute. Add broccoli; sauté for 4 to 5 minutes.

Add red pepper, mango, orange juice, red pepper flakes and cashews; sauté for another 2 to 3 minutes or until heated through. Serve warm over rice.

NUTRITION
Per serving: 398 cal, 33 g pro, 10 g total fat (2 g saturated fat), 46 g carb, 6 g fibre, 63 mg chol, 91 mg sodium

Ginger Tomato Chicken Pasta

Tomatoes are high in vitamins A, C and K, but it's their lycopene content that has helped them gain superfood status. Lycopene is a phytochemical that gives tomatoes their bright red colour and helps guard against prostate cancer and heart disease. Cooking tomatoes breaks down the fibres in the fruit and increases the amount of lycopene available.

Serves 4

2 tbsp (25 ml) olive oil

1 lb (454 g) skinless, boneless chicken breast, cubed

1/2 cup (125 ml) sliced green onions (about 4)

4 cloves garlic, crushed

4 cups (1 L) diced fresh tomatoes

1 cup (250 ml) sliced mushrooms

2 cups (500 ml) sliced zucchini, in medallions

2 tbsp (25 ml) grated fresh ginger root

1/4 tsp (1 ml) dried red pepper flakes

1/2 tsp (2 ml) coarse sea salt, or to taste

Freshly ground black pepper, to taste

4 cups (1 L) cooked whole wheat pasta, such as linguine

2 tbsp (25 ml) freshly squeezed lemon juice

Heat 1 tbsp (15 ml) of the oil in a skillet over medium heat. When pan is hot, add chicken and sauté for 12 to 15 minutes, or until cooked through.

Remove chicken from skillet and set aside.

Heat the remaining 1 tbsp (15 ml) oil in the skillet over medium heat. Add green onions and garlic; sauté for 2 minutes until fragrant. Add tomatoes, mushrooms, zucchini, half of the ginger root, red pepper flakes, salt, pepper and diced chicken.

Cover and simmer over medium-low heat for 20 minutes.

Remove from heat. Add cooked pasta to the skillet with vegetables. Add lemon juice and the rest of the fresh ginger root, and toss to coat. Serve hot.

NUTRITION

Per 1 cup (250 ml) pasta and 2 cups (500 ml) sauce: 427 cal, 38 g pro, 10 g total fat (2 g saturated fat), 50 g carb, 8 g fibre, 67 mg chol, 382 mg sodium

Grilled Chicken and Mixed Vegetable Pasta

This colourful pasta is loaded with flavour and just as good whether it's eaten warm or cold.

Serves 4

3 tbsp (50 ml) extra-virgin olive oil

3 cloves garlic, crushed

2 cups (500 ml) broccoli florets

1 cup (250 ml) asparagus tips

1 cup (250 ml) shredded carrot

2 cups (500 ml) halved cherry tomatoes

12 oz (350 g) grilled skinless, boneless chicken breast, thinly sliced

1 cup (250 ml) shredded spinach

1/4 cup (50 ml) chopped basil

1/4 tsp (1 ml) red pepper flakes, or to taste

1/4 tsp (1 ml) coarse sea salt, or to taste

Freshly ground black pepper, to taste

2 cups (500 ml) cooked whole wheat pasta

Heat olive oil in a large skillet over medium heat. Add garlic; sauté for 1 minute.

Add broccoli and asparagus; continue to sauté for 4 to 5 minutes.

Add carrots, cherry tomatoes, chicken breast, and spinach; sauté until heated through and spinach begins to wilt.

Remove from heat; toss with basil, red pepper flakes, salt, pepper and cooked pasta. Serve warm.

NUTRITION

Per 2 cup (500 ml) serving: 379 cal, 34 g pro, 14 g total fat (2 g saturated fat), 31 g carb, 7 g fibre, 71 mg chol, 274 mg sodium

Grilled Chicken with Tomato Cilantro Citrus Salsa

Choosing skinless chicken breast is a simple way to cut calories and saturated fat. Gram for gram, skinless chicken breast has 36% fewer calories and 86% less saturated fat than chicken with the skin on. But skinless chicken breast doesn't have to be boring. This recipe combines skinless chicken breast with antioxidant-rich tomatoes and heart-healthy avocado for a perfect mid-summer meal.

Serves 4

4 4-oz (120 g) boneless, skinless chicken breasts

2 tbsp (25 ml) freshly squeezed lime juice

2 tsp (10 ml) canola oil

2 cups (500 ml) diced fresh tomato

1 avocado, diced

1/2 cup (125 ml) coarsely chopped cilantro

2 tbsp (25 ml) freshly squeezed lime juice

1/4 tsp (1 ml) coarse sea salt, or to taste

Freshly ground black pepper, to taste

In a shallow dish, toss chicken breasts with lime juice and canola oil. Set aside for 10 to 20 minutes.

Meanwhile, preheat grill over medium-low heat.

Place chicken on grill and cook for 7 to 8 minutes per side, or until cooked through, flipping every 4 minutes.

Meanwhile, in a small mixing bowl combine tomato, avocado, cilantro, lime juice, salt and pepper. Toss to combine.

Remove chicken from grill and cover with tomato mixture. Serve immediately.

NUTRITION
Per chicken breast with 1/2 cup (125 ml) salsa: 307 cal, 26 g pro, 19 g total fat (4 g saturated fat), 8 g carb, 4 g fibre, 77 mg chol, 218 mg sodium

Tip: This recipe is designed for the barbecue but can be easily brought indoors to your kitchen oven. Bake the chicken at 375°F (190°C) for 20 to 22 minutes or until cooked through.

Grilled Lemon Garlic Chicken

Want a quick weeknight dinner that's ready to go? Then this is the recipe for you. Combine the chicken and tangy marinade in a resealable freezer bag and pop it in the freezer. For dinner in a hurry, put the chicken in the fridge to thaw in the morning and grill it when you get home in the evening. You'll have a delicious meal with little effort.

Serves 4

1/4 cup (50 ml) freshly squeezed lemon juice

1/2 tbsp (7 ml) granulated sugar

1/2 tbsp (7 ml) sodium-reduced soy sauce

3 cloves garlic, crushed

1 tbsp (15 ml) canola oil

Zest of 1 lemon

1/4 tsp (1 ml) coarse sea salt, or to taste

Freshly ground black pepper, to taste

4 4-oz (120 g) skinless, boneless chicken breasts

In a shallow dish, combine lemon juice, sugar, soy sauce, garlic, oil, lemon zest, salt and pepper. Add chicken; toss to coat. Cover and refrigerate for 1 to 2 hours.

Preheat grill.

Place chicken breasts on grill. Grill for 18 to 20 minutes or until cooked through.

NUTRITION
Per serving: 169 cal, 25 g pro, 6 g total fat (1 g saturated fat), 4 g carb, 0 g fibre, 64 mg chol, 275 mg sodium

Honey Mustard Chicken

This chicken dish is an old standby that tastes great and is so easy to make. For a taste variation, I sometimes use dried or chopped fresh rosemary instead of sage.

Serves 4

3 tbsp (50 ml) cider vinegar

2 tbsp (25 ml) honey

1 tbsp (15 ml) Dijon mustard

1 tsp (5 ml) canola oil

1/4 tsp (1 ml) dried sage

4 4-oz (120 g) boneless, skinless chicken breasts

In a shallow dish, combine vinegar, honey, mustard, oil and sage. Add chicken; marinate for 20 minutes.

Meanwhile, preheat grill to medium. Transfer chicken to the grill; cook for 7 to 8 minutes per side, or until cooked through, flipping every 4 minutes.

NUTRITION

Per serving: 184 cal, 28 g pro, 3 g total fat (1 g saturated fat), 11 g carb, 0 g fibre, 107 mg chol, 162 mg sodium

Jerk Chicken

This recipe is one of my husband's favourites, and the hotter the better! This chicken is a mainstay on my summer cottage menu—I like to serve it with corn on the cob and coleslaw.

Serves 4

1 tsp (5 ml) each ground ginger, garlic powder and thyme

1/2 tsp (2 ml) each cinnamon and salt

1/4 tsp (1 ml) each ground nutmeg and allspice

1/8 tsp (0.5 ml) cayenne pepper

1 tsp (5 ml) canola oil

4 4-oz (120 g) boneless, skinless chicken breasts

Preheat grill to medium.

In a shallow bowl, combine ginger, garlic powder, thyme, cinnamon, salt, nutmeg, allspice and cayenne. Lightly oil chicken and pat spice mixture onto chicken breasts.

Transfer chicken to the grill; cook for 7 to 8 minutes per side, or until cooked through, flipping every 4 minutes.

NUTRITION
Per serving: 148 cal, 28 g pro, 3 g total fat (1 g saturated fat), 2 g carb, 0 g fibre, 107 mg chol, 401 mg sodium

Kasha Cabbage Rolls

This recipe is a new take on an old classic that uses kasha, a whole grain with a distinct nutty flavour. These cabbage rolls freeze well after they've been baked—they're ideal to have on hand for quick, stress-free dinners and brown bag lunches.

Serves 6

12 medium green cabbage leaves

1 lb (454 g) ground chicken or turkey

2 cups (500 ml) cooked, cooled kasha

2 cups (500 ml) chopped onion

1/4 cup (50 ml) ground flaxseed

1 tbsp (15 ml) basil

1 tsp (5 ml) red pepper flakes, or to taste

1/2 tsp (2 ml) salt, or to taste

3 cloves garlic, crushed

2 eggs

2 cans (28 oz/796 ml each) diced tomatoes

Freshly ground pepper, to taste

Preheat oven to 375°F (190°C).

Blanch cabbage leaves by plunging them into a pot of boiling water; remove them once they're slightly softened and wilted. Shake off any water, and set aside.

In a large bowl, combine ground poultry, kasha, onion, flaxseed, basil, red pepper flakes, salt, garlic and eggs.

Cover the bottom of a large Dutch oven with one can of tomatoes.

Scoop 1/2 cup (125 ml) of the kasha mixture onto one end of a cabbage leaf and roll up, firmly folding the ends under. Place roll in the Dutch oven over the tomatoes.

Continue making the rolls in this way until all the cabbage and kasha mixture is used, arranging the rolls in the bottom of the pot in a snug single layer.

Pour remaining can of tomatoes over rolls. Season with black pepper.

Cover and bake for 2 to 2-1/2 hours or until tomato mixture is bubbling and meat is cooked through.

Makes 12 rolls.

NUTRITION
Per 2 cabbage rolls: 377 cal, 26 g pro, 6 g total fat (1 g saturated fat), 63 g carb, 13 g fibre, 56 mg chol, 626 mg sodium

Lemon Chicken

This simple recipe adds a subtle lemon flavour to chicken. To take it up a notch, add grated lemon zest to the marinade.

Serves 4

1/4 cup (50 ml) freshly squeezed lemon juice

1 clove garlic, crushed

1 tbsp (15 ml) honey

1 tsp (5 ml) Worcestershire sauce

1 tsp (5 ml) canola oil

Zest of 1 lemon

4 4-oz (120 g) boneless, skinless chicken breasts

In a shallow baking dish, combine lemon juice, garlic, honey, Worcestershire sauce, oil and lemon zest. Add chicken, cover with plastic wrap and marinate for 20 minutes (or longer) in the fridge. (Alternatively, marinate in a resealable plastic bag.)

Meanwhile, preheat grill to medium. Transfer chicken to the grill; cook for 7 to 8 minutes per side, or until cooked through, flipping every 4 minutes.

NUTRITION
Per serving: 166 cal, 28 g pro, 3 g total fat (1 g saturated fat), 7 g carb, 0 g fibre, 107 mg chol, 127 mg sodium

Lemon Sesame Chicken Stir-Fry

This colourful stir-fry is an excellent way to boost your intake of cancer-fighting vegetables; it's also a great way to use leftover grilled or roasted chicken. Low in saturated fat, this meal is an excellent source of vitamins A and C, potassium and dietary fibre.

Serves 4

1 tbsp (15 ml) sesame oil

2 cloves garlic, crushed

1 tbsp (15 ml) grated fresh ginger root

2 cups (500 ml) broccoli florets

2 cups (500 ml) chopped cauliflower

1 cup (250 ml) chopped red pepper

16 oz (480 g) cooked skinless, boneless chicken breast, diced

2 tbsp (25 ml) sodium-reduced soy sauce

3 tbsp (50 ml) freshly squeezed lemon juice

1 tbsp (15 ml) sesame seeds

1/4 cup (50 ml) cilantro to garnish

2 cups (500 ml) cooked brown rice

Heat sesame oil in a skillet over medium heat. Add garlic and ginger root; sauté for 1 minute.

Add broccoli, cauliflower and red pepper; sauté for 4 to 5 minutes.

Add chicken, soy sauce and lemon juice; heat through.

Sprinkle with sesame seeds and garnish with cilantro. Serve over rice.

NUTRITION

Per serving: 473 cal, 47 g pro, 9 g total fat (2 g saturated fat), 56 g carb, 12 g fibre, 84 mg chol, 449 mg sodium

Moroccan Turkey Meat Loaf

This is a low-fat twist on traditional meat loaf made with ground beef. This low-calorie version uses lean ground turkey and is infused with a variety of Moroccan-style spices. Serve with whole-grain couscous.

Serves 8

1/2 cup (125 ml) finely diced onion

1 clove garlic, crushed

1 tsp (5 ml) grated fresh ginger root

1-1/4 lb (570 g) lean ground turkey

1 tsp (5 ml) cinnamon

1/2 tsp (2 ml) ground cumin

1 tbsp (15 ml) tomato paste

1/2 cup (125 ml) large-flake rolled oats

1/2 tsp (2 ml) coarse sea salt, or to taste

Freshly ground black pepper, to taste

1/4 cup (50 ml) sliced almonds

Preheat oven to 375°F (190°C).

In a mixing bowl, combine onion, garlic, ginger root, turkey, cinnamon, cumin, tomato paste, oats, salt and pepper. Mix well.

Grease a 9 × 5 inch (2 L) loaf pan. Firmly press turkey mixture into loaf pan. Top with sliced almonds.

Bake uncovered for 60 to 70 minutes or until loaf begins to brown and pull away from sides of pan.

Preheat broiler. Place loaf under broiler for about 4 to 5 minutes or until almonds begin to brown.

NUTRITION

Per 1-inch (2.5 cm) slice: 157 cal, 17 g pro, 7 g total fat (2 g saturated fat), 6 g carb, 1 g fibre, 46 mg chol, 196 mg sodium

Pasta with Chicken, Sautéed Cherry Tomatoes and Basil

Store-bought pasta sauce is usually high in sodium, with some brands having upwards of 600 milligrams per half-cup serving (almost half a day's worth!). This recipe uses a medley of fresh ingredients, resulting in a light and healthy pasta meal with less than 250 milligrams of sodium per serving.

Serves 4

2 tsp (10 ml) canola oil

1 lb (454 g) thinly sliced chicken breast

2 tbsp (25 ml) extra-virgin olive oil

3-1/2 cups (875 ml) halved cherry tomatoes

4 cloves garlic, crushed

4 cups (1 L) cooked whole wheat pasta, such as linguine or spaghetti

1/2 cup (125 ml) coarsely chopped fresh basil

1/4 tsp (1 ml) coarse sea salt

Pinch red pepper flakes, or to taste

Freshly ground black pepper, to taste

Heat canola oil in a skillet over medium heat. When pan is hot, add chicken and sauté until cooked through and golden brown, about 12 to 15 minutes. Remove chicken from pan and set aside.

Heat 1 tbsp (15 ml) olive oil in a skillet over medium heat. When pan is hot, add cherry tomatoes and sauté for 3 minutes. Add garlic and sauté another minute. Add chicken and pasta to skillet and cook until pasta and chicken are heated through. Remove from heat; add basil, salt, red pepper flakes and pepper. Drizzle with additional 1 tbsp (15 ml) olive oil; toss to combine. Serve warm.

NUTRITION
Per 1-1/2 cup (375 ml) serving: 463 cal, 46 g pro, 12 g total fat (2 g saturated fat), 44 g carb, 6 g fibre, 96 mg chol, 242 mg sodium

Tip: If you don't have cherry tomatoes, you can substitute an equal amount of freshly diced tomatoes.

Pesto and Grilled Chicken Thin Crust Pizza

Once you try this mouth-watering pizza, you'll want to throw out those take-away menus! Making your own pizza is a lot easier than you might think. One of the best things about homemade pizza is that you can mix and match toppings to your liking. While this recipe combines pesto, grilled chicken, mushrooms and goat cheese, it also tastes great with a handful of fresh arugula, sliced tomatoes and black olives.

Serves 2

1 tsp (5 ml) active dry yeast

1/2 tsp (2 ml) granulated sugar

1/2 cup (125 ml) lukewarm water

3/4 cup (175 ml) all-purpose flour

1/2 cup (125 ml) whole wheat flour

1 tbsp (15 ml) extra-virgin olive oil

1/4 tsp (1 ml) coarse sea salt

2 tbsp (25 ml) pesto (from jar or homemade)

1/2 cup (125 ml) sliced brown mushrooms, such as cremini

4 oz (120 g) shredded grilled chicken breast

2 oz (60 g) crumbled goat cheese (about 1/3 cup/75 ml)

Preheat oven to 450°F (230°C).

Lightly grease a large baking sheet.

In a large mixing bowl, whisk together yeast, sugar and water. Set aside for 10 minutes.

Add all-purpose and whole wheat flour, olive oil and salt; stir to combine. When most of the flour is combined into the dough, empty dough onto a lightly floured surface. Knead dough for 8 minutes, adding extra flour as necessary to prevent it from sticking. Dough should be smooth and slightly damp, but not sticky.

Place dough back in bowl and cover with a warm, damp tea towel. Set aside to rest for 30 minutes.

Place dough on a lightly floured surface and use a rolling pin to gently roll out dough to about 12 inches (30 cm) square. Place onto prepared baking sheet and spread with pesto; arrange mushrooms and grilled chicken on pizza and sprinkle with crumbled goat cheese. Bake for 18 to 22 minutes, or until crust is golden brown and slightly crispy.

NUTRITION
Per 1/2 pizza: 589 cal, 37 g pro, 22 g total fat (8 g saturated fat), 61 g carb, 6 g fibre, 66 mg chol, 563 mg sodium

Tip: Use a pizza stone instead of a baking sheet for a crisper crust.

Rosemary Mustard Chicken

I've made this chicken recipe for years and still love it. If you like, add chopped fresh garlic to the marinade.

Serves 4

1/2 cup (125 ml) grainy Dijon mustard

1/3 cup (75 ml) lemon juice

2 tsp (10 ml) honey

1 tsp (5 ml) dried rosemary or 2 tablespoons (25 ml) fresh chopped rosemary

1/4 tsp (1 ml) black pepper

Zest of 1 lemon

4 4-oz (120 g) boneless, skinless chicken breasts

In a shallow baking dish, combine mustard, lemon juice, honey, rosemary, pepper and lemon zest. Add chicken; cover with plastic wrap, and marinate for 20 minutes (or longer) in the fridge. (Alternatively, marinate in a resealable plastic bag.)

Meanwhile, preheat grill to medium. Transfer chicken to the grill; cook for 7 to 8 minutes per side, or until cooked through, turning every 4 minutes.

NUTRITION
Per serving: 172 cal, 27 g pro, 5 g total fat (1 g saturated fat), 4 g carb, 0 g fibre, 66 mg chol, 175 mg sodium

Thai Peanut Chicken

This recipe is a favourite among my private practice clients. It's got so much flavour for so few calories. Serve it with steamed brown basmati rice and sautéed snow peas and red pepper strips.

Serves 4

4 4-oz (120 g) boneless, skinless chicken breasts

2 tbsp (25 ml) peanut butter

1 tbsp (15 ml) sodium-reduced soy sauce

1 tbsp (15 ml) lime juice

2 tsp (10 ml) sesame oil

1 clove garlic, crushed

1/8 tsp (0.5 ml) cayenne pepper, or to taste

Preheat oven to 375°F (190°C).

Arrange chicken in a shallow baking dish.

In a small bowl, whisk together peanut butter, soy sauce, lime juice, sesame oil, garlic and cayenne pepper until smooth.

Drizzle peanut sauce over chicken; toss to coat.

Cover and bake for 20 to 22 minutes, or until cooked through.

NUTRITION
Per serving: 202 cal, 30 g pro, 8 g total fat (1 g saturated fat), 3 g carb, 1 g fibre, 107 mg chol, 272 mg sodium

Turkey Burgers

These burgers are always a hit because they're so flavourful. It doesn't hurt that they're also low in fat and even have a little fibre. I like to serve them in whole wheat pita pockets with sliced tomato and avocado.

Serves 4

12 oz (340 g) lean ground turkey

1/2 cup (125 ml) whole wheat bread crumbs

1 medium egg

2 tbsp (25 ml) ground flaxseed

2 tbsp (25 ml) lemon juice

1 clove garlic, crushed

1 green onion, finely chopped

1 tsp (5 ml) chili powder

1/4 tsp (1 ml) dried sage

1/2 tsp (2 ml) coarse sea salt

Freshly ground black pepper, to taste

In a large mixing bowl, combine ground turkey, bread crumbs, egg, flaxseed, lemon juice, garlic, onion, chili powder, sage, salt and pepper; mix thoroughly.

Form mixture into 4 patties.

Preheat grill over medium heat. Grill burgers for a total of 7 to 8 minutes per side or until cooked through, flipping every 4 minutes.

NUTRITION
Per burger: 206 cal, 21 g pro, 9 g total fat (2 g saturated fat), 12 g carb, 2 g fibre, 90 mg chol, 327 mg sodium

Turkey Lasagna with Spinach, Eggplant and Zucchini

Who says lasagna has to be high in fat and calories? This incredibly healthy—and great tasting—version replaces beef with lean turkey, calls for low-fat cheese and includes spinach, eggplant, zucchini and red pepper.

Serves 9

2 tsp (10 ml) canola oil

2 cups (500 ml) chopped onion

1 lb (454 g) lean ground turkey

4 cloves garlic, crushed

1 jar (24 oz/700 ml) tomato and herb pasta sauce

2 tsp (10 ml) dried oregano

1 tsp (5 ml) dried basil

1/4 tsp (1 ml) black pepper

12 cooked whole wheat lasagna noodles

1 tub (18 oz/500 g) low-fat (1% MF or less) cottage cheese

2 eggs, whisked

3 cups (750 ml) coarsely chopped spinach

1 medium eggplant, ends trimmed and thinly sliced lengthwise

1 large zucchini, ends trimmed and thinly sliced lengthwise

1 cup (250 ml) diced red pepper

1 cup (250 ml) partly skimmed shredded mozzarella

Heat oil in a large skillet over high heat. When skillet is hot, add onions and turkey and reduce heat to medium. Continue to cook until turkey is cooked through and onions are soft, about 10 to 12 minutes. Add garlic, sauté for another minute. Remove from heat. Stir in pasta sauce, oregano, basil and pepper. Set aside.

Preheat oven to 350°F (180°C).

Lightly coat a 13 × 9 inch (3.5 L) baking dish. Spread one-quarter of the meat sauce in bottom of dish. Arrange 4 noodles on top and cover with half of the cottage cheese, egg, spinach, eggplant, zucchini and peppers as well as one-quarter of the meat sauce.

Repeat layers once more, topping with noodles, remaining meat sauce and mozzarella. Cover and bake for 45 minutes.

Note: If lasagna seems dry when cooking, pour 1 cup (250 ml) water over lasagna.

NUTRITION
Per serving: 380 cal, 29 g pro, 11 g total fat (3 g saturated fat), 42 g carb, 9 g fibre, 86 mg chol, 615 mg sodium

Vegetable Side Dishes

Balsamic Grilled Bell Peppers

This recipe plays up the bright colours and sweet taste of bell peppers. I recommend using a mix of red, orange and yellow peppers—they're so colourful and also provide plenty of vitamin C. Each serving delivers 284 milligrams of vitamin C—almost four days' worth!

Serves 4

4 bell peppers, red, yellow or orange

2 tsp (10 ml) olive oil

1 tbsp (15 ml) balsamic vinegar

1/8 tsp (0.5 ml) coarse sea salt, or to taste

Freshly ground black pepper, to taste

Preheat grill over low heat.

Cut peppers in half lengthwise; remove tops, inner ribs and seeds.

In a small mixing bowl, combine olive oil, vinegar, salt and pepper. Add peppers and toss to coat. Set aside for 10 minutes.

Place peppers on grill; reserve any leftover marinade. Cook peppers for 8 to 10 minutes, turning two or three times.

Remove from heat; toss with reserved marinade. Serve warm.

NUTRITION
Per 2 pepper halves: 64 cal, 2 g pro, 3 g total fat (0 g saturated fat), 10 g carb, 2 g fibre, 0 mg chol, 80 mg sodium

Balsamic Roasted Asparagus

Some vegetables taste even better when they're roasted and asparagus is definitely one of them. You might even get non–asparagus eaters to like these!

Serves 4

1 large bunch asparagus, washed and trimmed (about 1 lb/454 g)

2 tbsp (25 ml) balsamic vinegar

1 tbsp (15 ml) olive oil

1/4 tsp (1 ml) coarse sea salt

Freshly ground black pepper, to taste

Preheat oven to 375°F (190°C).

Lay asparagus on a baking sheet; drizzle with vinegar and oil. Sprinkle with salt and pepper. Bake for 15 to 20 minutes or until tender.

NUTRITION

Per serving: 60 cal, 3 g pro, 4 g total fat (1 g saturated fat), 6 g carb, 2 g fibre, 0 mg chol, 150 mg sodium

Balsamic Swiss Chard

Swiss chard is one of my favourite leafy green vegetables—it's a side I serve often. Swiss chard with pale green stems is the most common type you'll find in grocery stores. But you can also find rainbow and ruby chard—with brightly coloured red and yellow stems, respectively—at farmers' markets during the summer. If you grow Swiss chard in your garden, double or triple this recipe and freeze the leftovers so you can enjoy it throughout the winter months.

Serves 4

1 tsp (5 ml) canola oil

2 cloves garlic, crushed

6 cups (1.5 L) chard (Swiss, rainbow or ruby), washed and trimmed

1 tbsp (15 ml) balsamic vinegar

1/4 tsp (1 ml) coarse sea salt

Freshly ground black pepper, to taste

Heat oil in a skillet over medium heat. Add garlic; sauté for 1 minute. Add Swiss chard; cover and steam for 4 to 5 minutes, until chard begins to wilt.

Remove from heat, sprinkle with vinegar. Season with salt and pepper.

NUTRITION
Per serving: 23 cal, 1 g pro, 1 g total fat (0 g saturated fat), 3 g carb, 1 g fibre, 0 mg chol, 266 mg sodium

Broccoli with Sesame Dressing

The combination of rice vinegar, sesame oil, ginger root and sesame seeds is a perfect match for broccoli. When sautéing the broccoli, be careful not to overcook it—it should be slightly crunchy.

Serves 6

1 tsp (5 ml) canola oil

3 cloves garlic, crushed

3 cups (750 ml) broccoli, cut into bite-sized pieces

1 tbsp (15 ml) rice vinegar

1 tbsp (15 ml) sesame oil

1 tsp (5 ml) minced fresh ginger root

1 tbsp (15 ml) sesame seeds

Heat oil in a skillet over medium heat. Add garlic and broccoli; sauté until garlic is fragrant and broccoli is tender, about 4 to 5 minutes.

Transfer broccoli to a large bowl; set aside to cool.

Meanwhile, in a small bowl, whisk together rice vinegar, sesame oil and ginger root. Drizzle over broccoli. Sprinkle sesame seeds on top. Serve warm or cold.

NUTRITION
Per serving: 127 cal, 10 g pro, 5 g total fat (1 g saturated fat), 18 g carb, 8 g fibre, 0 mg chol, 86 mg sodium

Tip: Look for a brand of rice vinegar with less than 60 mg of sodium per tablespoon (15 ml).

Cilantro-Stuffed Grilled Avocados

This attractive dish pairs well with grilled chicken, white fish or steak. Although avocado is technically a fruit, this side dish can be served in lieu of a vegetable. Use medium-firm avocados for best results.

Serves 6

AVOCADO
3 avocados

2 tsp (10 ml) olive oil

TOMATO FILLING
1 tomato, diced

2 cloves garlic, crushed

1/4 cup (50 ml) finely chopped cilantro

2 tsp (10 ml) freshly squeezed lime juice

1/4 tsp (1 ml) red pepper flakes

1/4 tsp (1 ml) coarse sea salt

Preheat grill to medium.

Halve and pit the avocados, but keep the skin on. Rub olive oil on flesh side of each avocado.

Gently place avocados face down on grill. Grill for 2 to 3 minutes or until lightly brown. Remove from heat; set aside to cool.

Meanwhile, in a small bowl, combine tomato, garlic, cilantro, lime juice, red pepper flakes and salt. Fill the hollow part of each avocado with the tomato mixture. Serve chilled or at room temperature.

NUTRITION
Per 1/2 stuffed avocado: 135 cal, 2 g pro, 12 g total fat (2 g saturated fat), 8 g carb, 5 g fibre, 0 mg chol, 105 mg sodium

Tip: Easily remove the large seed from an avocado by firmly striking it with a sharp knife and lifting it away.

Garlic Roasted Cauliflower

If you're looking for a new way to cook cauliflower, look no further. Roasting the cauliflower gives it a delicious nutty flavour and crispy texture. I like to use plenty of freshly ground black pepper to give the cauliflower extra spice.

Serves 4

1 medium cauliflower, cut into bite-sized pieces (about 4 cups/1 L)

1 tbsp (15 ml) canola oil

1 clove garlic, crushed

1/4 tsp (1 ml) coarse sea salt

Freshly ground black pepper, to taste

Preheat oven to 375°F (190°C).

In a large bowl, toss cauliflower, oil, garlic, salt and pepper.

Spread cauliflower mixture on a baking sheet. Bake for 22 to 25 minutes or until edges begin to brown and the cauliflower is tender-crisp when pierced with a fork.

NUTRITION

Per serving: 68 cal, 3 g pro, 4 g total fat (1 g saturated fat), 8 g carb, 3 g fibre, 0 mg chol, 190 mg sodium

Garlic Sautéed Spinach

Although 8 cups (2 L) of spinach may sound like a lot, it wilts quickly and reduces in volume when it's cooked. If you have other leafy greens on hand, like Swiss chard or kale, substitute for a portion of the spinach for variety. Keep in mind, however, that kale and chard take a little longer to cook than spinach, so add them to the pan two minutes before the spinach.

Serves 4

1 tbsp (15 ml) olive oil

2 cloves garlic, crushed

8 cups (2 L) spinach

1/4 tsp (1 ml) coarse sea salt

Freshly ground black pepper, to taste

Heat oil in a skillet over medium heat. Add garlic; sauté for 1 minute. Add spinach; cover and steam for 3 to 4 minutes or until spinach begins to wilt.

Remove from heat. Season with salt and pepper.

NUTRITION
Per serving: 48 cal, 2 g pro, 4 g total fat (1 g saturated fat), 3 g carb, 0 g fibre, 0 mg chol, 292 mg sodium

Grilled Balsamic Portobello Mushrooms

Portobello mushrooms have a meaty texture and rich flavour, making them a tasty vegetarian alternative to a steak or beef burger. I also like to add these mushrooms to a platter of mixed grilled vegetables—they're delicious. In fact, you might want to barbecue extra for lunch the next day.

Serves 4

4 portobello mushrooms, washed and trimmed

1 tbsp (15 ml) olive oil

1 tbsp (15 ml) balsamic vinegar

1/4 tsp (1 ml) coarse sea salt

Freshly cracked pepper, to taste

Preheat grill over medium heat.

In a bowl, toss mushrooms with olive oil, vinegar, salt and pepper.

Place mushrooms on grill; cook for 4 to 5 minutes, turning once or twice, or until mushrooms begin to brown.

NUTRITION
Per grilled mushroom: 55 cal, 2 g pro, 4 g total fat (1 g saturated fat), 5 g carb, 1 g fibre, 0 mg chol, 152 mg sodium

Grilled Corn on the Cob with Cajun and Lime Rub

Corn on the cob without butter or salt? Absolutely! Fresh lime juice and a spicy Cajun rub turn corn on the cob into a healthy side dish you'll want to make again and again.

Serves 4

1 tbsp (15 ml) paprika

1/2 tbsp (7 ml) garlic powder

1 tsp (5 ml) freshly ground black pepper

1/8 tsp (0.5 ml) cayenne pepper

1 lime, cut into quarters

4 corn on the cob, husked

In a small bowl, combine paprika, garlic powder and peppers.

Bring a pot of water to a boil. Add corn; boil for 3 to 4 minutes. Remove from heat.

Rub each cob with a slice of lime and sprinkle with Cajun seasoning.

NUTRITION

Per cob of corn with seasoning: 94 cal, 3 g pro, 1 g total fat (0 g saturated fat), 22 g carb, 3 g fibre, 0 mg chol, 14 mg sodium

Grilled Zucchini with Lemon and Garlic

You can't go wrong with this classic summer dish. It's low in calories and sodium and high in vitamin C. Look for locally grown yellow and green squash during the summer months at your nearest farmers' market.

Serves 4

2 tbsp (25 ml) freshly squeezed lemon juice

1 tbsp (15 ml) olive oil

1 tbsp (15 ml) rice vinegar

2 cloves garlic, crushed

3 green and yellow zucchini, quartered lengthwise

1/8 tsp (0.5 ml) coarse sea salt, or to taste

Freshly ground black pepper, to taste

Preheat grill over low heat.

In a shallow dish, combine lemon juice, olive oil, rice vinegar and garlic. Gently place zucchini in lemon juice mixture; toss to coat. Season with salt and pepper.

Place zucchini on the grill; reserve any leftover marinade. Grill zucchini for 8 to 10 minutes, turning every 2 to 3 minutes.

Remove zucchini from grill and drizzle with reserved marinade. Serve warm.

NUTRITION
Per 3 zucchini strips: 58 cal, 2 g pro, 4 g total fat (1 g saturated fat), 6 g carb, 2 g fibre, 0 mg chol, 86 mg sodium

Honey Dijon Carrots

This quick beta carotene–rich side dish feeds a crowd. If you're a mustard fan, try making this recipe with different variations of mustard, such as whole grain or honey Dijon.

Serves 8

4 cups (1 L) carrots sliced into medallions

1 tbsp (15 ml) honey

1 tsp (5 ml) Dijon mustard

Freshly ground black pepper, to taste

Fill a medium saucepan with water. Add carrots and bring to a boil. Reduce heat; simmer until carrots are tender, about 8 to 10 minutes.

Drain carrots. Stir in honey and mustard until well combined. Season with black pepper.

NUTRITION
Per 1/2 cup (125 ml) serving: 55 cal, 1 g pro, 0 g total fat (0 g saturated fat), 13 g carb, 3 g fibre, 0 mg chol, 44 mg sodium

Lemon Roasted Asparagus

Nothing says spring like fresh asparagus! Low in calories and packed with vitamin K, folate and vitamin C, asparagus tastes great whether it's roasted, grilled or steamed. Here it's roasted with lemon juice, sea salt and pepper for an easy and delicious side.

Serves 4

1 lb (454 g) asparagus, washed and trimmed (about 28 medium spears)

2 tbsp (25 m) freshly squeezed lemon juice

1 tbsp (15 ml) olive oil

1/4 tsp (1 ml) coarse sea salt, or to taste

Freshly ground black pepper, to taste

Preheat oven to 375°F (190°C).

In a large mixing bowl toss asparagus with lemon juice, olive oil, salt and pepper.

Lay asparagus on a large baking sheet; bake for 15 to 18 minutes, or until tender but still crisp. Serve warm.

NUTRITION
Per serving (about 7 spears): 54 cal, 3 g pro, 4 g total fat (1 g saturated fat), 5 g carb, 2 g fibre, 0 mg chol, 149 mg sodium

Lemon Swiss Chard

I love to serve Swiss chard with a little lemon juice; it really brings out the flavour of the chard. To amp up the flavour, I sometimes like to add a little grated lemon zest before serving.

Serves 4

1 tsp (5 ml) canola oil

1 clove garlic, crushed

6 cups (1.5 L) Swiss chard, washed and trimmed

1 tbsp (15 ml) lemon juice

1/4 tsp (1 ml) coarse sea salt, or to taste

Freshly ground black pepper, to taste

In a large skillet, heat oil over medium heat. Add garlic; sauté for 1 minute.

Add Swiss chard; cover and steam for several minutes, until the chard is wilted. Remove from heat; sprinkle with lemon juice, salt and pepper. Serve warm.

NUTRITION
Per serving: 22 cal, 1 g pro, 1 g total fat (0 g saturated fat), 2 g carb, 1 g fibre, 0 mg chol, 266 mg sodium

Maple Mashed Sweet Potatoes

I'm convinced orange zest and sweet potatoes were meant to be together, and I think you'll agree after tasting this dish. For a version that's lower in sugar, substitute the maple syrup with orange juice.

Serves 4

2 large sweet potatoes, peeled and quartered

1 tsp (5 ml) olive oil

2 tbsp (25 ml) maple syrup

Zest of 1/2 orange

Preheat oven to 375°F (190°C).

In a bowl, toss sweet potatoes with oil to coat. Transfer to a baking sheet. Bake for 45 minutes or until tender.

Transfer potatoes to a large bowl. Add maple syrup and orange zest. With a potato masher, mash potatoes to a smooth consistency.

NUTRITION

Per serving: 92 cal, 1 g pro, 1 g total fat (0 g saturated fat), 20 g carb, 2 g fibre, 0 mg chol, 37 mg sodium

Oven Roasted Brussels Sprouts

If your family turns up their noses at Brussels sprouts, I think this recipe will change their opinion. It's the way I serve them most often because they taste so great. Roasting Brussels sprouts mellows their earthy flavour—they taste almost like an entirely different vegetable.

Serves 4

4 cups (1 L) Brussels sprouts, ends trimmed and halved

1-1/2 tbsp (22 ml) olive oil

1/2 tsp (2 ml) coarse sea salt

Freshly ground black pepper, to taste

Preheat oven to 400°F (200°C).

In a bowl, toss Brussels sprouts with oil, salt and pepper.

Transfer to a baking sheet. Bake for 20 to 25 minutes or until Brussels sprouts are golden brown and tender when pierced with a fork.

NUTRITION
Per serving: 83 cal, 3 g pro, 5 g total fat (1 g saturated fat), 8 g carb, 4 g fibre, 0 mg chol, 168 mg sodium

Tip: Cooking time depends largely on the size of the sprouts, so keep an eye on them. They're done when they can be easily pierced with a fork and start to get brown and crispy around the edges.

Oven Roasted Root Vegetables

This is a basic recipe for roasted vegetables—feel free to substitute or add any other root vegetables you have on hand. Before serving, add grated lemon zest for extra flavour.

Serves 6

4 carrots

2 parsnips

1 sweet potato

1/2 turnip

2 stalks celery

12 scrubbed baby red potatoes

2 small onions, quartered

1 tsp (5 ml) peppercorns

5 cloves garlic

2 bay leaves

2 tbsp (25 ml) olive oil

2 tbsp (25 ml) chopped fresh rosemary

1/2 tsp (2 ml) coarse sea salt, or to taste

Freshly ground black pepper, to taste

Preheat oven to 375°F (190°C).

Peel the carrots, parsnips, sweet potato and turnip. Cut, along with the celery, into 1-inch (2.5 cm) pieces.

In a 13 × 9 (3.5 L) glass baking dish, toss red potatoes and onions with the carrots, parsnips, sweet potato, turnip, celery, peppercorns, garlic and bay leaves. Sprinkle oil and rosemary on top and toss vegetables again to coat. Season with salt and pepper.

Bake, uncovered, for 50 to 55 minutes or until vegetables are tender when pricked with a fork. If the baking dish begins to dry out during cooking, add a little water.

NUTRITION
Per serving: 190 cal, 4 g pro, 5 g total fat (1 g saturated fat), 35 g carb, 6 g fibre, 0 mg chol, 281 mg sodium

Roasted Beets with Honey Balsamic Glaze

The same pigment that gives beets their vibrant colour is also responsible for many of the vegetable's potent cancer-fighting properties. Preparing beets can be messy—use lemon juice to remove any stains that beet juice leaves on your hands, countertop and cutting board.

Serves 6

2 large beets, trimmed and peeled (about 1-3/4 lb/800 g)

2 tbsp (25 ml) olive oil

1/8 tsp (0.5 ml) coarse sea salt, or to taste

2 tbsp (25 ml) balsamic vinegar

2 tbsp (25 ml) honey

Preheat oven to 375°F (190°C).

Slice peeled and washed beets in half lengthwise; cut into 1/4-inch (0.5 cm) slices. Place beets in a large mixing bowl and toss with 1 tbsp (15 ml) olive oil and sea salt.

Arrange beets in a single layer on a baking sheet. Place them in the oven and bake until the beets are firm but can easily be pierced with a fork, about 45 to 55 minutes.

Meanwhile, in a small saucepan whisk 1 tbsp (15 ml) olive oil together with the balsamic vinegar and honey. Bring the mixture to a rolling boil over medium-high heat, then remove from heat.

When beets are cooked, remove baking sheet from the oven and transfer the beets to a serving dish; drizzle the honey balsamic glaze over them. Serve warm.

NUTRITION
Per serving: 123 cal, 2 g pro, 5 g total fat (1 g saturated fat), 19 g carb, 3 g fibre, 0 mg chol, 154 mg sodium

Roasted Broccoli

If you're looking for ways to get the kids—or even the adults—in your family to eat their green vegetables, try this recipe! Roasting broccoli in the oven gives it a delicious nutty flavour and crispy texture. You may never go back to plain steamed broccoli after tasting this side dish—it's that good!

Serves 4

6 cups (1.5 L) broccoli florets (about 1 large head of broccoli)

2 tbsp (25 ml) olive oil

1/4 tsp (1 ml) coarse sea salt, or to taste

Freshly ground black pepper, to taste

Preheat oven to 450°F (230°C).

Put broccoli florets in a large mixing bowl. Drizzle with olive oil. With clean hands, rub the olive oil into the broccoli to evenly coat it.

Season with salt and pepper.

Lay broccoli in a single layer on a large baking sheet.

Place in the oven and roast for 18 to 20 minutes, or just until the edges of the broccoli are brown and crispy and the stems are tender but not soft. Remove from heat; serve warm.

NUTRITION
Per serving: 105 cal, 4 g pro, 7 g total fat (1 g saturated fat), 9 g carb, 3 g fibre, 0 mg chol, 190 mg sodium

Tip: Cooking time can vary by a few minutes depending on your oven, so keep an eye on the broccoli to make sure it doesn't burn. If you're doubling the recipe, be sure to use a large baking sheet. Crowding the broccoli will prevent it from roasting properly.

Roasted Gingered Squash

Roasting the squash with ginger root and orange zest adds plenty of flavour. It's a delicious way to get your beta carotene.

Serves 4

2 cups (500 ml) butternut squash, diced (about 1 medium squash)

2 tbsp (25 ml) grated fresh ginger root

2 tbsp (25 ml) honey

1 tbsp (15 ml) orange zest

1 tbsp (15 ml) olive oil

1/4 tsp (1 ml) coarse sea salt

Preheat oven to 375°F (190°C).

Cut squash into 1-inch (2.5 cm) cubes. In a large bowl, toss squash with ginger root, honey, orange zest, oil and salt.

Spread squash on a baking sheet and bake for 30 to 40 minutes, or until tender.

NUTRITION
Per serving: 96 cal, 1 g pro, 4 g total fat (1 g saturated fat), 17 g carb, 1 g fibre, 0 mg chol, 150 mg sodium

Roasted Tomatoes with Herbes de Provence

This roasted tomato dish, inspired by my fellow dietitian Michelle Gelok's recent trip to France, is delicious when served with Pepper-Crusted Salmon (page 226). Best of all, it's low in calories and high in vitamin C. If you don't have Herbes de Provence on your spice rack, you can make your own blend using equal parts savory, fennel, basil and thyme.

Serves 4

4 large beef tomatoes

2 tsp (10 ml) olive oil

1/4 tsp (1 ml) coarse sea salt, or to taste

1 tsp (5 ml) Herbes de Provence

Preheat oven to 350°F (180°C).

Using a small knife, remove stems from tomatoes. Cut tomatoes in half widthwise. Gently place tomatoes, cut side up, on a baking sheet.

Drizzle tomatoes with olive oil; sprinkle with sea salt and Herbes de Provence.

Bake for 40 to 45 minutes, or until the tomatoes are soft but still hold their shape. Serve warm.

NUTRITION
Per 2 tomato halves: 42 cal, 1 g pro, 3 g total fat (0 g saturated fat), 5 g carb, 2 g fibre, 0 mg chol, 152 mg sodium

Sautéed Cherry Tomatoes with Garlic and Fresh Basil

This side dish takes less than five minutes to cook and is delicious eaten warm or cold. For the best flavour, use fresh, locally grown cherry tomatoes when in season.

Serves 4

2 tbsp (25 ml) extra-virgin olive oil

4 cups (1 L) cherry tomatoes

2 cloves garlic, crushed

1/4 cup (50 ml) fresh basil, roughly chopped

2 tbsp (25 ml) pine nuts

Freshly ground black pepper, to taste

Heat olive oil in a skillet over medium heat. Add tomatoes; sauté for about 3 to 4 minutes or until warm. Add garlic; sauté for another minute.

Remove from heat; stir in basil and pine nuts and season with pepper. Serve warm.

NUTRITION
Per 1 cup (250 ml) serving: 95 cal, 1 g pro, 10 g total fat (1 g saturated fat), 2 g carb, 1 g fibre, 0 mg chol, 2 mg sodium

Simple Sautéed Spinach with Lemon

Spinach gets two thumbs up when it comes to nutrition. It's high in vitamin C, vitamin K, folate, iron, magnesium and potassium and low in calories. And it's loaded with lutein, an antioxidant that helps keeps your eyes healthy as you age.

Serves 4

1 tbsp (15 ml) olive oil

2 cloves garlic, crushed

8 cups (2 L) spinach

2 tbsp (25 ml) freshly squeezed lemon juice

1/4 tsp (1 ml) coarse sea salt, or to taste

Freshly ground black pepper, to taste

Pinch red pepper flakes, or to taste

Heat oil in a large skillet over medium heat. Add garlic; sauté for 1 minute.

Add spinach, lemon juice, salt, pepper and red pepper flakes to skillet; cover and steam for 3 to 4 minutes, or until spinach is wilted. Remove from heat and serve immediately.

NUTRITION
Per serving: 60 cal, 3 g pro, 4 g total fat (1 g saturated fat), 5 g carb, 3 g fibre, 0 mg chol, 236 mg sodium

Spicy Sautéed Kale

With its unmistakable dark green, curly leaves, kale is as attractive as it is nutritious. Gram for gram, kale outshines most other leafy green vegetables when it comes to vitamins A, C, E and K. This recipe is a great way to introduce kale into your diet if you're not familiar with it.

Serves 4

1 tbsp (15 ml) olive oil

2 cloves garlic, crushed

8 cups (2 L) kale, washed and trimmed, stems removed and torn into bite-sized pieces

1/3 cup (75 ml) water

1 tbsp (15 ml) red wine vinegar

1/4 tsp (1 ml) red pepper flakes, or to taste

1/4 tsp (1 ml) coarse sea salt, or to taste

Freshly ground black pepper, to taste

Heat oil in a skillet over medium heat; add garlic and sauté for 1 minute.

Add kale, water, red wine vinegar, red pepper flakes, salt and pepper to skillet.

Cover and steam for 10 to 12 minutes, or until kale is wilted and tender. Remove from heat and serve immediately.

NUTRITION
Per serving: 100 cal, 5 g pro, 4 g total fat (1 g saturated fat), 14 g carb, 3 g fibre, 0 mg chol, 205 mg sodium

Spicy Sesame Swiss Chard

Swiss chard has big green leaves and stalks that may be green, red or yellow in colour. It's a versatile vegetable that can be added to soups, stir-fries and casseroles, or sautéed and enjoyed on its own. This recipe is simple to make and big on flavour.

Serves 4

2 tsp (10 ml) sesame oil

1 clove garlic, crushed

8 cups (2 L) Swiss chard, washed and trimmed

1/8 tsp (0.5 ml) red pepper flakes, or to taste

2 tsp (10 ml) toasted sesame seeds

Heat sesame oil in a skillet over medium heat. Add garlic; sauté for 1 minute. Add Swiss chard; cover and sauté for 6 to 8 minutes or until chard is wilted and soft.

Remove from heat. Sprinkle with pepper flakes and sesame seeds.

NUTRITION
Per serving: 32 cal, 1 g pro, 3 g total fat (0 g saturated fat), 1 g carb, 0 g fibre, 0 mg chol, 23 mg sodium

Spicy Sweet Potato Wedges

This is one of those easy-to-make recipes that your guests of all ages will love. Turn the potatoes once or twice while baking to prevent them from burning. If you like, serve them with Guacamole (page 88) as a dipping sauce.

Serves 4

2 medium sweet potatoes, peeled

1 tbsp (15 ml) olive oil

2 tsp (10 ml) cumin seeds

1/8 tsp (0.5 ml) cayenne pepper, or to taste

1/4 tsp (1 ml) coarse sea salt

Freshly ground black pepper, to taste

Preheat oven to 375°F (190°C).

Cut each sweet potato into 8 wedges. In a bowl, toss sweet potato wedges with oil to coat. Add cumin seeds, cayenne pepper and sea salt. Season with black pepper. Toss to mix.

Spread potato wedges on a baking sheet. Bake for 30 to 40 minutes, turning once or twice, until potatoes are slightly crispy and tender.

NUTRITION

Per 4 wedges (1/2 sweet potato): 90 cal, 1 g pro, 4 g total fat (1 g saturated fat), 14 g carb, 2 g fibre, 0 mg chol, 184 mg sodium

Spinach with Spicy Peanut Sauce

The peanut sauce in this recipe tastes wonderful on spinach, but it can also be used on grilled vegetables or chicken breast. Or try it as a dipping sauce for Tempeh Vegetable Summer Rolls (page 198).

Serves 4

1 tsp (5 ml) canola oil

2 cloves garlic, crushed

1 tbsp (15 ml) grated fresh ginger root

8 cups (2 L) spinach

2 tbsp (25 ml) peanut butter

2 tsp (10 ml) freshly squeezed lime juice

1 tsp (5 ml) sodium-reduced soy sauce

Pinch cayenne pepper, or to taste

Heat oil in a large skillet over medium heat. When skillet is hot, add garlic and ginger root and sauté for 1 minute. Add spinach, cover pan and let steam for 2 to 3 minutes until wilted.

Meanwhile, in a small bowl, whisk together peanut butter, lime juice, soy sauce and cayenne pepper.

When spinach is just wilted, remove from heat and drizzle with peanut sauce. Serve immediately.

NUTRITION
Per serving: 88 cal, 5 g pro, 6 g total fat (1 g saturated fat), 7 g carb, 4 g fibre, 0 mg chol, 168 mg sodium

Muffins & Quick Breads

QUICK BREADS

Apple Blueberry Bran Muffins

Bran muffins have never tasted so good! These dense muffins are packed with blueberries and apples, and make for a healthy breakfast or midday snack. Other fresh or frozen berries work just as well as blueberries—try sliced strawberries or raspberries.

Serves 16

1 cup (250 ml) all-purpose flour

1 cup (250 ml) whole wheat flour

1 cup (250 ml) oat bran

1 tsp (5 ml) baking powder

1 tsp (5 ml) baking soda

2 tsp (10 ml) cinnamon

1 cup (250 ml) unsweetened applesauce

3/4 cup (175 ml) brown sugar

1/4 cup (50 ml) canola oil

2 medium eggs

2 tbsp (25 ml) low-fat (1% MF or less) milk or soy milk

1-1/2 tsp (7 ml) vanilla extract

1 cup (250 ml) diced apple (about 1 medium apple)

1/2 cup (125 ml) blueberries, fresh or frozen

Preheat oven to 375°F (190°C).

In a large mixing bowl, combine all-purpose and whole wheat flour, oat bran, baking powder, baking soda and cinnamon.

In a separate bowl, whisk together applesauce, sugar, oil, eggs, milk and vanilla until well combined.

Add wet ingredients to dry ingredients; whisk together until combined.

Gently fold apples and blueberries into the batter.

Spoon batter into 16 paper-lined muffin cups.

Bake for 22 to 25 minutes or until cooked through (when a knife inserted in the centre comes out clean).

NUTRITION
Per muffin: 161 cal, 4 g pro, 5 g total fat (1 g saturated fat), 29 g carb, 3 g fibre, 21 mg chol, 111 mg sodium

Chocolate Zucchini Muffins

Yes, chocolate is heart healthy! The cocoa beans used to make cocoa powder are an excellent source of antioxidants that, studies suggest, help keep blood pressure in check. Freeze these muffins in individual freezer bags for a grab-and-go breakfast when you're short on time.

Serves 16

1 cup (250 ml) all-purpose flour

1 cup (250 ml) whole wheat flour

1/3 cup (75 ml) cocoa powder

1 tsp (5 ml) baking powder

1 tsp (5 ml) baking soda

1/2 cup (125 ml) low-fat (1% MF or less) milk or soy milk

2 medium eggs

1/4 cup (50 ml) canola oil

3/4 cup (175 ml) brown sugar

2 tsp (10 ml) vanilla extract

2 cups (500 ml) shredded zucchini (about 1 large zucchini)

Preheat oven to 375°F (190°C).

In a large mixing bowl, combine all-purpose and whole wheat flour, cocoa, baking powder and baking soda.

In a separate bowl, whisk together milk, eggs, oil, sugar and vanilla. Add zucchini and stir to combine.

Add wet ingredients to dry ingredients; whisk together until combined.

Spoon batter into 16 paper-lined muffin cups.

Bake for 18 to 20 minutes or until cooked through (when a knife inserted in the centre comes out clean).

NUTRITION
Per muffin: 138 cal, 3 g pro, 5 g total fat (1 g saturated fat), 23 g carb, 2 g fibre, 21 mg chol, 111 mg sodium

Jalapeno Cornmeal Muffins

These muffins are a cinch to make! They're a great snack to enjoy on their own or extra delicious paired with my mouth-watering Chipotle Chili (page 180).

Serves 12

1 medium egg

1 cup (250 ml) low-fat (1% MF or less) milk or soy milk

2 tbsp (25 ml) canola oil

3/4 cup (175 ml) cornmeal

1-1/2 cups (375 ml) whole wheat flour

4 tsp (20 ml) baking powder

1/2 tsp (2 ml) salt

2 tsp (10 ml) minced jalapeno

1/2 tsp (2 ml) chili powder

1 tbsp (15 ml) freshly squeezed lime juice

1 tbsp (15 ml) granulated sugar

Preheat oven to 425°F (220°C).

In a large mixing bowl, whisk together egg, milk and oil.

Add cornmeal, flour, baking powder, salt, jalapeno, chili powder, lime juice and sugar. Mix just enough to combine. Note: Batter will be very thick.

Spoon batter into 12 paper-lined muffin cups.

Bake for 13 to 15 minutes or until cooked through (when a knife inserted in the centre comes out clean).

NUTRITION

Per muffin: 119 cal, 4 g pro, 4 g total fat (1 g saturated fat), 19 g carb, 2 g fibre, 19 mg chol, 229 mg sodium

Tip: Chopping a fresh jalapeno can cause mild skin irritation. Consider wearing gloves while chopping, or be sure to wash your hands very well to remove any oil.

Lemon, Blueberry and Millet Muffins

Millet, a whole grain, is characterized by its small, round shape and pale yellow colour. Like other whole grains, millet is high in fibre and is a good source of manganese and magnesium. When added to baked goods, like these muffins, it gives a lovely crunchy texture and nutty taste.

Serves 16

3/4 cup (175 ml) all-purpose flour

3/4 cup (175 ml) whole wheat flour

1/4 cup (50 ml) millet

1 tsp (5 ml) baking powder

1 tsp (5 ml) baking soda

1/4 tsp (1 ml) salt

1 medium egg

3/4 cup (175 ml) granulated sugar

1 cup (250 ml) low-fat (1% MF or less) plain yogurt

1/4 cup (50 ml) canola oil

1/4 cup (50 ml) freshly squeezed lemon juice

1 tsp (5 ml) freshly grated lemon zest

3/4 cup (175 ml) fresh or frozen blueberries

Preheat oven to 375°F (190°C).

In a large bowl, combine all-purpose flour, whole wheat flour, millet, baking powder, baking soda and salt.

In a separate bowl, whisk together egg, sugar, yogurt, canola oil, lemon juice and lemon zest.

Add wet ingredients to dry ingredients, whisk together to combine. Gently fold in blueberries.

Spoon batter into 16 paper-lined muffin cups.

Bake for 20 to 22 minutes or until cooked through (when a knife inserted in the centre comes out clean).

NUTRITION
Per muffin: 136 cal, 3 g pro, 4 g total fat (0 g saturated fat), 23 g carb, 1 g fibre, 11 mg chol, 150 mg sodium

Pumpkin Quinoa Muffins

Quinoa is an ancient grain from South America that's higher in protein than brown rice. Even better, it takes less than 15 minutes to cook. While it's a great side dish on its own, quinoa also works well in baked goods like these muffins, where it adds a slightly nutty flavour. Quinoa is usually available in a pale yellow colour; however, some specialty food stores carry a dark reddish-brown variety. Either one works well in this recipe.

Serves 20

1 cup (250 ml) water

1/2 cup (125 ml) quinoa

1 cup (250 ml) all-purpose flour

1 cup (250 ml) whole wheat flour

1-1/2 tsp (7 ml) baking powder

1 tsp (5 ml) baking soda

2 tsp (10 ml) cinnamon

1-1/2 tsp (7 ml) allspice

1 cup (250 ml) pure pumpkin purée

1/4 cup (50 ml) canola oil

1/2 cup (125 ml) low-fat (1% MF or less) milk or soy milk

1 medium egg

1 medium egg white

3/4 cup (175 ml) brown sugar

1 tsp (5 ml) vanilla extract

1/2 cup (125 ml) raisins

1/4 cup (50 ml) unsalted, dry pumpkin seeds, coarsely chopped

Bring water to a boil in a small saucepan. Add quinoa, stir and bring back to a boil. Cover, reduce heat and simmer for 12 minutes or until all of the water is absorbed. Remove from heat and cool.

Preheat oven to 375°F (190°C).

In a large mixing bowl, combine all-purpose flour, whole wheat flour, baking powder, baking soda, cinnamon and allspice.

In a separate bowl, whisk together pumpkin, oil, milk, egg, egg white, brown sugar and vanilla.

Add wet ingredients to dry ingredients; whisk until well combined. Fold in cooked quinoa and raisins.

Spoon batter into 20 paper-lined muffin cups. Sprinkle chopped pumpkin seeds on top of muffins.

Bake for 18 to 20 minutes or until cooked through (when a knife inserted in the centre comes out clean).

NUTRITION
Per muffin: 148 cal, 3 g pro, 4 g total fat (1 g saturated fat), 25 g carb, 2 g fibre, 9 mg chol, 100 mg sodium

Tip: If you don't have pumpkin seeds, unsalted sunflower seeds work equally well.

Pumpkin Spice Muffins with Carrots and Blueberries

It's hard to believe these muffins have only 150 calories per serving. They're moist, colourful and taste great! And they're low in saturated fat and, of course, trans fat–free. Be sure to use pure pumpkin purée, not pumpkin pie filling, to keep the calories and sugar in check. Sold in cans at the grocery store, pumpkin purée has about one-third of the calories of the pie filling, without added sugar, fat or spices.

Makes 16 muffins

1 cup (250 ml) all-purpose flour

1 cup (250 ml) whole wheat flour

2 tsp (10 ml) baking powder

1 tsp (5 ml) baking soda

1/2 tsp (2 ml) salt

1 tsp (5 ml) nutmeg

1 tsp (5 ml) ground cloves

1 medium egg

1 egg white

3/4 cup (175 ml) brown sugar

1 cup (250 ml) pure pumpkin purée

1 cup (250 ml) shredded carrot (about 1 large)

1/2 cup (125 ml) low-fat (1% MF or less) milk or soy milk

1/4 cup (50 ml) canola oil

1 tsp (5 ml) vanilla extract

1 cup (250 ml) blueberries

1 tbsp (15 ml) brown sugar

Preheat oven to 375°F (190°C).

In a large mixing bowl, combine all-purpose flour, whole wheat flour, baking powder, baking soda, salt, nutmeg and cloves. Set aside.

In a separate large mixing bowl, whisk together egg and egg white until frothy, about 30 seconds. Add brown sugar and whisk until ingredients are combined. Add pumpkin, carrots, milk, canola oil and vanilla; whisk together.

Add wet ingredients to dry ingredients and whisk until ingredients are combined. Gently fold blueberries into batter.

Spoon batter into 16 paper-lined muffin cups; sprinkle top of each muffin with brown sugar.

Bake for 20 to 22 minutes, or until cooked through (when a knife inserted in the centre comes out clean).

NUTRITION
Per muffin: 149 cal, 3 g pro, 4 g total fat (1 g saturated fat), 26 g carb, 2 g fibre, 11 mg chol, 211 mg sodium

Tip: Fresh or frozen blueberries work equally well in these muffins.

Raspberry Ginger Muffins

The combination of raspberries and fresh ginger makes these muffins irresistible! Unlike most store-bought muffins, these contain low-fat milk, egg whites and just a touch of canola oil. As a result they have fewer than 150 calories each. Consider making extra—they won't last long!

Makes 16 muffins

1 cup (250 ml) all-purpose flour

1 cup (250 ml) whole wheat flour

3/4 cup (175 ml) granulated sugar

1-1/2 tsp (7 ml) baking powder

1/2 tsp (2 ml) baking soda

1/2 tsp (2 ml) salt

1 medium egg

1 egg white

1 cup (250 ml) low-fat (1% MF or less) milk or soy milk

1/4 cup (50 ml) canola oil

1 tbsp (15 ml) grated fresh ginger root

1 tsp (5 ml) vanilla extract

1-1/3 cups (325 ml) raspberries

2 tbsp (25 ml) quick cooking oats

1 tbsp (15 ml) granulated sugar

Preheat oven to 375°F (190°C).

In a large mixing bowl combine all-purpose flour, whole wheat flour, sugar, baking powder, baking soda and salt. Set aside.

In a separate large mixing bowl, whisk together egg and egg white until frothy, about 30 seconds. Add milk, canola oil, ginger and vanilla, and whisk together.

Add wet ingredients to dry ingredients, whisking until all the ingredients are combined. Add raspberries, gently folding them into the batter.

In a small bowl, combine oats and sugar. Set aside.

Spoon batter into 16 paper-lined muffin cups; sprinkle top of each muffin with oat and brown sugar mixture.

Bake for 20 to 22 minutes, or until cooked through (when a knife inserted in the centre comes out clean).

NUTRITION
Per muffin: 144 cal, 3 g pro, 4 g total fat (1 g saturated fat), 24 g carb, 2 g fibre, 11 mg chol, 155 mg sodium

Tip: Swap raspberries with other berries such as blueberries or blackberries for an easy variation.

Strawberry Rhubarb Muffins

If you're lucky enough to have a rhubarb patch in your backyard, this is a great way to use the famously tart vegetable. If you're buying rhubarb for this recipe, clean and chop what you don't use and store it in the freezer to make these homemade muffins year-round.

Serves 12

3/4 cup (175 ml) all-purpose flour

3/4 cup (175 ml) whole wheat flour

1/2 cup (125 ml) oat bran

2 tsp (10 ml) baking powder

1/2 tsp (2 ml) baking soda

1 tsp (5 ml) cinnamon

3/4 cup (175 ml) low-fat (1% MF or less) milk or soy milk

1 medium egg

1/2 cup (125 ml) granulated sugar

1/4 cup (50 ml) canola oil

1 tsp (5 ml) vanilla extract

1 cup (250 ml) sliced rhubarb, cut into 1/2-inch (1 cm) pieces

1 cup (250 ml) sliced strawberries

Preheat oven to 375°F (190°C).

In a large mixing bowl, combine all-purpose and whole wheat flour, oat bran, baking powder, baking soda and cinnamon.

In a separate bowl, whisk together milk, egg, sugar, oil and vanilla.

Add wet ingredients to dry ingredients; whisk together to combine. Fold in rhubarb and strawberries.

Spoon batter into 12 paper-lined muffin cups.

Bake for 20 to 22 minutes or until cooked through (when a knife inserted in the centre comes out clean).

NUTRITION

Per muffin: 156 cal, 4 g pro, 6 g total fat (1 g saturated fat), 25 g carb, 2 g fibre, 14 mg chol, 116 mg sodium

Applesauce Oat Loaf

This dense quick bread is packed with oats and is incredibly moist thanks to the applesauce. Enjoy it as a mid-afternoon snack when your energy levels are sagging or as a quick breakfast during the week. I like to eat it with a dollop of apple or pear butter.

Serves 12

1 cup (250 ml) all-purpose flour

1/2 cup (125 ml) whole wheat flour

1-1/2 cups (375 ml) large-flake rolled oats

1 tsp (5 ml) baking powder

1 tsp (5 ml) baking soda

1 tsp (5 ml) cinnamon

1/2 tsp (2 ml) allspice

1 cup (250 ml) sweetened applesauce

1/2 cup (125 ml) brown sugar

1/3 cup (75 ml) canola oil

2 medium eggs

1-1/2 tsp (7 ml) vanilla extract

1 tbsp (15 ml) large-flake rolled oats

Preheat oven to 350°F (180°C).

Grease and flour a 9 × 5 inch (2 L) loaf pan.

In a large mixing bowl, combine all-purpose flour, whole wheat flour, oats, baking powder, baking soda, cinnamon and allspice.

In a separate bowl, whisk together applesauce, brown sugar, canola oil, eggs and vanilla.

Add wet ingredients to dry ingredients; mix until combined. Pour batter into prepared loaf pan and sprinkle top with 1 tbsp (15 ml) oats.

Bake for 30 minutes, or until bread is cooked through (when a knife inserted in the centre comes out clean).

NUTRITION

Per 3/4-inch (2 cm) slice: 223 cal, 5 g pro, 8 g total fat (1 g saturated fat), 34 g carb, 3 g fibre, 27 mg chol, 145 mg sodium

Berry Almond Loaf

This loaf is packed with raspberries and blueberries, although just about any kind of fresh or frozen berry would work well. I like to freeze fresh, locally grown berries when they're in season in the summer and use them year-round in baked goods and smoothies.

Serves 9

3/4 cup (175 ml) all-purpose flour

3/4 cup (175 ml) whole wheat flour

1 cup (250 ml) sliced almonds

1 tsp (5 ml) baking soda

1 tsp (5 ml) baking powder

1 cup (250 ml) low-fat (1% MF or less) plain yogurt

3/4 cup (175 ml) granulated sugar

1/4 cup (50 ml) canola oil

1 medium egg

1 tsp (5 ml) vanilla extract

1/2 cup (125 ml) raspberries, fresh or frozen

1/2 cup (125 ml) blueberries, fresh or frozen

Preheat oven to 350°F (180°C).

Grease and flour a 9 × 5 inch (2 L) loaf pan.

In a large mixing bowl, combine all-purpose flour, whole wheat flour, sliced almonds, baking soda and baking powder.

In a separate bowl, whisk together yogurt, sugar, oil, egg and vanilla.

Add wet ingredients to dry ingredients; mix until combined. Gently fold raspberries and blueberries into batter.

Pour batter into prepared loaf pan; bake for 40 to 45 minutes, or until loaf is cooked through (when a knife inserted in the centre comes out clean).

NUTRITION

Per 1-inch (2.5 cm) slice: 212 cal, 5 g pro, 9 g total fat (1 g saturated fat), 29 g carb, 3 g fibre, 15 mg chol, 150 mg sodium

Tip: Swap regular yogurt with soy yogurt for a lactose-free version of this loaf.

Carrot Walnut Bread

This delicious bread is a great way to increase your intake of alpha-linolenic acid (ALA), an omega-3 fatty acid plentiful in walnuts that's linked with protection from heart disease.

Serves 9

3/4 cup (175 ml) all-purpose flour

1/2 cup (125 ml) whole wheat flour

1/2 cup (125 ml) quick cooking oats

1/4 cup (50 ml) walnuts, coarsely chopped

1 tsp (5 ml) baking soda

1 tsp (5 ml) baking powder

1 tsp (5 ml) cinnamon

1/2 tsp (2 ml) cloves

1/4 tsp (1 ml) salt

1 medium egg

1/4 cup (50 ml) canola oil

1/2 cup (125 ml) brown sugar

1/2 cup (125 ml) low-fat (1% MF or less) milk or soy milk

1 cup (250 ml) shredded carrot

Preheat oven to 375°F (190°C).

Grease and flour a 9 × 5 inch (2 L) loaf pan.

In a large mixing bowl, combine all-purpose flour and whole wheat flour, oats, walnuts, baking soda, baking powder, cinnamon, cloves and salt.

In a separate bowl, whisk together egg, oil, brown sugar and milk. Fold in carrots.

Add wet ingredients to dry ingredients; whisk together to combine.

Pour batter into prepared loaf pan.

Bake for 30 to 35 minutes or until cooked through (when a knife inserted in the centre comes out clean).

NUTRITION

Per 1-inch (2.5 cm) slice: 217 cal, 4 g pro, 9 g total fat (1 g saturated fat), 31 g carb, 2 g fibre, 19 mg chol, 266 mg sodium

Cinnamon Orange Loaf

Adding mild beans such as navy beans to muffins and quick breads helps boost the fibre content. The combination might sound strange, but once it's baked you can't even tell what the secret ingredient is. If you don't have navy beans, other mild beans such as romano or white kidney beans work equally well.

Serves 12

3/4 cup (175 ml) all-purpose flour

3/4 cup (175 ml) whole wheat flour

1 tsp (5 ml) baking soda

1 tsp (5 ml) baking powder

2 tsp (10 ml) cinnamon

1/4 tsp (1 ml) salt

2 medium eggs

2/3 cup (150 ml) brown sugar

1 cup (250 ml) canned navy beans, drained, rinsed well and mashed

1/4 cup (50 ml) canola oil

1/4 cup (50 ml) low-fat (1% MF or less) milk or soy milk

2 tbsp (25 ml) frozen orange juice concentrate

1 tbsp (15 ml) grated orange zest

2 tsp (10 ml) vanilla extract

Preheat oven to 350°F (180°C).

Grease and flour a 9 × 5 inch (2 L) loaf pan.

In a large mixing bowl, combine all-purpose and whole wheat flour, baking soda, baking powder, cinnamon and salt.

In a separate bowl, whisk together eggs, sugar, beans, oil, milk, orange juice concentrate, orange zest and vanilla.

Add wet ingredients to dry ingredients; whisk to combine.

Pour batter into prepared loaf pan.

Bake for 35 to 40 minutes or until cooked through (when a knife inserted in the centre comes out clean).

NUTRITION
Per 3/4-inch (2 cm) slice: 182 cal, 4 g pro, 6 g total fat (1 g saturated fat), 29 g carb, 2 g fibre, 28 mg chol, 196 mg sodium

Cranberry Orange Bread with Toasted Flaxseed

I love the combination of cranberries and orange. This delicious, moist and lower-calorie quick bread is the perfect accompaniment to a cup of coffee on Saturday morning.

Serves 12

1/3 cup (75 ml) ground flaxseed

3/4 cup (175 ml) all-purpose flour

1/2 cup (125 ml) whole wheat flour

2/3 cup (150 ml) granulated sugar

1-1/2 tsp (7 ml) baking powder

1 tsp (5 ml) baking soda

3/4 cup (175 ml) low-fat (1% MF or less) plain yogurt

1 medium egg

1 medium egg white

1/4 cup (50 ml) canola oil

2 tbsp (25 ml) frozen orange juice concentrate

2 tsp (10 ml) vanilla extract

2 tsp (10 ml) orange zest

1/2 cup (125 ml) dried cranberries

2 tsp (10 ml) ground flaxseed

Preheat oven to 350°F (180°C).

Place 1/3 cup (75 ml) ground flaxseed on a baking sheet; place in oven for 5 minutes, or until flaxseed is lightly brown and fragrant. Remove and cool.

Grease and flour a 9 × 5 inch (2 L) loaf pan.

In a large bowl, combine all-purpose flour, whole wheat flour, sugar, toasted flaxseed, baking powder and baking soda.

In a separate bowl, whisk together yogurt, egg, egg white, canola oil, orange juice concentrate, vanilla and orange zest.

Add wet ingredients to dry ingredients; whisk together until combined. Add dried cranberries and fold into batter. Pour batter into prepared loaf pan. Sprinkle 2 tsp (10 ml) ground flaxseed on top.

Bake for 35 to 40 minutes or until cooked through (when a knife inserted in the centre comes out clean).

NUTRITION
Per 3/4-inch (2 cm) slice: 184 cal, 4 g pro, 7 g total fat (1 g saturated fat), 28 g carb, 2 g fibre, 14 mg chol, 165 mg sodium

Tip: Swap soy yogurt for regular yogurt for a lactose-free version of this loaf.

Lemon Poppy Seed Loaf

The combination of lemon and poppy seeds in a quick bread is a favourite of mine. Here's my heart-healthy version that's low in saturated fat and cholesterol.

Serves 12

1 cup (250 ml) all-purpose flour

1/2 cup (125 ml) whole wheat flour

3/4 cup (175 ml) granulated sugar

1 tbsp (15 ml) poppy seeds

1 tsp (5 ml) baking powder

1/2 tsp (2 ml) baking soda

1/4 tsp (1 ml) salt

1 cup (250 ml) low-fat (1% MF or less) plain yogurt

1 medium egg

1/4 cup (50 ml) canola oil

1/4 cup (50 ml) freshly squeezed lemon juice

1 tbsp (15 ml) lemon zest

1 tsp (5 ml) vanilla extract

Preheat oven to 350°F (180°C).

Grease and flour a 9 × 5 inch (2 L) loaf pan.

In a large mixing bowl, combine all-purpose and whole wheat flour, sugar, poppy seeds, baking powder, baking soda and salt.

In a separate bowl, whisk together yogurt, egg, oil, lemon juice, lemon zest and vanilla.

Add wet ingredients to dry ingredients; whisk together until ingredients are combined.

Pour batter into prepared loaf pan.

Bake for 35 to 40 minutes or until cooked through (when a knife inserted in the centre comes out clean).

NUTRITION
Per 3/4-inch (2 cm) slice: 168 cal, 3 g pro, 6 g total fat (1 g saturated fat), 26 g carb, 1 g fibre, 15 mg chol, 146 mg sodium

Marbled Chocolate Banana Bread

This recipe is a hit with kids (and adults too). If you have bananas that are starting to turn brown, peel them and pop them into a resealable freezer bag and then into the freezer. They're ready to use when you want to make this recipe—just mash the frozen bananas with the back of a fork.

Serves 12

1 cup (250 ml) all-purpose flour

1/2 cup (125 ml) whole wheat flour

1 tsp (5 ml) baking powder

1 tsp (5 ml) baking soda

3/4 cup (175 ml) granulated sugar

1/4 cup (50 ml) canola oil

1 tbsp (15 ml) low-fat (1% MF or less) milk or soy milk

2 medium eggs

1 cup (250 ml) mashed banana (about 2 medium)

2 tbsp (25 ml) cocoa powder

Preheat oven to 350°F (180°C).

Grease and flour a 9 × 5 inch (2 L) loaf pan.

In a large mixing bowl, combine all-purpose flour, whole wheat flour, baking powder and baking soda.

In a separate bowl, whisk together sugar, oil, milk, eggs and mashed banana.

Add banana mixture to flour mixture; whisk together until combined.

Remove 1/4 cup (50 ml) of the batter and mix with cocoa powder in a separate bowl. Set aside.

Pour the batter into the prepared loaf pan.

Drizzle the cocoa mixture over the batter in the pan, and then drag a knife through the batter to create a marbled effect.

Bake for 40 to 45 minutes or until cooked through (when a knife inserted in the centre comes out clean).

NUTRITION
Per 3/4-inch (2 cm) slice: 175 cal, 3 g pro, 6 g total fat (1 g saturated fat), 29 g carb, 2 g fibre, 27 mg chol, 141 mg sodium

Rosemary Beer Bread

Beer isn't just for drinking anymore! This simple recipe uses beer instead of yeast, and the result is a dense bread with a ton of flavour. I like to spread it with roasted garlic, and serve it with Squash and Apple Soup (page 116) or Three Bean Garden Chili (page 189).

Serves 12

BREAD

1-1/2 cups (375 ml) all-purpose flour

1-1/2 cups (375 ml) whole wheat flour

1 tsp (5 ml) coarse sea salt

5 tsp (25 ml) baking powder

3 tbsp (50 ml) granulated sugar

1 tbsp (15 ml) dried rosemary

1 (12 oz/375 ml) can beer

TOPPING

1 tbsp (15 ml) olive oil

1/4 tsp (1 ml) coarse sea salt

Preheat oven to 375°F (190°C).

Grease and flour a 9 × 5 inch (2 L) loaf pan.

In a large mixing bowl, combine all-purpose flour, whole wheat flour, salt, baking powder, sugar and dried rosemary. Add beer, and quickly mix until combined and all the flour is absorbed.

Add batter to prepared loaf pan; drizzle with olive oil and sprinkle with sea salt.

Bake for 45 minutes or until bread is cooked through (when a knife inserted in the centre comes out clean).

Let the bread cool for at least 15 minutes before serving.

NUTRITION
Per 3/4-inch (2 cm) slice: 194 cal, 5 g pro, 2 g total fat (0 g saturated fat), 37 g carb, 3 g fibre, 0 mg chol, 497 mg sodium

Tip: The type of beer you choose will change the flavour and colour of the bread, so try a few different kinds to see what you prefer. Light and dark beer work equally well.

Desserts

Apple Raspberry Crisp with Maple Oat Topping

Apple crisp has always been my favourite dessert! As a kid, I loved it warm from the oven with a scoop of vanilla ice cream. (Now I serve it with vanilla frozen yogurt!) This recipe is delicious made with all types of seasonal fruit. Try locally grown peaches or pears in place of apples, and blueberries or strawberries instead of raspberries.

Serves 6

1/2 cup (125 ml) whole wheat flour

3/4 cup (175 ml) large-flake rolled oats

1/2 cup (125 ml) oat bran

1 tsp (5 ml) cinnamon

1 tsp (5 ml) ground cloves

1 tsp (5 ml) vanilla extract

3 tbsp (50 ml) maple syrup

2 tbsp (25 ml) canola oil

8 cups (2 L) peeled and sliced apples

1 cup (250 ml) raspberries

Preheat oven to 375°F (190°C).

In a large bowl, combine flour, oats, oat bran, cinnamon, cloves, vanilla, maple syrup and oil. Mix until crumbly.

In an 8 × 8 inch (2 L) glass baking dish, combine apples and raspberries. Sprinkle crumble mixture over fruit.

Bake for 40 to 50 minutes or until fruit is soft and the top begins to brown.

NUTRITION
Per serving: 235 cal, 5 g pro, 7 g total fat (1 g saturated fat), 45 g carb, 7 g fibre, 0 mg chol, 3 mg sodium

Tip: Double the recipe for the crumble topping and freeze half in a resealable freezer bag. When you want to make this recipe, all you have to do is slice the fruit and add the topping directly from the freezer.

Baked Summer Berries with Almond Oat Topping

I can't think of a better dessert to make when fresh, locally grown berries are in season at the height of summer in June, July and August. Somewhere between a crustless pie and a fruit crumble, this dish is a guaranteed crowd pleaser. Serve it on its own or with low-fat vanilla frozen yogurt.

Serves 6

2 cups (500 ml) fresh or frozen blueberries

2 cups (500 ml) fresh or frozen raspberries

2 cups (500 ml) fresh or frozen sliced strawberries

2 tbsp (25 ml) granulated sugar

1-1/2 tbsp (22 ml) cornstarch

1 tsp (5 ml) lemon zest

1/2 cup (125 ml) brown sugar

1/2 cup (125 ml) large-flake rolled oats

1/2 cup (125 ml) sliced almonds

1/4 cup (50 ml) all-purpose flour

1/4 cup (50 ml) whole wheat flour

3 tbsp (50 ml) non-hydrogenated margarine

1/2 tsp (2 ml) vanilla extract

1/4 tsp (1 ml) salt

Preheat oven to 350°F (180°C).

In a large bowl, combine blueberries, raspberries, strawberries, sugar, cornstarch and lemon zest. Stir until cornstarch is thoroughly mixed through berries. Pour berries into a 9 × 9 (2.5 L) metal baking dish.

In a mixing bowl, combine brown sugar, oats, almonds, flours, margarine, vanilla and salt. Using clean hands, combine ingredients until mixture begins to hold together and form large clumps when squeezed. Sprinkle oat mixture over berries.

Bake for 25 minutes, or until berry mixture is bubbling and oat topping begins to brown.

NUTRITION
Per serving: 324 cal, 5 g pro, 11 g total fat (2 g saturated fat), 55 g carb, 8 g fibre, 0 mg chol, 184 mg sodium

Tip: The bottom layer of berries will be runny if you serve this hot out of the oven. Instead, I recommend you make it in advance and chill it in the fridge for a few hours before you serve it to allow the berries to firm up so they hold together.

Bean Brownies

Beans in brownies, you ask? You won't even know you're eating heart-healthy legumes when you taste these yummy brownies! My taste-testers couldn't tell that this dessert was made with navy beans—they loved it!

Serves 20

1/2 cup (125 ml) all-purpose flour

1/4 cup (50 ml) whole wheat flour

1/2 cup (125 ml) dark cocoa

1/4 tsp (1 ml) baking soda

1/4 tsp (1 ml) salt

1 cup (250 ml) canned or boiled navy beans,
    drained and mashed

1 cup (250 ml) granulated sugar

1/3 cup (75 ml) canola oil

2 medium eggs

2 medium egg whites

2 tsp (10 ml) vanilla extract

Preheat oven to 350°F (180°C).

Grease and flour a 9 × 9 inch (2.5 L) metal cake pan.

In a large mixing bowl, combine all-purpose and whole wheat flour, cocoa, baking soda and salt.

In a separate bowl, whisk together mashed beans, sugar, oil, eggs, egg whites and vanilla.

Add bean mixture to dry ingredients; whisk for 20 to 30 seconds until ingredients are well combined. Pour batter into prepared cake pan.

Bake for 30 minutes, or until brownies are cooked through or until a knife inserted in the centre comes out clean.

NUTRITION
Per brownie: 114 cal, 3 g pro, 4 g total fat (1 g saturated fat), 17 g carb, 2 g fibre, 16 mg chol, 56 mg sodium

Blueberries Topped with Candied Almonds

You'll be lucky if these candied almonds last until dessert—they're so good, you can't help but nibble on them. The candied almonds can be made up to one week in advance and stored in an airtight container in the refrigerator.

Serves 4

1 egg white

1-1/2 tbsp (22 ml) granulated sugar

3/4 cup (175 ml) sliced almonds

1 tsp (5 ml) almond extract

2 cups (500 ml) fresh blueberries

Lemon zest or sprigs fresh mint, as garnish

Preheat oven to 350°F (180°C).

In a small bowl, whisk egg white until frothy. Add sugar, continuing to whisk until egg white is light and airy. Add almonds and almond extract. Gently fold ingredients together until almonds are coated in egg whites.

Spread almond mixture onto a baking sheet lined with parchment paper. Bake for 10 to 12 minutes or until almond mixture begins to harden and brown. Remove from heat; set aside to cool.

When almonds are cool, break up into small pieces.

Divide blueberries into 4 bowls, sprinkle with almond mixture and garnish with lemon zest or sprigs of fresh mint.

NUTRITION
Per 1/2 cup (125 ml) blueberries and 2 tbsp (25 ml) candied almonds: 221 cal, 7 g pro, 14 g total fat (1 g saturated fat), 20 g carb, 5 g fibre, 0 mg chol, 25 mg sodium

Carrot Cake with Lemon Cream Cheese Frosting

Though carrot cake sounds healthier than most desserts, it's notorious for being very high in calories and fat. This version uses a fraction of the oil usually called for and just a light coating of frosting. Compared with standard carrot cake recipes, my version serves up half the calories and two-thirds less fat. Best of all, it's irresistibly moist and flavourful—your guests will love it!

Serves 12

CARROT CAKE

1 cup (250 ml) all-purpose flour

1/2 cup (125 ml) whole wheat flour

1-1/2 tsp (7 ml) cinnamon

1 tsp (5 ml) baking powder

1 tsp (5 ml) baking soda

1/4 tsp (2 ml) salt

1/4 tsp (2 ml) cloves

1/2 cup (125 ml) brown sugar

1/2 cup (125 ml) granulated sugar

2 medium eggs

1/4 cup (50 ml) canola oil

2 cups (500 ml) grated carrot

1 cup (250 ml) coarsely chopped fresh pineapple

2 tsp (10 ml) vanilla extract

FROSTING

1/4 cup (50 ml) low-fat cream cheese

1 cup (250 ml) icing sugar

1/2 tsp (2 ml) chopped lemon zest

Few drops vanilla extract

Preheat oven to 350°F (180°C).

Lightly grease and flour a 9 × 9 inch (2.5 L) metal cake pan.

In a mixing bowl, combine all-purpose and whole wheat flour, cinnamon, baking powder, baking soda, salt and cloves.

In a separate mixing bowl, whisk together brown sugar, granulated sugar, eggs and canola oil. Stir in carrot, pineapple and vanilla.

Add dry ingredients to wet ingredients; stir until combined. Pour batter into the prepared cake pan and bake for 35 minutes, or until a knife inserted in the centre comes out clean. Remove from heat; set aside to cool.

Meanwhile, in a mixing bowl, whisk together cream cheese, icing sugar, lemon zest and vanilla until just combined. Be careful not to overmix, otherwise the frosting will be too runny.

When cake is cool, spread frosting over cake.

NUTRITION
Per slice: 241 cal, 4 g pro, 6 g total fat (1 g saturated fat), 43 g carb, 2 g fibre, 30 mg chol, 221 mg sodium

Tip: Fresh pineapple is used in this recipe because it gives a delicious burst of flavour. However, if you're in a pinch, you can substitute 1 cup (250 ml) diced, drained, canned pineapple.

Chocolate Fruit Fondue

This is a healthy, delicious and fun dessert to serve when you're entertaining! The recipe skips the cream that's usually added to chocolate fondue, making it a little thicker but considerably lower in saturated fat. Buy dark chocolate with at least 70% cocoa solids: the higher the cocoa solids, the greater the concentration of antioxidants.

Serves 4

1 cup (250 ml) finely chopped dark chocolate (about 5 oz/140 g)

4 cups (1 L) mixed fresh fruit, cut into 1-inch (2.5 cm) chunks (such as strawberries, mango, apples, banana, kiwi or pineapple)

Using a double boiler (see Tip), and stirring constantly, melt chocolate until warm and smooth.

Remove from heat; pour into a heat-resistant bowl. Serve immediately with fresh fruit for dipping.

NUTRITION
Per serving: 302 cal, 5 g pro, 18 g total fat (10 g saturated fat), 44 g carb, 4 g fibre, 0 mg chol, 4 mg sodium

Tip: A double boiler is two saucepans that stack on top of each other. The bottom saucepan is filled with simmering water, while the top saucepan is filled with food that is cooked, or in this case melted, by the heat from below. If you don't have a double boiler, make your own: In a small saucepan, bring 1 to 2 inches (2.5 to 5 cm) of water to a boil, then place a stainless steel bowl over the mouth of the saucepan to hold the chocolate.

Chocolate Ginger Cake

Who doesn't love chocolate? This decadent chocolate cake is made using antioxidant-rich cocoa powder. It's delicious served on its own or topped with fresh blueberries and strawberries.

Serves 10

1 cup (250 ml) all-purpose flour

1/3 cup (75 ml) whole wheat flour

1/3 cup (75 ml) unsweetened cocoa

1 tsp (5 ml) baking powder

1 tsp (5 ml) baking soda

1/8 tsp (0.5 ml) salt

2 medium eggs

2/3 cup (150 ml) granulated sugar

1/3 cup (75 ml) low-fat (1% MF or less) milk or soy milk

1/3 cup (75 ml) applesauce

1/4 cup (50 ml) canola oil

3 tbsp (50 ml) grated fresh ginger root

2 tsp (10 ml) vanilla extract

1 tbsp (15 ml) icing sugar, optional

Preheat oven to 350°F (180°C).

Lightly grease and flour a 9-inch (23 cm) round metal cake pan.

In a large mixing bowl, combine all-purpose and whole wheat flour, cocoa, baking powder, baking soda and salt.

In a separate bowl, whisk together eggs, sugar, milk, applesauce, oil, ginger and vanilla.

Add the dry ingredients to the wet ingredients; whisk together until ingredients are well combined.

Pour batter into prepared cake pan and bake for 25 to 30 minutes or until a knife inserted in the centre comes out clean.

Let cake cool for 5 minutes before gently removing it from the pan. When the cake has cooled completely, dust it with icing sugar by placing icing sugar in a fine sieve and gently tapping it a few inches above the surface of the cake.

NUTRITION
Per slice: 191 cal, 4 g pro, 7 g total fat (1 g saturated fat), 30 g carb, 2 g fibre, 33 mg chol, 203 mg sodium

Chocolate Walnut Cookies

These delicious cookies combine two heart-healthy foods—walnuts and dark chocolate. Look for a dark chocolate bar with at least 70% cocoa, such as Lindt Excellence 70% Cocoa Dark or Nestlé Noir Intense.

Makes 20 cookies

1/2 cup (125 ml) non-hydrogenated margarine

3/4 cup (175 ml) brown sugar

1/4 cup (50 ml) granulated sugar

1 medium egg

2 medium egg whites

1 tsp (5 ml) vanilla

1-3/4 cups (425 ml) all-purpose flour

1/2 cup (125 ml) whole wheat flour

1/2 tsp (2 ml) baking soda

1/4 tsp (1 ml) salt

1/3 cup (75 ml) coarsely chopped dark chocolate (about 50 g)

1/3 cup (75 ml) coarsely chopped walnuts

Preheat oven to 350°F (180°C).

In a large mixing bowl, use an electric mixer or whisk to beat together margarine and both sugars until light and fluffy. Beat in egg, egg whites and vanilla.

In a separate mixing bowl, combine all-purpose flour, whole wheat flour, baking soda and salt. Add flour mixture to egg and sugar mixture. Mix ingredients together until well combined. Fold in chocolate and walnuts.

Fill a small bowl with water.

Drop 2 tbsp (25 ml) batter onto a baking sheet lined with parchment paper; dip your fingers into the bowl of water and then gently press down on each cookie, spreading dough slightly. Repeat with each cookie.

Bake for 12 minutes, or until cookies are golden brown on the bottom.

NUTRITION
Per cookie: 160 cal, 3 g pro, 7 g total fat (2 g saturated fat), 23 g carb, 1 g fibre, 8 mg chol, 136 mg sodium

Cinnamon Pecan Baked Apples

Baked apples conjure up thoughts of cool autumn days; however, I recommend you enjoy these apples year-round. It's important to use a firm variety of apple that will hold its shape after cooking, such as Granny Smith, Spy or Ida Red.

Serves 4

4 apples

1/4 cup (50 ml) brown sugar

1 tbsp (15 ml) chopped pecans

1 tsp (5 ml) cinnamon

1 tbsp (15 ml) dried cranberries

1/2 tsp (2 ml) vanilla extract

Preheat oven to 375°F (190°C).

Using an apple corer, remove most of the core of each apple, leaving about 1/2 inch (1 cm) at the bottom.

In a small bowl, combine sugar, pecans, cinnamon, cranberries and vanilla.

Place the apples in a glass baking dish.

Place equal portions of sugar mixture in the hollow centre of each apple.

Cover the bottom of the dish with 1/4 inch (0.5 cm) of water.

Bake for 40 to 50 minutes or until apples are soft, but still hold their shape.

NUTRITION
Per baked apple: 166 cal, 1 g pro, 3 g total fat (0 g saturated fat), 37 g carb, 3 g fibre, 0 mg chol, 6 mg sodium

Coconut Almond Macaroons

I love coconut, so macaroons are a favourite of mine. But not all macaroons are made with coconut. In France they're often made with ground almonds, in Spain they're made with hazelnuts and honey, and in India they're made with cashews. This recipe yields unbelievably light macaroons that literally melt in your mouth.

Serves 16

3 egg whites

1/3 cup (75 ml) granulated sugar

1-1/2 cups (375 ml) unsweetened shredded coconut

1/4 tsp (1 ml) vanilla extract

1/4 tsp (1 ml) lemon zest

2 tbsp (25 ml) sliced almonds

Preheat oven to 350°F (180°C).

Lightly grease a baking sheet, or cover with parchment paper.

In a large mixing bowl, use an electric mixer or whisk to beat egg whites until they are light and fluffy and form stiff peaks. Add sugar and continue beating until mixture holds stiff peaks.

Gently fold in coconut, vanilla and lemon zest just until combined, being careful not to overmix.

Using a spoon, drop about 1-1/2 tbsp (22 ml) batter onto baking sheet. Gently press 3 pieces of sliced almond into each cookie.

Bake for 12 minutes, or until macaroons are golden brown on the bottom; remove from heat. Gently run a spatula under each cookie before they cool to separate from the baking sheet or parchment paper. Set aside to cool.

NUTRITION
Per macaroon: 79 cal, 1 g pro, 6 g total fat (5 g saturated fat), 6 g carb, 2 g fibre, 0 mg chol, 13 mg sodium

Fresh Berries with Chocolate and Toasted Coconut

This easy-to-prepare dessert is a great way to showcase fresh, locally grown berries when they're in season during the summer. Toasted coconut, grated dark chocolate and a hint of lemon zest are the ultimate accompaniment to sweet, succulent berries. Feel free to use other fresh berries such as blackberries or Saskatoon berries—a dark purple berry native to western Canada.

Serves 4

1/3 cup (75 ml) unsweetened shredded coconut

2 cups (500 ml) quartered strawberries

1 cup (250 ml) fresh raspberries

1 cup (250 ml) fresh blueberries

1 tsp (5 ml) grated lemon zest

40 g dark chocolate, grated (about 3–4 tbsp)

Preheat oven to 350°F (180°C).

Place coconut on a baking sheet; bake for 5 to 7 minutes until light golden brown and fragrant. Remove from heat and cool.

Meanwhile, in a large bowl toss together strawberries, raspberries, blueberries and lemon zest. Add coconut and combine until fruit is coated with coconut. Garnish with grated chocolate. Serve immediately.

NUTRITION
Per 1 cup (250 ml) serving: 160 cal, 2 g pro, 8 g total fat (7 g saturated fat), 23 g carb, 6 g fibre, 0 mg chol, 15 mg sodium

Tip: For more antioxidants, use dark chocolate with at least 70% cocoa solids.

Ginger Flax Cookies

To enjoy freshly baked cookies any day of the week, portion 1/2-inch (1 cm) balls of dough onto a baking sheet and place them in the freezer. Once frozen, transfer them into a resealable freezer bag and put them back in the freezer. When your kids want cookies, place a few frozen balls on a baking sheet and pop them in the oven.

Makes 28 cookies

1 cup (250 ml) all-purpose flour

1 cup (250 ml) whole wheat flour

1/4 cup (50 ml) ground flaxseed

2 tbsp (25 ml) whole flaxseed

2 tsp (10 ml) baking soda

2 tsp (10 ml) cinnamon

2/3 cup (150 ml) brown sugar

1/4 cup (50 ml) non-hydrogenated margarine

1/4 cup (50 ml) molasses

2 medium eggs

1 tbsp (15 ml) grated fresh ginger root

1 tsp (5 ml) vanilla extract

2 tbsp (25 ml) granulated sugar

Preheat oven to 350°F (180°C).

In a large mixing bowl, combine all-purpose and whole wheat flour, ground flaxseed, whole flaxseed, baking soda and cinnamon.

In a separate bowl, use an electric mixer or whisk to beat together brown sugar and margarine until light and fluffy. Add molasses, eggs, ginger root and vanilla and stir to combine.

Add dry ingredients to wet ingredients; mix just enough to combine.

Place granulated sugar in a small, shallow bowl.

Using moist hands, roll dough into 28 balls and roll in granulated sugar; place on a baking sheet. Bake for 12 minutes or until lightly brown.

Remove from pan; let cool on a wire rack before serving.

NUTRITION
Per cookie: 92 cal, 2 g pro, 3 g total fat (1 g saturated fat), 15 g carb, 1 g fibre, 12 mg chol, 120 mg sodium

Ginger-Flax Fruit Crisp

The ground flaxseed gives this dessert an infusion of fibre, while the ginger root adds some bite. Feel free to use whatever locally grown fruit is available in place of the berries, apples or peaches, including pears, rhubarb and apricots.

Serves 6

1/2 cup (125 ml) large-flake rolled oats

1/3 cup (75 ml) all-purpose flour

1/3 cup (75 ml) whole wheat flour

1/4 cup (50 ml) brown sugar

2 tbsp (25 ml) ground flaxseed

2 tbsp (25 ml) whole flaxseed

1 tsp (5 ml) cinnamon

1/4 tsp (1 ml) ground nutmeg

3 tbsp (50 ml) canola oil

1/2 cup (125 ml) mixed berries, fresh or frozen, such as blueberries, raspberries or blackberries

4 apples, peeled, cored and sliced

2 peaches, peeled, pitted and sliced

1 tbsp (15 ml) grated fresh ginger root

Preheat oven to 375°F (190°C).

In a large bowl, combine oats, all-purpose and whole wheat flour, brown sugar, ground and whole flaxseed, cinnamon and nutmeg. Add canola oil and mix until moist and crumbly.

In an 8 × 8 inch (2 L) glass baking dish, combine berries, apples, peaches and ginger root. Sprinkle oat flaxseed mixture over fruit.

Bake for 40 to 50 minutes or until fruit is soft and the topping begins to brown. Serve warm.

NUTRITION

Per serving: 274 cal, 5 g pro, 10 g total fat (1 g saturated fat), 44 g carb, 6 g fibre, 0 mg chol, 7 mg sodium

Grilled Pineapple
with Maple Lime Glaze

Grilled fresh fruit is the perfect way to end a summer dinner. Grilled pineapple is a favourite of mine—its firm texture fares well on the grill and its natural sugars caramelize perfectly. It's delicious drizzled with maple syrup and lime juice, but also tastes great with a small bowl of low-fat vanilla ice cream.

Serves 4

1 large pineapple

2 tbsp (25 ml) maple syrup

2 tbsp (25 ml) freshly squeezed lime juice

Trim, peel and core a large pineapple by placing it on its side and removing the stem and 1/2 inch (1 cm) from the top and 1/2 inch (1 cm) from the base. Standing the pineapple upright on its base, use a sharp knife to vertically cut down, removing the skin in strips. Continue cutting strips around the pineapple until you have removed all the skin.

Place the pineapple on its side, and cut into 8 slices, about 3/4-inch (2 cm) thick. Use a small paring knife to remove the hard core from each slice. Place pineapple rings in a shallow dish.

In a small bowl, whisk together maple syrup and lime juice. Pour over pineapple rings, and set aside for 20 minutes.

Preheat well-cleaned and lightly oiled grill over medium heat. When grill is hot, reduce heat to medium-low. Place pineapple rings on grill, reserving any extra marinade. Grill pineapple for 3 to 4 minutes per side, until grill marks appear.

Remove pineapple from grill; drizzle with remaining marinade. Serve warm.

NUTRITION

Per 2 rings with marinade: 142 cal, 1 g pro, 0 g total fat (0 g saturated fat), 37 g carb, 3 g fibre, 0 mg chol, 3 mg sodium

Lemon Squares

I love these squares because they're not too heavy; they're a light and refreshing dessert. They also go very well with a cappuccino or latte. For the best-tasting squares, use freshly squeezed lemon juice, not bottled lemon juice.

Serves 12

CRUST

1 cup (250 ml) all-purpose flour

1/2 cup (125 ml) non-hydrogenated margarine

1/4 cup (50 ml) granulated sugar

1 tsp (5 ml) vanilla

1/4 tsp (1 ml) salt

LEMON TOPPING

2 medium eggs

3 medium egg whites

3/4 cup (175 ml) granulated sugar

1 tbsp (15 ml) all-purpose flour

2 tsp (10 ml) lemon zest

1/4 tsp (1 ml) baking powder

1/3 cup (75 ml) freshly squeezed lemon juice

Preheat oven to 350°F (180°C).

Lightly grease a 9 × 9 inch (2.5 L) square metal cake pan.

In a mixing bowl, use a pastry cutter (or large fork) to combine flour, margarine, sugar, vanilla and salt until margarine is well combined, flour is absorbed and mixture is moist.

Use your hands to firmly press dough into bottom of cake pan.

Bake for 15 minutes, or until light golden brown. Remove from oven and set aside.

Meanwhile, in a large mixing bowl, use an electric mixer or whisk to beat together eggs and egg whites for 30 seconds until foamy. Add sugar and whisk for another minute until egg and sugar mixture is pale yellow, light and foamy. Whisk in flour, lemon zest and baking powder. Pour lemon juice into egg mixture, while whisking vigorously.

Pour egg and lemon mixture into prebaked shell; bake for 20 minutes, or until lemon topping is golden brown and firm (that is, the lemon topping doesn't jiggle when the pan is gently shaken).

Remove from heat; while pan is still hot, use a knife to gently cut around edges of squares to prevent them from sticking when they cool.

NUTRITION
Per square: 189 cal, 3 g pro, 8 g total fat (2 g saturated fat), 26 g carb, 0 g fibre, 27 mg chol, 179 mg sodium

Oatmeal Raisin Cookies

When I was a kid, these were my favourite cookies. Still are. This recipe uses large-flake rolled oats and has just the right amount of raisins. They're a hit with adults and kids. For variety, substitute dark chocolate chips (or coarsely chopped dark chocolate) or dried cranberries for the raisins.

Serves 16

1/2 cup (125 ml) all-purpose flour

1/2 cup (125 ml) whole wheat flour

1-1/2 cups (375 ml) large-flake rolled oats

1 tsp (5 ml) cinnamon

1/2 tsp (2 ml) baking soda

1/4 tsp (1 ml) baking powder

1/4 tsp (1 ml) salt

Pinch nutmeg, or to taste

1/2 cup (125 ml) non-hydrogenated margarine

3/4 cup (175 ml) brown sugar

2 medium eggs

1 tsp (5 ml) vanilla

1/3 cup (75 ml) raisins

Preheat oven to 375°F (190°C).

In a mixing bowl, combine all-purpose flour, whole wheat flour, oats, cinnamon, baking soda, baking powder, salt and nutmeg.

In a large mixing bowl, use an electric mixer or whisk to cream margarine with sugar until light and fluffy, about 1 minute. Beat in eggs and vanilla.

Add flour mixture to egg mixture and mix until combined. Add raisins and fold into batter.

Fill a small bowl with water. Scoop about 2 tbsp (25 ml) batter onto a baking sheet lined with parchment paper; dip your fingers into the bowl of water and then gently press down on each cookie, spreading dough until about 2-1/2 inches (6 cm) across.

Bake for 10 minutes, or until bottoms of cookies begin to turn golden brown.

NUTRITION
Per cookie: 174 cal, 3 g pro, 7 g total fat (2 g saturated fat), 25 g carb, 2 g fibre, 21 mg chol, 169 mg sodium

Roasted Fruit Kebabs with Lemon Ginger Dip

This is a refreshing dessert to cap off a summer barbecue. The fruit needs only to be heated, so cooking time is short. For a variation on this recipe, soak the fruit in orange juice or brush with rum before grilling. Be sure to clean the grill well before barbecuing the fruit kebabs.

Serves 6

KEBABS

12 bamboo skewers

2 apples, peeled, cored and cut into 1-inch (2.5 cm) chunks

2 pears, peeled, cored and cut into 1-inch (2.5 cm) chunks

2 cups (500 ml) strawberries

1 large orange, peeled and sectioned

LEMON GINGER DIP

1-1/2 cups (375 ml) low-fat (1% MF or less) vanilla yogurt

2 tbsp (25 ml) honey

1 tsp (5 ml) minced fresh ginger root

Zest of 1/2 lemon

Fill a shallow dish with water; soak skewers for 30 minutes.

Meanwhile, prepare Lemon Ginger Dip by combining yogurt, honey, ginger root and lemon zest in a small bowl. Cover and refrigerate until ready to serve.

Preheat clean grill to medium-low.

Thread 5 to 6 pieces of fruit onto each skewer, alternating types of fruit.

Lightly coat the grill with cooking spray. Grill kebabs, rotating every few minutes to prevent sticking, until lightly brown. Allow to cool before serving.

Serve with Lemon Ginger Dip.

NUTRITION
Per 2 undressed kebabs: 87 cal, 1 g pro, 1 g total fat (0 g saturated fat), 22 g carb, 4 g fibre, 0 mg chol, 1 mg sodium
Per 2 kebabs with 1/4 cup (50 ml) Lemon Ginger Dip: 144 cal, 4 g pro, 1 g total fat (0 g saturated fat), 33 g carb, 4 g fibre, 1 mg chol, 45 mg sodium

Tropical Fruit Salad
with Lemon Maple Glaze

This is a simple and healthy dessert to end a meal but it's also delicious at breakfast. Even better, it doesn't take much time to prepare. Make this one day in advance if you can: the fruit tastes even better after it sits in the marinade overnight.

Serves 4

1/4 cup (50 ml) maple syrup

1/4 cup (50 ml) freshly squeezed lemon juice

2 cups (500 ml) diced mango

1 cup (250 ml) sliced kiwi

1 cup (250 ml) diced pineapple

4 mint leaves

Combine maple syrup and lemon juice in a saucepan; bring to a boil over high heat. Boil for 3 minutes. Remove from heat and cool.

In a large bowl, toss together mango, kiwi and pineapple. Drizzle with cooled lemon maple glaze; garnish with mint leaves. Serve immediately.

NUTRITION
Per 1 cup fruit with 1 tbsp (15 ml) glaze: 156 cal, 1 g pro, 1 g total fat (0 g saturated fat), 40 g carb, 3 g fibre, 0 mg chol, 5 mg sodium

Index